STANDING UPON THE
MOUTH OF A VOLCANO

Cotton Porter, Savannah, c. 1890
Photograph by J. N. Wilson, Private Collection

STANDING UPON THE MOUTH OF A VOLCANO

New South Georgia

A DOCUMENTARY HISTORY

EDITED BY MILLS LANE

A Beehive Press Book

LIBRARY OF GEORGIA

SAVANNAH · 1993

Contents

THE NEW SOUTH

THE COLOR LINE

Introduction

IN late January, 1865, General William T. Sherman and his victorious Union army crossed the Savannah River to South Carolina, leaving Georgia behind in a sea of confusion. On April 30th, General Joseph E. Johnston telegraphed Governor Joseph E. Brown that hostilities with the United States had ceased. After the fall of Richmond, members of the Confederate government fled south, holding a final meeting at Washington, Georgia, and Jefferson Davis was arrested near Irwinville on May 10th. The shattered remains of Lee's army began straggling back home on foot, eating raw turnips, meat skins, parched corn, anything they could find, sometimes looting government stores and stealing the last precious supplies from private citizens who had already been plundered by the Union army. Eliza Andrews wrote from Washington, Georgia, in May: "The props that held society up are broken. Everything is in a state of disorganization and tumult. We have no currency, no law save the primitive code that might makes right. The suspense and anxiety in which we live are terrible."[1] John Kennaway, a reporter who followed Sherman's tracks in 1865, found ruins of houses at Calhoun, blank walls and skeleton buildings at Marietta, a landscape littered with broken wagons, spent ammunition, abandoned breastworks, hastily dug graves and the carcasses of rotting animals. But the gravest evidence of disaster was not the ravaged countryside but the devastated people of Georgia. "I do not remember to have seen," Kennaway wrote, "a smile upon a single human face."[2]

Federal authority, already established at Macon and Savannah, was extended throughout Georgia during April, May and June. Several prominent Georgians—Governor Brown, Vice President Alexander H. Stephens, Senator Benjamin H. Hill and General Howell Cobb—were arrested. Senator Robert Toombs fled to Europe until it was safe to return to Georgia. In May, President Andrew Johnson proclaimed James Johnson, a lawyer from Columbus, the provisional governor and instructed him to call a convention of "loyal" Georgians—mostly native-born Georgians who had not been secessionists—to form a new government. In October, the legislature repealed the secession ordinance, abolished slavery and repudiated the Confederate war debt. In November, Charles Jenkins, a judge who had been a Unionist before the war, was elected governor. A new legislature ratified the Thirteenth Amendment, which had freed the slaves, and passed laws intended to guarantee the civil equality of freedmen.

In March, 1867, Congress, defying a presidential veto, passed the military reconstruction act. Georgia's new government was abolished, the state was returned to military rule and again the state government was reorganized, this time with more blacks and fewer white legislators. In August, 1867, Reuben S. Norton, a merchant in Rome, Georgia, observed that educated whites were denied the right to vote, while illiterate blacks were enfranchised: "An old Negro man I had owned and who could neither read nor write [or] count ten, having not sense enough to take care of himself, will be allowed to vote! I, with a number of others, was refused, because we had before the war held the office of alderman. The Negroes had a free barbecue, forming a procession and marching through town with flags and banners. The procession had over nine hundred in it, and the whole number in attendance including women and children was about three thousand. This is a free country with a vengeance!"[3] A group of irreconcilable Georgia rebels sailed to Brazil, where they hoped to escape the wreckage of the Confederacy and transplant their plantation system.

In April, 1868, Rufus Bullock, a New Yorker who had come to Georgia four years before the war and served in the Confederate army, was elected governor; and in July the new legislature ratified the Fourteenth Amendment, guaranteeing civil rights of the freedmen. In December, 1869, the U.S. Congress, outraged by Ku Klux Klan violence against blacks, once again imposed military rule upon Georgia, and the government was reorganized a third time. The new legislature, now including many blacks and Republicans who had been previously excluded, finally ratified the Fifteenth Amendment, guaranteeing voting rights for all black and white male adults. Georgia was finally readmitted to the United States in July, 1870.

Thoughtful Northerners who came to Georgia immediately after the war acknowledged that the sudden emancipation and enfranchisement of nearly one-half of the population, many of whom were unprepared to except the responsibilities of citizenship, created tremendous economic and political difficulties. Most plantations lay idle during the first two growing seasons after the war, while freedmen wandered into cities to test their independence. Whites, having lost their steady supply of farm laborers, picked up the plough for themselves. During the summer of 1865 Robert Battey, a physician at Rome, Georgia, described the situation: "The merchants, clerks, lawyers and many doctors are upon farms in their shirt-sleeves, scratching the soil for bread. Many girls and ladies labor day by day with the hoe in the corn fields."[4] Tunis G. Campbell from New York collected a small army of black followers on the sea islands, accompanied by a self-styled "professor" named Tower who showed magic lantern slides of Negro degradation under slavery, inflaming the resentments of the freedmen. Ella Thomas, a housewife at Augusta, heard that blacks were preparing to burn down white people's houses in 1868: "The South feels instinctively that she is standing upon the mouth of a volcano, expecting every moment an eruption. Four or five colored men said that the white folks was scared of the niggers, that things wasn't like they used to be and that they was gwine to have fine times!"[5]

Though it took more than five years for Georgia to return to the Union, conservatives were surprisingly powerful in the late 1860's. After a winter or two of starvation and homelessness in cities, most freedmen returned to plantations—often to the same plantations where they had been slaves, again working for the same bosses, again under a task system and again dependent on the good will of a white man. A Savannah man predicted a gloomy future for blacks under freedom: "What sort of freedom? He has freedom in name, but not in fact. In many respects he is worse off than he was before, for then the property interest of his master protected him, and now . . . everybody . . . is against him. He's only partially protected now. Take the troops away, and his chances wouldn't be as good as a piece of lightwood in a house on fire." Blacks, he said, had freedom but no land; they could raise no crops without the permission of a white man; they could get no wood, draw no water or occupy a house without a white man's permission. "What sort of freedom is that?"[6]

Though freedmen exercised their political rights in 1867 and 1868, contrary to popular tradition, they never dominated the government of Georgia during Reconstruction. An independent black vote was largely eliminated by the threats and floggings inflicted by the Ku Klux Klan. In the December, 1870, election, the Democrats won overwhelming control of the legislature. Governor Bullock, a Republican facing almost certain impeachment, resigned his office in October, 1871. The next year a regular Democrat was elected Governor. In 1873 the legislature effectively curtailed black voting by extending residency requirements for state and county elections.

Nevertheless, a real economic and political revolution had already commenced in Georgia. The 1857 election of Governor Joseph E. Brown, a pugnacious, self-made north Georgia lawyer who appealed to the common people for support, signalled a shift of power from the aristocratic planters of middle and coastal Georgia to a new professional middle class. The Civil War brought the industrial revolution to the South, which was finally compelled by wartime necessity to manufacture rather than import. The reorganization of state government specifically eliminated most of the old leading class—military officers above the rank of colonel, Confederate officials and men worth more than $20,000. Meanwhile, the war destroyed the value of stocks, bonds and slaves, while rapid inflation and currency depreciation benefitted people with debts and penalized people with money in the bank. Plantations—the other wealth of rich men—had lost much of their value, because planters lacked capital and their labor supply had been disrupted.

Atlanta, a city created and destroyed by the war, was a scene of amazing recovery, fast rebuilding amidst crumbling walls, solitary chimneys and charred timbers. The journalist Sidney Andrews described Atlanta in November, 1865: "The streets are alive from morning 'till night, with drays and carts and hand-barrows and wagons, hauling teams and shouting men, with loads of lumber and loads of brick and loads of sand, with piles of furniture and hundreds of packed boxes, with mortar-makers and carpenters and masons, with rubbish removers and house-builders, with a never-ending throng of pushing and crowding and scrambling and eager and excited and enterprising men, all bent on building and trading and swift fortune-making."[7] A Milledgeville newspaper complained in 1867: "Atlanta is certainly a fast place, and our friends in Atlanta are a fast people. They live fast, they make money fast, and they spend it fast. To a stranger, the whole city seems to be running on wheels and all of the inhabitants continually blowing off steam."[8] The following year, Elizabeth Sterchi, a middle-aged Swiss school teacher, lamented: "Atlanta is crowded with poor people piled one upon the other, perfect heathen in a civilized country, with the most savage tastes, fighting, murdering, stealing, quarreling, begging, swearing, drinking, and possessing the most abject ideas of life. . . . The god of Atlanta is money!"[9] Atlanta's population increased from 37,000 in 1880 to 90,000 in 1900.

A lesson of defeat seemed to be that tangible success mattered more than abstract principles. "Now that money is acknowledged to be the ruling power in the country," a Savannah man wrote, "it is clear that so long as the South remains under the ban of poverty, so long will she remain in the minority of government. The answer, Get rich!"[10] When it was necessary, Georgia's post-war leaders were pragmatic, opportunistic men, who conspired for a time with the Republicans. The military governor moved his regional headquarters from Montgomery, Alabama, to Atlanta in 1867, and the Republican government moved the state capital from Milledgeville to Atlanta in 1868. Joe Brown urged Georgians to accept each new plan of reconstruction and announced that his state wanted a great importation of "Yankee energy, Yankee enterprise, Yankee education and Yankee business sense."[11] An 1881 International Cotton Exposition in Atlanta was designed to promote industry and investment in Georgia. The most famous stockholder of that venture, and its most celebrated visitor, was former General William T. Sherman. At last, the forces of economic and social change that came to Georgia during war and Reconstruction had produced this ironic reconciliation.

Henry Grady, the energetic and optimistic editor of the Atlanta *Constitution* in the 1880's, may not have invented the phrase, but he became the most acclaimed Southerner of his day to proclaim a "New South" of reconciliation and reform. Grady preached political harmony to a generation of Georgians who had suffered conquest and occupation, economic achievement in a poverty-stricken land and justice for blacks where slavery had been ended only recently and, for most whites, reluctantly. Grady prophesied: "A vision of surpassing beauty unfolds before my eyes . . . a South, the home of fifty millions of people, who rise up every day from blessed cities, vast hives of industry and of thrift, her streams vocal with whirring spindles, her valleys tranquil in the white and gold of the harvest, her rulers honest and her people loving, her homes happy, her wealth diffused and poor-houses empty, her two races walking together in peace and contentment!"[12]

How could Georgians escape the burden of their impoverished farm economy and the racial prejudices that had helped justify slavery for several generations? "I write to you," scrawled Oscar Wilde from Augusta in 1882, "from the beautiful, pasionate, ruined South, the land of magnolias and music, of roses and romance, picturesque, too, in her failure to keep pace with your keen Northern pushing intellect, living chiefly on credit and on the memory of crushing defeats."[13] Despite the New South's promotion of agricultural reform and industrial development, most Southerners remained farmers, producing cotton and too much of it. In 1900 eighty-five per cent of Georgia's population still lived on farms or in small villages and sixty per cent worked in agriculture. Between 1880 and 1900, the number of people working at manufacturing jobs in the South rose only from 4.6 per cent to 6.3 per cent of the population. The region's per capita wealth was 56.8 per cent below the national average in 1880 and remained 56.3 per cent below the national average in 1900; per capita income in the Southern states was 49.7 per cent below the national average in 1880, still 49.8 per cent below in 1900. Georgia's per capita income showed no increase at all between 1880 and 1900. Northern cotton mills did not come to Georgia in significant numbers until after 1900, and industrial diversification did not materialize until after World War II. The "industries" that came to Georgia before 1945 were cotton, lumber and paper mills, which paid low wages and exploited the region's natural resources.

The war left the South with a chronic shortage of capital and labor. Sharecropping evolved to accommodate the needs of landowners who did not have the money to hire laborers and landless farmers who did not have money to rent farms. If a black farmer had no money and few implements of agriculture, his white landlord could furnish him not only land and a house to live in, but also food, tools and mules in return for a share of the harvest. At the end of the planting season, the worker would be credited with his share of the crop and charged with the cost of supplies he had received during the year plus the rent of the land. By 1870 sharecropping had already become common in middle Georgia and spread across the cotton belt, first among blacks and later among whites. At least three-quarters of the farmers in Georgia were sharecroppers in the late nineteenth century.

The farms of the New South tended to be less sufficient than the plantations of the Old South, which had produced most of their subsistence needs. The urgent hope of sharecroppers was to get out of debt by raising a little more cotton and selling it at a little higher price. But most of these farmers continued to raise cotton by a primitive technique that had not changed since the early nineteenth century: one man and his family and a mule devoting all of their energies to raising a small patch of cotton. A handful of letters written by J. M. Pearson, a sharecropper of Gwinnett County, record his quiet despair in the 1880's: "As to our crop last year, we made a failure for various causes. In the first place, we had to keep the boys hired to get supplies. Two, our horse power wasn't able to do the plowing needed. Three, it was late before we could get a stand . . . on the ground. Four, the early drought injured our crop and, five, the long continued rains in July and August almost ruined it. Then in Christmas week we lost a mule that died . . . for which we owe $50 that we can't pay."[14] Meanwhile, vast new areas of cotton production were opened in the Southwestern states and beyond American borders; as production increased, prices declined from twenty-five cents in 1868, to twelve cents in the 1870's, to nine cents in the 1880's, to seven cents in the 1890's. Debts that could have been repaid with ten bales of cotton in 1880 had to be repaid with eighteen bales five years later.

A larger harvest might mean only a smaller income, accumulating debts and ultimate disaster. As cotton prices declined and debts mounted, more and more whites were forced to sell their land, then rent another man's land and finally to become sharecroppers like the blacks they despised and feared. A tenant cabin might house a black family one year and a white family the next. By 1900 there were more white tenant farmers than black tenants in Southern agriculture, a situation that worsened as blacks began to move into cities and to the North. Thus a land tenure system that had helped control black labor after the Civil War came to dominate more whites than blacks.

The Democrat party that dominated state government until 1906 was itself dominated by an alliance of businessmen in Atlanta and other cities. Former Governor Joe Brown, Confederate General John B. Gordon and planter-businessman Alfred Colquitt were the evergreen personalities of Georgia politics from the end of Reconstruction into the 1890's. Colquitt and Gordon each served two terms as governor; between 1872 and 1890 Brown or Gordon held one of Georgia's Senate seats; after the end of his second term as governor in 1882, Colquitt held the other Senate seat. Unhappy farmers, represented by William H. Felton's Independents, were easily defeated by Democrat appeals for unity against the threat of black domination. Fifteen years later, farmers led by Congressman Tom Watson mounted a more formidable challenge to the regular Democrats. In the 1890 election, the Farmers Alliance unseated conservative Democrats in six of the ten Congressional districts, took control of the state party convention, chose the governor, wrote the party platform, elected three-fourths of the state senators and four-fifths of the state representatives. The legislature then proposed to extend the powers of the railroad commission, prohibit monopolistic business practices, regulate banking, reform the crop lien laws and prohibit speculation in farm products and extend the public school system.

In 1892 these reformers, now calling themselves Populists, bolted from the Democrat party, and their leader, Tom Watson, appealed to the common interests of all Georgia farmers, black as well as white. Until 1890 the conservative Democrats, who controlled the major newspapers and had the most money to buy the most votes, usually pocketed the black vote. When William H. Felton's Independents championed honest government and appealed to black voters by attacking the convict lease system in the 1870's, they had been beaten back by accusations that they were threatening to divide the white vote and throw the balance of power to the blacks. This was more than theory in a state with 816,906 whites and 723,133 blacks in 1880. In 1894 Tom Watson's more radical program of economic reform and his appeal to the discontent shared by black and white farmers provoked the regular Democrats to wholesale election frauds. Sandy Beaver recalled how blacks were driven to polling places after receiving free liquor and barbecue: "I remember seeing wagonloads of Negroes brought into the wagon yards the night before the election. There was whiskey for them, and all night many drank, sang and fought. The next morning they were herded to the polls and openly paid . . . each man as he handed in his ballot."[15] A black, paid ten cents a vote, could make six dollars by voting sixty times. Thus, in the Tenth District, the Democrat candidate for Congress achieved a literally unbelievable victory by receiving a majority of 13,780 votes out of a total possible poll of only 11,240! The total vote cast in Augusta was twice the number of registered voters. Tom Watson, defeated for relection to Congress, later lamented: "The argument against the independent movement in the South may be boiled down to one word—niggers!"[16]

New England schoolmarms and agents of the Freedmen's Bureau began giving aid to blacks immediately after the war. Within the first year, sixty-two schools with eighty-nine teachers for 6600 black students were established in larger Georgia towns. By 1900 seven colleges for blacks had been established in Georgia. At first they offered only elementary subjects but over the years became complete colleges and universities with graduate programs. Illiteracy among Georgia blacks dropped from 92.1 per cent in 1870 to 52.4 per cent in 1900. By 1906 they owned 1,400,000 acres of land and total property worth $28,000,000. You could express all of these statistics by saying that freedmen in Georgia were able to increase their land holdings by over a million acres and reduced their rate of illiteracy by fifty per cent in one generation.

Since the Civil War, most white people of Georgia wanted as much as possible to return to the world they had known before 1865. William J. Northen, one of Georgia's governors in the late nineteenth century, wrote with unintended irony: "The people of the South stand, all the time, ready to serve, in any way they may, the old-time Negro of slave memories and slave devotion."[17] In 1879, the traveller Sir George Campbell described the views of a representative Georgian: "He thinks the negro first-rate to 'shovel dirt,' a function for which he was made, but not good for much else. He must be 'kept in his place,' as it is the fashion to say in Georgia."[18] By the 1890's, whites began to view the progress of blacks with alarm. Before his death in 1885, Robert Toombs pronounced: "As long as a Negro keeps his place I like him well enough. As a race, they are vastly inferior to whites and deserve pity. This pity I am willing to extend as long as they remain Negroes, but the moment a nigger tries to become a white man, I hate him like hell!" Forrest Pope, a working man in Atlanta, wrote in 1906: "All the genuine Southern people like the Negro as a servant, and so long as he remains strictly in what we choose to call his place, everything is all right. But when ambition, prompted by real education, causes the Negro to grow restless and bestir himself to get out of that servile condition, then there will be sure enough trouble . . . and I will kill him!"[19]

Segregation, a relatively late development, paralleled the collapse of the South's agrarian empire and the movement of displaced whites and blacks into Southern cities. As long as there was no pressure or opportunity for blacks to cross accepted lines and as long as old traditions of social relations prevailed, there was no need for rigid segregation laws. But as the lives of blacks and whites began to converge, especially in the cities where landless whites and blacks were competing for jobs but also in rural districts where black and white sharecroppers lived side by side, lines began to be drawn to separate the races. Though the first public schools, started just after the Civil War, had always been segregated, custom and choice regulated most aspects of daily living. In 1875 blacks could ride streetcars in Augusta and Atlanta but not in Savannah. Railroads usually provided one car for ladies and nonsmokers and another car for blacks and people who smoked. About 1870 second-class passengers were described as "Negroes and others desiring to travel cheap." Georgia's first statewide segregation law was not passed until 1891—a comprehensive bill that separated whites and blacks on the railroads. More laws in 1891, 1897 and 1908 separated convicts on the chain gang. The Separate Parks Law of 1905 was the first state legislation to segregate public amusements.

As poor whites and blacks began abandoning their farms and moving into Georgia cities about 1900, cities began to pass municipal ordinances against blacks. Augusta was the first to segregate its street cars in 1900.

Canton, population 847, allowed no blacks except nurses with white children to enjoy its public park in 1906. Savannah did not establish segregated streetcars until 1906, though such laws had been proposed earlier. In 1905 the Southern Bank of Savannah began labelling its teller windows by race, and in 1906 the journalist Ray Stannard Baker found elevators in Atlanta marked: "This car for Colored Passengers, Freight, Express and Packages."[20] Blacks began to move into a separate world, with separate Bibles for court swearings, side entrances and separate waiting rooms in railroad stations, seats in the backs of buses and balconies of theaters. Most Georgians were poor, but blacks tended to receive less than their separate but equal share. These disadvantages tended to make many blacks seem to be what many whites had always believed—unaspiring, ignorant, childlike, amoral, criminal and unequipped for full citizenship.

Blacks, most of them poor and uneducated and often confused by vagrancy laws, crop liens and contracts, tended to receive harsh justice —often harsher justice than whites, because blacks did not serve on juries. At the end of the Civil War, the penitentiary at Milledgeville had been burned but the impoverished government could not rebuild it. In the late 1860's the State began to lease its prisoners to private companies—entrusting their care and reform to people who only wished to make money from their cheap and unrelenting labor in quarries or brick yards. By 1900, despite several investigations of abuse, the State was leasing some 2500 prisoners, about eighty-five per cent of them black, for terms up to twenty years at the rate of $20 per year per man. George Clarke described the Georgia chain gang in 1906: "When a new recruit for the gang arrives, he is provided with two striped cotton suits; iron manacles are riveted about his ankles and connected with chains two and a half feet long. The convict is then given a pick or shovel and required to work every weekday from sunrise to sundown. Guards stand by armed with rifles and shotguns, and at closer quarters walked the whipping boss, whose badge of office is a broad, thick strap."[21] The leasing of prisoners to private companies was ended in

1908; subsequently, each county began to work its convicts on public roads.

A dramatic outbreak of lynchings, reflecting the poverty and frustrations of many white Georgians, paralleled the collapse of the cotton economy and the failure of Populist reforms. Scholars have shown a direct relationship between the per acre value of the cotton harvest and the number of lynchings in nine cotton states of the South each year during this period. When the price of cotton was high, lynchings were few; when the price was low, lynchings increased. The Panic of 1893, when prices declined to less than five cents a pound, below the cost of production, was followed by the political debacle of 1894. Between 1889 and 1918 Georgians lynched at least 386 people—more than any other state—and 360 of those were blacks.

As the South's cotton empire approached collapse, white farmers, most of them sharecroppers, were sinking economically and socially under the failure of one-crop cotton, sterile and eroded soil, overproduction, declining prices, low cash incomes and culmulative debts. They grew alarmed when they observed black progress, comparing it with their own declining standard of living. The regular Democrats, who represented cities and businessmen, had stifled popular reform by appealing to party unity against the threat of Negro domination—and using that threat to justify election fraud. By 1906, when reformers at last staged a successful revolt against the regular Democrats, most white people had come to feel that subordination of the Negro would be essential to a recovery of freedom for themselves. Tom Watson, the embittered Populist of 1890's, returned to politics, recanted his radical appeal to blacks and now pledged to support any gubernatorial candidate who would pledge to disfranchise the Negro.

In the aftermath of a lurid campaign that was punctuated with denunciations of blacks as criminal and unfit for full citizenship, Atlanta exploded in a four-day race riot. In September, 1906, a mob of five thousand whites killed ten blacks and wounded sixty more. Though the successful gubernatorial candidate, Hoke Smith, was a genuine reformer who had served as Secretary of Interior in President Grover Cleveland's second administration, he had pledged to disfranchise the Negro—and this was done by constitutional amendment in 1908, making Georgia the seventh state to do so. To vote, a person would have to be a Confederate veteran or descended from one, of good character and citizenship, who could read or write any part of the U.S. or Georgia constitutions or the owner of forty acres of fix land or property worth $500, with all poll taxes paid back to 1877. Disfranchisement closed the door of progress to half of Georgia's population, for inevitably the whole system of public service, education and justice would become unresponsive to the needs of people who could not vote. A half century after emancipation, Georgians had put the black back "in his place."

NOTES

1. Eliza Frances Andrews, *The War-Time Journal of a Georgia Girl* (New York, 1908).

2. John H. Kennaway, *On Sherman's Track* (London, 1867), 106. Selections appear as Document 1 in the present volume.

3. Diary of Reuben S. Norton is at Georgia Archives, Atlanta.

4. Robert S. Battey to Mary Halsey, July 19, 1865, Emory University. Document 5 in the present volume.

5. Journal of Ella G. Thomas, Duke University Library. Document 9 in the present volume.

6. Sidney Andrews, *The South Since the War* (Boston, 1866). Document 2 in the present volume.

7. *Ibid.*

8. Milledgeville, *Federal Union*, February 12, 1867.

9. Adelaide L. Fries, "The Elizabeth Sterchi Letters," *Atlanta Historical Bulletin* (1940), 123, 198, 200. In the 1880's, embittered by the failure of his law practice in Atlanta, Woodrow Wilson complained about "the shoddy, new-wealth damsels of Atlanta" and the "humdrum life down here in slow, ignorant, uninteresting Georgia . . . where the chief aim of men is certainly to make money." Ray Stannard Baker, *Woodrow Wilson, Life and Letters* (New York, 1946).

10. Savannah, *Morning News*, November 5, 1880.

11. Atlanta, *Constitution*, January 25, 1881.

12. Mills Lane, The New South, *Writings and Speeches of Henry Grady* (Savannah, 1971).

13. Rupert Hart-Davis, *Selected Letters of Oscar Wilde* (Oxford, 1979), 46.

14. J. M. Pearson to Andrew and Elizabeth Reeves, January 8, 1888, Georgia Archives.

15. Election frauds are detailed in C. Vann Woodward, *Tom Watson, Agrarian Rebel* (New York, 1938, and Savannah, 1973).

16. *Ibid.*

17. See Mills Lane, *The People of Georgia* (Savannah, 1975).

18. George Campbell, *White and Black* (London, 1879). Document 5 in the present volume.

19. Mills Lane, *The People of Georgia*, 292.

20. Ray Stannard Baker, *Following the Color Line* (New York, 1908). Document 28 in the present volume.

21. The extensive literature on the convict lease system includes Rebecca A. Felton, "The Convict Lease System of Georgia," *Forum*, II (January, 1887); Selena S. Butler, *The Chain-Gang System* (Tuskegee, 1897); George H. Clarke, "Georgia and the Chain Gang," *Outlook* (January 13, 1906); Benjamin F. Blackburn, "Farming Out Convicts," *Leslie's* LIII (April, 1908); Alfred C. Newell, "Georgia's Barbarous Convict Lease System," *World's Work* (October, 1908); A. Elizabeth Taylor, "The Convict Lease System in Georgia, 1866–1908," M.A. Thesis, University of North Carolina, 1940.

Aftermath of War

IN late January, 1865, General William T. Sherman's army crossed the Savannah River, leaving behind a strip of devastation sixty miles wide—towns and plantations in ruins, farms stripped of crops, houses stripped of food and possessions—stretching across Georgia from the Tennessee border to the coast. It was not until April that hostilities finally ended; Georgians observed white flags waving from passing freight trains. Some 125,000 Georgians had fought, and some 25,000 died. Now the survivors began straggling home, most on foot, plundering whatever they could find not already taken by Union forces. George Pepper saw the desperately poor Georgians, civilians and returning soldiers, on the roadsides: "Barefooted and barelegged, with scarcely as many tatters hung round them as covered their naked limbs, with misery and wretchedness pictured on their countenances, [they] trudged along on their weary way."

The Englishman John H. Kennaway visited Georgia in November, 1865. Travelling southeast from Chickamauga through Atlanta and Augusta to Savannah, he found ruins of houses at Calhoun, blank walls and skeleton buildings at Marietta, a landscape littered with broken wagons, spent ammunition, abandoned breastworks, fresh graves and the rotting carcasses of animals. "I do not remember to have seen a smile upon a single human face." [Document One]

The Massachusetts-born newspaperman Sidney Andrews toured Georgia in September-November, 1865—across the central and eastern counties through Fort Valley, Newnan, Atlanta, Greensboro, Augusta, Waynesboro and Savannah. He found bitterness toward the Yankees and general contempt toward the freedmen—but saw Atlanta already springing back to life. Andrews recognized the central problem of the era, especially for the black man: "What is the 'freedom' that war has brought? He can make no crops except the white man gives him a chance. He can't get a pail of water, a stick of wood without asking a white man for the privilege. What sort of freedom is that?" [Document Two]

Another Massachusetts journalist, John R. Dennett, exploring defeated Georgia in December, found signs of optimism and recovery amidst ruins, as Georgians began to rebuild their homes, cities and plantations. Atlanta, particularly, was a scene of life and energy—"the middle of the city a wilderness of mud . . . with unfinished houses, scaffolding, piles of lumber and brick and sand, the noise of carpenters and masons." [Document Three]

John T. Trowbridge came to Georgia from New York in the summer of 1865 and winter of 1866—visiting Atlanta, Macon, Eatonton, Madison and Augusta. He observed the extreme poverty of the whites, the activities of the Freedmen's Bureau and the mingled feelings of affection and resentment between the races. "Everywhere were ruins and rubbish, mud and mortar and misery." [Document Four]

[1]

---

*I do not remember to have seen a smile upon a single human face. . . .
The ladies could speak of no subject but the war, and there was a settled
grief, a heart-broken expression about them. How their eyes flashed
when they mentioned a Yankee!*

JOHN H. KENNAWAY, 1865

JOHN H. KENNAWAY (1837–1910), an Oxford-educated hereditary baronet who would serve
in Parliament from 1870 to 1910, visited Georgia in November, 1865. These excerpts from his
tour appear in his *On Sherman's Track or the South after the War* (London, 1867), pp. 105–163.

We found ourselves in the heavily-wooded country of the Chickamauga creeks.
The condition of the people may be imagined from the account of one who had
traversed the distance by road a short time before and says, "Between Chattanooga and Atlanta I do not remember to have seen a smile upon a single
human face." We found the stations destroyed or gutted all along the line, and
charred ruins met the gaze wherever human habitations had been. At Resaca, as
elsewhere, remains of camp huts and earthworks were to be seen. At Calhoun,
ruins of houses met the view far and near. "How can we forgive," a Reb in our
car said, "with those ruins staring us in the face?" The line presented the usual
signs of having been torn up and hastily replaced. Marietta, which we reached
about 5, was considered one of the prettiest and most rising towns in Cherokee
Georgia. Little now remained of it but blank walls and skeleton houses.

Reaching Atlanta, we were landed among an inextricable labyrinth of rails
that centered in what had once been the station. Under the guidance of a nigger
and with the help of a lantern, we picked our way as we best could through the
deep and sticky mud to a lodging called the Sassein House. Here we found fair
quarters and Southern fare—beefsteaks of the consistency of leather, pork fixings,
molasses, cornbread and rye coffee. Life and property are notoriously insecure
in Atlanta, and outrages are of frequent occurrence, notwithstanding that a military guard patrols the streets at night. No one is permitted to be out after
10 o'clock.

Colonel S—— was in command here. He was a rough specimen of a Federal officer. He considered the Southern people to be the laziest set upon earth and wished that the North had given them another year of the war and driven them all into the sea. About a mile from the town we came upon an encampment of Negro troops. An officer who came out to us said that they made excellent soldiers and were more obedient to command than the whites. They seemed, however, to need pretty sharp discipline, as we gathered from the character of the punishments in use, viz. flogging, tying up by the thumbs and ears with the tips of the toes touching the ground, which our guide described to us with great vivacity. A little further on was a camp containing 1000 freedmen, seemingly in wretched plight, who, together with 800 white families on the other side of the town, were being supported by government on the surplus rations of the war. Close by was a wood where the fight must have raged fiercely. Not a tree but had been scathed by shot, hardly a stick which had not been cut off by grape or canister.

It was not a year from the date of Sherman's leaving Atlanta a prey to the flames that we entered the city, and we left it next day, hardly knowing whether to wonder most at the completeness of the ruin which had swept over it or at the rapidity with which its restoration was being effected. The five railways which centered there were all in operation, though the station buildings had been destroyed. A few battered brick walls and an occasional chimney, looking grim and gaunt, were all that remained to attest the former existence of the great mills and foundries. But wooden frame workhouses were springing up on all sides, and along the main street, where frontage was fetching $40 a foot, buildings of a more substantial character were beginning to rise.

We decided to move on at once to Augusta, notwithstanding the dismal account we heard of the car, which was the only accommodation provided in the night train on the Georgia Railway. Imagine a long box upon wheels, with a board seat running along the sides as in an omnibus, a door, of course, at each end—the glass broken in every third or fourth window—every inch of space occupied by a most promiscuous crowd of workmen and darkies, the latter chattering and grinning. The prospect of a seventeen hours' journey was not an inviting one. Not very assuring either was the following printed notice, which we discovered posted up in one of the corners: "Passengers are positively forbidden to ride upon the tops or platforms of cars. From the defective condition of the track the cars are very likely to run off, in which case the danger to passengers is much increased in such a position."

By midnight we had the car pretty well to ourselves and were able to lie at full length along the seat and try to court sleep in spite of the bitter draughts rushing in on all sides. We got into conversation during the course of the evening with some of the natives, and how they did execrate Sherman! "He had robbed them of everything." "Sherman has taken all the cows," was the answer to our application for milk with the rye coffee, when we stopped for supper. That they spoke only the truth, there can be no doubt. The long night wore away, as we turned uneasily from side to side on our hard couch or roused ourselves to try and stuff up the windows—or heaped on logs till the round stove glowed red hot.

Towards morning the number of residences on either side the line indicated that we were approaching the neighborhood of Augusta, and before 11 o'clock we were delighted to be free and safely located at the Planters' Hotel. Augusta was spared a visit from Sherman, and the city stands as it did before the war. Outwardly all is as before. Nothing at least appears upon the surface to indicate the change, except the presence of an idle crowd of niggers in the streets. Business seems to be going on as usual, grocery, dry goods and tobacco stores driving a brisk trade. Express companies are in full swing, and bales of cotton, the last remains of the crop of 1860 are lying about on the banks of the river ready for shipment or peeping out of the warehouses. But unless the promise of a share in the crop will induce the Negroes to work or white labor can be procured by immigration, the lands will lie uncultivated this year as they were last, and, no more cotton being forthcoming, the warehouses will be closed, the wharves empty, the stores shut.

We paid a visit to a large plantation belonging to General ——, who at the beginning of the war was a very rich man. The Yankees, he said, had robbed him of all. He had returned home only the week before our visit, having just been pardoned by the President. There, after a separation of three years, he found his family, who had not quitted the place (they knew not indeed where to go) in spite of all the annoyances to which they were subjected. Deserted by their servants, watched at every turn, they were liable at any moment to have to throw open their house to the inspection of Yankee soldiers, searching nominally for arms but in reality carrying off everything they could lay hands on.

We left our carriage at the gate and walked about twenty yards through an avenue to the house, delivered our letter, and were at once asked by the lady of the house to come in. We were introduced to her three daughters, with whom she was sitting working in a room of good size, but scantily and poorly furnished. The carpet was worn out, the paper, once gilt, was faded and old, and the only ornaments, a small bronze clock which had stopped, and some pieces of plate on the table in the middle of the room. The ladies were sitting around in the plainest cotton dresses, and two little boys, in a sort of Confederate uniform, were playing in front of the great log fire. They all welcomed us or tried to do so. But they could speak of no subject but the war, and there was a settled grief, a heart-broken expression about them, that was most painful. And how their eyes flashed, and they ground their teeth, when they mentioned the name of a Yankee! "You seem to have a very bad opinion of us," said a Federal officer to one of them the other day. "If you want my opinion, I think you the meanest of the mean," was the reply.

Presently came in the son from squirrel hunting. He had been in the Confederate army all through the war and seemed none the worse for the hardships he had undergone. At our request he took us 'round the place, for we were glad to escape the melancholy atmosphere of the drawing room. There was little to show—the old nigger quarters, a little village of wooden huts, neat in appearance but now almost tenantless. The stables, in which were kept in old times fifteen carriage horses besides riding horses for everyone that came, now only contained a few mules. Horses, dogs, carriages, everything had disappeared, but one child's pony. We passed on through a paddock much trampled by cavalry, into what had been a large flower garden but was now utterly neglected and overgrown, and into a glass house, which had contained a number of exotics but now was cold and empty. On our return to the house we were shown into another room, in which a few relics of rich furniture strengthened the impression left on our minds of departed grandeur. We drank whiskey in silver cups but poured from a broken decanter.

The general came home just as we were about to leave—a handsome, pleasant old man, who made us heartily welcome and insisted on our staying to dinner. He was busily engaged in the work of reconstruction and, as we afterwards heard, with every prospect of success. A grand sight it was to see the grey-headed old gentleman setting to work, with such pluck and determination, to retrieve the shattered fortunes of his family, and quite affecting to see him stand up before dinner and thank God for the blessings still remaining to him, as he might have done in the times when he had fifty servants about his house in the place now occupied by two little nigger boys. The food was plain but plentiful. We tasted squirrel for the first time. We left towards evening with a grateful remembrance of Southern hospitality but oppressed and pained by the grief and desolation of which we had been made somewhat intrusive witnesses—a scene very different from the plantation we had expected to see.

Augusta is a good specimen of one of the chief inland Southern towns with 19,000 inhabitants, a number which has been increased to a large extent lately by the influx of Negroes from the country districts. If a notice which appeared in a daily paper one morning during our stay be a true indication of the manners and customs of the place and of the state of order prevailing, there would be little reason to delay our departure. The advertisement read as follows: "Notice to Loafers—You are respectfully requested to keep your knives in your pockets while about our door and not to stay longer than a quarter of a second—Central Hotel." We were anxious to be moving on!

Savannah and Charleston were both within reach. The railways which connected them with Augusta had been partially restored, but by either route there was a break in the communications which involved fifty miles—a matter of twelve or thirteen hours—of travelling by road in old military ambulances purchased from government at the end of the war. The misery and discomfort of a night so spent were vividly portrayed to us by a traveller fresh from the experience of them, who told us that twenty-four hours in bed were insufficient to rid him of the aches which the cruel jolting had caused him to suffer in every limb. One other alternative remained: to look out for a berth in one of the steamboats running on the Savannah River. By good fortune, we heard of the unexpected arrival of a favorite little steamer, the *Helen*, just come up on an extra trip from Savannah and about to return as soon as her cargo could be put on board.

The loading was all but finished when we reached the ship. Every inch of space seemed already to be occupied, so that it was with difficulty that we squeezed our way between the huge cotton bales which blocked up all the passages and gangways. It was "cotton, cotton, everywhere." The lower deck was occupied with upland cotton made up in square bales, tight-corded and bursting, the average size of a chest of drawers. Sea island cotton, sewn up in huge sacks, covered all the upper part of the ship and the roof of the little cabin. A spare corner was luckily found for the luggage, and the passengers, who numbered about twenty, settled themselves as best they could.

But what is all this excitement which is bringing everybody to the lookout? See, we are approaching an obstruction—a line of piles stretching across the river, which have been driven in during the war to bar the passage of the Yankee gunboats. A breach has been made this summer, but in the wrong place—close to one of the banks, where the current is strong and the stream shallow. We hold our breath as we just clear the narrow opening! A wretched spectacle was presented by the remains of the bridge of the Savannah and Charleston Railway, an unmistakable piece of Sherman's handiwork. No attempt has as yet been made to restore it. The brick piers were still standing, but the iron bridge which rested upon them seemed to have been cut in two places and the ends tilted down in helpless, almost ludicrous impotence, into the river.

We reached Savannah after a very quick passage at 10 A.M. and ran alongside the quay, already crowded with vessels waiting for cotton freight or unloading the bales brought down from the interior. The wharves and warehouses were many of them fine and seemed not to have suffered. Indeed the whole scene was a busy one, full of life and interest, and all the inlets and creeks were swarming with niggers in canoes.

⌈ 2 ⌉

What is the "freedom" that war has brought this dusky race? He can make no crops except the white man gives him a chance. He can't get a pail of water without asking a white man for the privilege. He can't get a stick of wood without leave from a white man. What sort of freedom is that?

SIDNEY ANDREWS, 1865

SIDNEY ANDREWS (1837–1880) was born in Massachusetts, attended the University of Michigan 1856–59, joined the gold rush in California and worked as an attendant in the U.S. Senate during the Civil War. From 1864 until 1869 Andrews was special correspondent for the Chicago *Tribune* and the Boston *Advertiser*. His visit to Georgia in September-November, 1865, was narrated in his book, *The South since the War as Shown by Fourteen Weeks of Travel and Observation in Georgia and the Carolinas* (Boston, 1866).

Fort Valley
November 15, 1865

This is a pleasant little town of some 1600 to 2000 inhabitants, situated thirty miles below Macon and about one hundred miles above the Florida line. The section of the state below here, constituting southwestern Georgia, is one of the finest cotton-growing regions of the South. It was not much traversed by either army, had no chance at running the blockade and could get very little shipment on the railroads; consequently the surrender of the Southern army found in the country about all the cotton that had been raised in five years. There was probably more cotton in Georgia at the close of the war than in any other Southern state.

The men who did the fighting are everywhere the men who most readily accept the issues of the war. "I can whip any three Yankees in town," blustered an ex-Rebel officer at Americus the other day, but when I inquired about his record in the army I found that he was generally "seriously unwell" on the day of battle! The late rebel privates of this section are generally doing quite well. They mourn over the defeat of their armies and are very fond of showing that but for this little mistake or that little accident or that other little blunder, the

8

Confederacy would now be a great nation. But they appear on the whole to accept the issue of the war in good faith and with a determination to do their duties hereafter as orderly citizens. An Americus merchant told me he was a hot secessionist all through 1860 and, though sixty years of age, shouldered his musket early in 1861 and saw two years of service before he broke down. "We staked everything on the result, and for my part I submit to the issue without a murmur."

There is a pretty general contempt everywhere for the "Yankees," the word standing for the resident of any Northern state. Passing by a piazza in Americus on which three or four men sat, I overheard one of them remark, "Well, hell's the place for Yankees, and I want 'em all to go thar as soon's possible, and take the niggers 'long with 'em!" Talking with a very intelligent Macon gentleman, I asked him how Northern men would be likely to succeed in business if they were to come into the state this winter, and his answer was, "I think they would get along well enough in the upper country but in the lower part of the state there is such ignorance and prejudice that I reckon they would see hard times a long while before they made a living." I must add that in a general way I hear much expression of a desire for an influx of Northern energy and Northern capital.

I found many Negroes below here who were run out of the northern part of the state and out of South Carolina on the approach of Sherman's army. These refugee Negroes generally seem anxious to return to their former homes. I saw a party of eleven one morning just starting out to walk over to Barnwell district, South Carolina, a distance of at least 250 miles. And the members of another gang of fourteen told me they were going to start for North Carolina so as to get there by Christmas.

The idea that the whites and the blacks cannot live together is unusually prevalent throughout all this section. "The Negroes were the ignorant cause of the war and are bound to be exterminated before the conflict closes," said one gentleman, and I have heard the same idea a dozen times expressed within a week. "We must go down or they must," says another man. And his associate responds, "Damned if it's *us*, though!"

I sat an hour or more in the Freedmen's Bureau agency office at Albany one day last week. A planter from Mitchell County came in with the stereotyped phrase, "Niggers won't work, and everything is all going to ruin." While he sat there, in came a planter from Lee County, an ex-rebel Colonel, who works twenty men and twelve women. He said he had found no trouble with his Negroes. As soon as he came home from the army he called them together, explained to them that they were free and could go where they pleased; said to them that he would like to have all of them remain on the place and would pay

9

them fairly for their work. He gave them a week for consideration, and then every one was ready to contract with him. The contract gives them house room, firewood, medical attendance, and one-third of the crop. None of his hands have left him, and all are ready to contract for the next year. Give the Negro fair treatment and there will be very little cause for complaint against him.

The cases in which the planters turn the Negroes off the plantation as soon as the crops are gathered are somewhat numerous. Here is one that comes under my own observation. The planter worked seven men and six women. I met the men on the street one forenoon, wandering aimlessly about. When I talked with them they told me their story. "Ole mass'r had 'greed to give we one tird de craps, an' we dun got 'em all up, got de corn shucked, an' de tatees digged, and de rice trashed. An' ole mass'r he dun gone sold all de craps, an' he bringed we all up yere yes'erday, an' gif we seven dollar fur der man an' he wife to buy de cloth wid to make we clofes, an' he say may be he gif we some shoes. An' he dun gif we'n none o' de craps, none o' de rice, none o' de corn, none o' de tatees, on'y de seven dollar fur de man an' he wife. An' den he tell we ter come on de plantation no mo'. An' he say we all bof mus' make livin' on we'ns freedom. An' we got not'ing fur all de work on'y de seven dollar fur de man an' he wife, an' we got no corn nor not'ing for de winter."

Newnan
November 20, 1865

As I looked up the streets of Newnan from the windows and platform of the railway car, it seemed a charming place—a gentle slope toward the east, three or four white stores, the corner of the courthouse, with its surroundings of luxuriant China trees, the hotel with its broad and high piazzas, a wealth of trees and shrubbery everywhere, on all sides handsome cottage houses embowered in greenness and rose blossoms, to the right and left numberless oaks with their crimson and golden frost-touched leaves, and then in the dim background the dreamy and uncertain outline of wooded hills with their blue beauty shimmering in the low sun of a glorious Indian summer afternoon! It is the home of very many rich planters, boasts numerous handsome suburban residences, is said to have a more elegant and cultured society than any other place in the western part of the state, prides itself on its early and constant devotion to the cause of secession, and has just elected radical secessionists and unconquered rebels to the legislature. Yet Newnan is just like every other Southern town— streets full of mud holes and wallowing swine, fences in every stage of tumble-down ruin, sidewalks in every condition of break-neck disorder, yards full of sticks and stones and bits of every conceivable rubbish, everywhere a grand carnival of sloth and unthrift and untidiness and slovenliness, that apathy of shiftlessness so pitiful to the soul of a New Englander!

Whether the North Carolina "dirt-eater" or the South Carolina "sand-hiller" or the Georgia "cracker" is lowest on the scale of human existence would be difficult to say. The ordinary plantation Negro seemed to me, when I first saw him in any numbers, at the very bottom of not only probabilities, but also possibilities, so far as they effect human relations. But these specimens of the white race must be credited with having reached a yet lower depth of squalid and beastly wretchedness. However poor or ignorant or unclean or improvident he may be, I never yet found a Negro who had not at least a vague desire for a better condition, an undefined longing for something called freedom, a shrewd instinct of self-preservation. These three ideas do not make the creature a man, but they lift him out of the bounds of brutedom. The Georgia "cracker," as I have seen him since leaving Milledgeville, seems to me to lack not only all that the Negro does but also even the desire for a better condition and the vague longing for an enlargement of his liberties and his rights. Such filthy poverty, such foul ignorance, such idiotic imbecility, such bestial instincts, such grovelling desires—no trick of words can make plain the scene in and around one of these "cracker" habitations, and the case is one in which even seeing itself is scarcely believing.

I also bear you sorrowful witness that every Georgian despises the Negro. As a slave he was well enough, but as a man he is only a poor, pitiful creature, from whom little or no good can be expected. Secessionists and Unionists are just alike, so far as I can see, in contempt for him and alike in wanting him out of the way. "I hope you will remain in the state long enough," said a very intelligent gentleman of northern Georgia to me, nearly a month ago. "I hope you will remain in the state long enough to see what a miserable thing the Negro is, the poor creature who brought on the war and is bound to be exterminated before it ends. For it won't end till they or we are gone." There spoke the true Georgian, a kindly man, a sober judge, and a professed Unionist.

From the average Georgia standpoint, he who talks of educating the Negro is half insane. "What, build school houses for the niggers!" exclaimed a citizen with whom I sat in the public room at the Macon hotel. Some of the leading men see and say that the interests of the state will be promoted by educating the freedmen, but nine-tenths of the people sneer just as the Macon man did. Yet within four blocks of that same hotel I saw the Negro porter of a store laboring at his spelling book in the corner and a young Negro woman with her spelling book fastened to the fence while at work over the wash tub. Still I'm everywhere told that the nigger can't learn and money spent in educating him would be money thrown away.

11

Atlanta was a city of about 14,000 inhabitants two years ago, and it was not more than half burned last fall. The entire business portion, excepting the Masonic Hall building and one block of six stores and a hotel, was laid in ruins, and not a few of the larger residences in all parts of the city were also burned. But the city hall and the medical college and all the churches and many of the handsomer and more stylish private dwellings and nearly all the houses of the middling and poorer classes were spared. And on the first of last June there was ample shelter for at least six or eight thousand persons.

The marks of the conflict are everywhere strikingly apparent. Crumbling walls and solitary chimneys, thousands of masses of brick and mortar, thousands of pieces of charred timber, thousands of half-burned boards, thousands of scraps of tin roofing, thousands of car and engine bolts and bars, thousands of ruined articles of hardware, thousands upon thousands of tons of debris of all sorts and shapes. Moreover, there are plenty of cannon balls and long shot lying about the streets with not a few shell-struck houses in some sections. From the courthouse square can be seen a dozen or more forts, and many a hillside from which the timber was cut so that the enemy might not come upon the city unawares.

From all this ruin and devastation a new city is springing up with marvellous rapidity. The narrow and irregular and numerous streets are alive from morning till night with drays and carts and hand-barrows and wagons, with hauling teams and shouting men, with loads of lumber and loads of brick and loads of sand, with piles of furniture and hundreds of packed boxes, with mortar-makers and hod-carriers, with carpenters and masons, with rubbish removers and house-builders, with a never-ending throng of pushing and crowding and scrambling and eager and excited and enterprising men, all bent on building and trading and swift fortune-making. The streets never were either neat or tasty. Now, what with the piles of building material and the greater piles of debris and rubbish, and the vast amount of teaming and hauling over them, they are simply horrible!

Every horse and mule and wagon is in active use. The four railroads centering here groan with the freight and passenger traffic, and yet are unable to meet the demand of the nervous and palpitating city. Men rush about the streets with little regard for comfort or pleasure and yet find the days all too short and too few for the work in hand. The sound of the saw and plane and hammer rings out from daylight till dark, and yet master-builders are worried with offered contracts which they cannot take. There are already over two hundred stores, so called, and yet every day brings some trader who is restless and fretful till he secures a place in which to display another stock of goods. The one sole idea first in every man's mind is to make money. The trade of the city is already thirty percent greater than it was before the war. Few of the present merchants were here before the war; few of them are yet to be considered as permanent residents of the city.

The northwestern counties were all strongly opposed to secession. Its disposition toward the government is now, as a whole, probably better than that of any other district in the state. Its slaves constituted less than one-fourth of its aggregate population before the war, and in general there is much less complaint here than elsewhere as to the disposition of the freedman. The people pretty generally quietly accept the decision of the sword, and the men who prate of state supremacy are far less in number than in the district below. The people of this section are generally hardy and industrious and in many respects are so much unlike those of some other sections of the state that "Cherokee Georgia" is a term of contempt and reproach with the aristocrats and land monopolists of the southern and southeastern parts. (I believe the contempt for labor and the laborer is strong in Georgia. In Americus, I met an ex-colonel, a man of forty-five years, who had a plantation and worked thirty-four Negroes. I asked him how he and his neighbors were getting on with the fall work. "I know nothing about the *work*, sir," said he with a lofty air, in which there was a fine sneer.) Poor they are, having little left but lean bodies and homespun garments, but I judge that the whites of these twenty counties in the northwest have done more work since the close of the war than the whites of any fifty counties below the middle line of the state.

Greensboro
November 25, 1865

Greensboro is the only place of thirty or forty in which I have stopped that may challenge comparison with Northern towns on the score of general appearance. It is the shire town of Greene County, has a population of 1600 to 2000 persons. Thousands of Negroes in this section, where slavery was less a burden than in almost any other part of the South, have left homes wherein they had every needful care and comfort for the uncertain chances of life by themselves. In Greensboro, in Madison, in Sparta, in Milledgeville, in Macon, in Athens, in Washington—go where you will in central Georgia and you cannot fail to come to this conclusion. I know very well that every white man, woman and child in the whole state is ready to swear that every Negro is worse off now than before he was freed. I accept no such evidence, but hundreds of conversations with Negroes in at least a dozen towns of this section have convinced me that the race is ignorantly sacrificing its own material good for the husks of vagabondage.

I went into the outskirts of Macon and hunted up many of the Negroes who had left old homes in the city and surrounding country. I did the same thing at Madison and Milledgeville. Hundreds and hundreds of them will feel the pangs of cold and hunger this winter who might have kept every necessity and many of the comforts of life, if they had chosen to remain with those who formerly held them as slaves. Who shall have the heart to blame them? For they were in search of nothing less noble and glorious than freedom.

Over by the half-built Confederate arsenal in Macon I found a little hut in which were eleven Negroes—an old man, a middle-aged man, three women and six children. There was, beside, in the hut only a couple of bundles of old rags, which answered, I suppose, for beds, three or four rude stools, a single chair, a bag of meal, four or five pounds of bacon, and half a dozen cooking utensils. "Well, uncle," said I, after he had told me that he was raised near Knoxville, some thirty miles away. "Well, uncle, what did you come to the city for? Why didn't you stay on the old place? Didn't you have a kind master?" "I's had a berry good master, mass'r," he said, "but ye see I's wanted to be free man." "But you were just as free there as you are here." "P'r'aps I is, but I's make a livin' up yer, I dun reckon, an' I likes ter be free man whar I's can go an' cum, an' nobody says not'ing." "But you would have been more comfortable on the old place. You would have had plenty to eat and plenty of clothes to wear." "Ye see, mass'r, de good Lo'd He know what's de best t'ing fer de brack, well as fur de w'ite, an' He say ter we dat we should cum up yer, an' I don't reckon He let we starve." I had some further talk with the family but could only get for answer to my many times varied questions that they came to the city to get freedom.

This morning I walked out to the little Negro village near Greensboro, where are living many blacks who were house servants in the town, as well as some who have come in from the country. "Well, auntie," said I to one of them, a weather-beaten old creature who looked as though she had seen at least sixty years. "Well, auntie, how do you get along in your freedom?" "No reason to make complaint, sah. I has sum soin' and some washin' and 'pears like I had nuf ter do." "What did you leave the old place for, auntie, any way?" "What fur? '*Joy my freedom!*'" The directness and exultation of this answer half puzzled and half disconcerted me. What is the "freedom" that war has brought this dusky race?

Augusta
November 28, 1865
Augusta is a fine point for business. "I hate the Yankees with my whole heart," said a genteely dressed woman who sat just behind me in the cars the other day

14

coming to the city. "And I hate them so bad that I'm going off to Texas to live," answered the gentleman with whom she talked. At Atlanta I saw a family of seven persons from the county above this on their way to that region. At Greensboro I saw a family of thirteen, including the old folks, with daughter, son-in-law, and grandchildren, and having a wagonload of trunks, bound for that state. At Berzelia, twenty miles west of here, I fell in with a man who had just returned from an inspection tour and would start for there next week at the head of a company of twenty. I asked him if he didn't like it in this state, to which he answered, "I am going to see if I can't get shet of the Yankees!" A man whom I sat opposite at breakfast this morning told his neighbor that a common acquaintance from Athens left last week, and he knew of another family near Washington who would go in a few days. I am convinced that in the central and eastern sections of Georgia there are many who purpose moving to Texas, and only in one or two instances have I heard any reason assigned but a desire to get away from the Yankees.

"I don't believe I'll ever vote again in my life," said a young man from Athens to me. "The first vote and the only vote I ever cast was for the revolution candidates from our county to the Convention of 1861. I left college and went into service two days after Sumter was fired on, and I stayed in the army to the bitter end. I've got enough of war, and if there is ever another in this country I shall emigrate." "I'm damn glad the war's over, anyhow," said a Madison gentleman to me. He was dressed like a gentleman and mostly spoke like one, but profanity is much more common down here than in the North. "I did all I could for the revolution, and now I'm going to do all I can for the Union. You mustn't ask me to give up my idea of state rights, that's in my bones and never can be got out. But I assure you it shall never give any more trouble, so far as I am concerned."

Waynesboro
November 29, 1865

"There are two places in the state," said an acquaintance to me at Augusta, "where they'd as soon shoot a man as a dog—Albany and Waynesboro!" Waynesboro isn't a lovely place by any means. In fact, I don't see why anybody should desire to live here, and a forced residence of half a year might very well make a man long to be shot. Happily, though the town is the county seat of Burke, but few persons do live here—five hundred perhaps. From Greensboro to Waynesboro is about one hundred miles, but those miles space the distance from civilization to barbarism!

There is hereabouts a strong hatred of the Yankees. In an adjoining county there is a public league of young women who have vowed not to speak to a Federal soldier under any circumstances whatever. Insolent treatment of soldiers and officers on the street is so common that it excites little or no remark. One of the drivers of the stage line tells me that only three days ago a man refused to ride in his coach because an officer of the army had a seat therein. In one neighboring county young ladies have been seen within a fortnight wearing little secession flags in their hats.

As a curious specimen of what one hears, take the following little speech made by an apparently intelligent man to a group of half a dozen persons, of whom I was one: "I've seen an advertisement to the paper for a job of overseeing some plantations next year. I reckon I could do that right lively. O, I tell you, I can do up some tall cussin' when I get started. Can't lick free niggers, but I don't know if there's any law ag'in cussin' 'em, and I believe it does 'em a heap o' good. It's next best to lickin'. Jest cuss one o' 'em right smart for 'bout five minutes, and he'll play off peart. Probably the Yankees don't like that style, but I ha'n't no use for a Yankee no how. I had a lot of likely Negroes, but they're all gone. Had Confederate money, but that's all gone. And I've got a heap o' Confederate bonds, but they a'n't worth a damn. I reckon God Almighty fought on the other side in this war. He used to smile on us, but He hasn't given us anything but frowns lately. I don't care a damn, but I don't like to see my friends all so cut up about it. I can git along well enough. I should like to lick a hundred free Negroes jest once all 'round. If I didn't bring 'em to know their places, I'd pay $10 apiece for all I failed on. But the Yankees give us our orders: we musn't lick the freedmen, they say. Free-damn-cusses I call 'em. I reckon 'ta'n't ag'in no law to swa'r at 'em, and damn me if I can't do that ar. Yes, sir. I 'low 'it won't be wrong to cuss the free niggers. Waal, I ha'n't no use for a Yankee. They're low-down, triflin' fellows, anyhow."

The planters hereabouts are not generally hopeful in regard to free Negro labor. I had some conversation with a knot of them in which the question of white labor came up. "We shall have to have control of the free Negroes or import white men to do the work," said one of them. I asked if the Negroes wouldn't work if they were treated exactly as white men would be in the same circumstances. "No, a free Negro is a free Negro, anyhow." "But," said I, "that way of talking and feeling cannot be beneficial either to him or to your interests. Why not use him fairly like a man?" "The trouble is jest here," said another, "He don't know his place. If you let us alone, we'll teach him, and then I reckon we'll git along with him better." "But what do you mean by teaching him his place?" I asked. A third man took up the question, and answered, "Our people are restive at what they call outside interference. The Negro isn't to blame for his freedom. He served us faithfully all through the war, and I

16

sincerely believe very few planters have any desire to see him injured. We know his ways, and if you give us time, I think we shall be able to get him back into his place again, not as a slave but as a good producer." They kept up a conversation among themselves till the first again responded, "A free Negro is a poor cuss, anyhow."

Savannah
December 2, 1865

There is much want and suffering among the residents of southeastern Georgia. I judge they did not very readily accept the situation last spring. However that may be, there is no question about two facts: they were despoiled of nearly all their property by the rebel army and have made but insignificant crops of all kinds during the present season. I am told that there are at least 2000 respectable white persons in and around Savannah alone who must live mainly on charity through the winter. I know, too, that there are numbers of such persons in nearly all the twenty-five or thirty nearest counties.

Of course, this general destitution effects the Negroes even more seriously than the whites. I shall not exaggerate if I say that hundreds of them have already died in and about Savannah of actual starvation. The Negroes are badly treated in some of the counties west and northwest of the city. I fell in, on yesterday, with a gentleman who has been making a horseback tour in six or eight of them, in search of cotton. He says hundreds of Negroes have been turned off the plantations during the month, with little or no money and but a few bushels of corn, and that many of them will be actually forced into thieving to support life. He saw one Negro woman horsewhipped very severely for some offence and saw a Negro man who had been shot in the arm for declining at first to be turned off the plantation where he had worked all summer. He also tells me that some of the members elect of the legislature are pledged to resist all efforts to give the Negro the right to sue or be heard as evidence in the courts.

The freedmen throughout this section are somewhat disinclined to make contracts for another season. The rice plantation Negroes are very slow to comprehend the fact that freedom does not mean idleness, being the most degraded specimens of the race I have anywhere found.

I have fallen in with a gentleman of middle age who was in the rebel army about three years. He claims to have been always a Union man and says his service in the army was compulsory. We fell into some talk on the condition of the state and the prospects of the future. This, almost word for word, is what he said: "The Negro's first want is, not the ballot, but a chance to live. You say the government has given him freedom and that many good men in the North believe he must have the ballot to secure that freedom. I tell you he's not got his freedom yet and isn't likely to get it right away. Why, he can't even live without the consent of the white man! He has no land. He can make no crops except the white man gives him a chance. He hasn't any timber. He can't get a stick of wood without leave from a white man. He can scarcely get work anywhere but in the rice fields and cotton plantations of a white man who has owned him and given up slavery only at the point of the bayonet. Even in this city he can't get a pail of water from a well without asking a white man for the privilege. He can hardly breathe, and he certainly can't live in a house, unless a white man gives his consent. What sort of freedom is that?

"He has freedom in name, but not in fact. In many respects he is worse off than he was before you made him free, for then the property interest of his master protected him, and now his master's hand as well as the hand of everybody else is against him. It isn't whippings that most wrong the Negro; it's the small, endless, mean little injustices of every day that's going to kill him off. He's only partially protected now. Take the troops away, and his chance wouldn't be as good as a piece of light wood in a house on fire."

⌈ 3 ⌋

Though Atlanta has a cheap and squalid look, it evinces much energy and life . . . the middle of the city a wilderness of mud with a confused jumble of railway sheds and rails, where engines constantly puff and whistle, unfinished houses, scaffolding, piles of lumber and brick and sand, the noise of carpenters and masons.

JOHN R. DENNETT, 1865

JOHN RICHARD DENNETT (1838–1874), born in New Brunswick, moved to Massachusetts as a child. After graduating from Harvard College in 1862, he served with Federal forces that occupied the sea island of South Carolina and returned to Harvard Law School in 1864–65. In the summer of 1865, Dennett began a nine-month tour of the defeated South as a reporter for *The Nation*, visiting Georgia in December. Dennett was later taught rhetoric at Harvard and was a staff member of *The Nation*. His reports from Georgia were published in *The Nation* in 1865 and 1866.

Augusta is a well-built town, well situated on the Savannah River. My stay there was only long enough for a walk through the principal streets, which are regularly laid out, level and so exceedingly wide as almost to dwarf the rows of buildings on either side. They were cheerful with a busy press of pedestrians of various colors and streams of vehicles. There was a vast display of goods in the warehouses and shops, and the newspapers were filled with advertisements of every kind. By its position Augusta is the seat of a large jobbing business, the river and the railroad connect it with the ports of Charleston and Savannah, and it is enabled to avail itself of these advantages, for it has received its full measure of the Northern capital which, since the surrender, has been poured into every Southern town.

There is apparent a willingness, often an anxiety even, to secure Northern men as lessees of plantations, and large tracts of land, well improved and productive, are everywhere offered for sale at low prices, sometimes at prices that may be called ruinously low. "These freedmen will work a heap better for a Yankee than they will for one of us," it is frequently said. Other causes of this sacrifice of lands and rents are to be found in the belief that the free labor of the Negroes cannot be made profitable, and in the fact that many men who have much land have no money with which to cultivate it. But although much land may still be bought cheap, there are some signs that these causes will not continue to operate so extensively as heretofore. Often I hear it predicted that cotton is going to command a very high price for some years to come, that therefore its culture may be profitable though the laborers should work a smaller number of acres than in old times, and occasionally some local newspaper announces that the gloomy prospects of the planters are brightening, that the Negroes who, after all, showed so commendable a spirit of devotion, faithfulness and obedience during the war are beginning in certain districts to make contracts and profess a willingness to receive a share of the crop as wages.

But however the case may be as regards the business relations of Northern men in the South, I should consider it advisable for the newcomer, if he desires agreeable social intercourse with his neighbors in almost any part of the South that I have yet seen, to restrain the free expression of any social or political opinions distinctively Northern.

It was on a Sunday that I made the journey, 171 miles long, between Augusta and Atlanta, and all day the rain was pouring steadily, so that we could see the country turning to mud as we passed and every stream growing yellower. We were able to ride all the way, however, for the bridges stood, and our train went on without delay. Among the passengers were Jews, drummers from New York, a few women and men from nearly every Southern state. Everybody seemed resolved to lighten as much as possible the fatigues of travelling. Some slept, there were many whiskey flasks in circulation, fowls were eaten, the news-papers of Chicago, Louisville and Nashville could be bought, a one-armed man in the rebel uniform sold cigars and it was assumed that the ladies would make no objection if they were smoked. In the course of the afternoon, two or three of my neighbors, who had told each other all the stories they knew, began comparing their pistols and disputing about the comparative merits of the patterns.

As we approached Atlanta, of course we saw burned buildings at the way stations, rails fantastically twisted and bent and ruined locomotives—remembrances of Sherman and Johnston. It was too dark when we arrived in the city to see anything but the lights and an occasional rocket shooting through the rain. It was Christmas Eve, and it appears to be usual in the South to celebrate the coming of this festival with Chinese crackers and other fireworks.

Atlanta, as I saw it on Christmas morning, was a most cheerless and mean-looking place. The sky was dropping rain, and underfoot the mud was almost ankle-deep. It had rained for three weeks. People walked slowly, treading with careful steps in the footprints—slowly getting narrower in the soft mud—of those who had ventured before them. The middle of the city is a great open space of irregular shape, a wilderness of mud, with a confused jumble of railway sheds, and traversed by numberless rails, rusted and splashed, where strings of dirty cars are standing and engines constantly puff and whistle. In one place I saw beside the track a heap of bones and skulls of animals, collected from battlefields and the line of march for some factory, moulding and blackening in the wet weather. Bricks and blocks of stone and other rubbish were everywhere. Around this central square the city was formerly built and is now again building. Unfinished houses are to be seen on every hand; scaffolding, mortar-beds and lime-barrels, piles of lumber and bricks and mounds of sand choke every street, and the whole place on working days resounds with the noise of carpenters and masons. The city is hardly less pleasing to the eye than the people. A great many rough-looking fellows hang about the numerous shops and the shanties among the ruins where liquor is sold, and a knot of them cluster at each street corner. The gray coats are almost as numerous as the blue uniforms, often very dirty, of the white and Negro soldiers, some of whom are always on guard in the streets. White women are but seldom seen, perhaps because the sidewalks are nearly impassable. The men are obliged to wear the bottoms of their trousers tucked in their boots. Negroes of all colors abound.

But though Atlanta, in spite of its newness, has a cheap and squalid look, which is depressing, it evinces much energy and life. Trade of all kinds is extremely active. The city is full of goods, and though the number of traders seems inordinately great, new ones are pushing into business. To a stranger it appears as if the feverish activity of the mercantile community must eventually bring on a crash, but the citizens indulge in glowing anticipations of the future prosperity and growth of their town. They point to the railroads centering here and say that if the country around to be supplied with goods was poorer than it is and less productive, the mere storage and trans-shipment of freight would suffice to make Atlanta a great city.

In walking about the town on Christmas morning my attention was attracted by a crowd of two hundred colored people and a few whites gathered about the door of the city hall. They were listening to an address from Colonel Curkendall of the Freedmen's Bureau. He had made many a horseshoe nail, he said, but he had never before made a speech. All his life he had been a working man, and he supposed that they, too, would be working men as long as they lived. He had the meanest kind of a camp close by, with about 650 colored people in it receiving rations from the government, and if anyone of his audience was not able-bodied and could get no work to do and was starving, he would put him into that camp and let him have a little hard tack and a poor place to sleep till he could find some work to do. There was no comfort for them anywhere without hard work for honest wages. No land would be given them. They knew that, it was responded from the crowd. Very well, then, they probably knew that some persons were expecting a Negro insurrection about this time. Yes, they said. Yes, Colonel, they knew that, too, and they agreed with him that, though he was not a very big man, he would be able to put down all the insurrectionary movements that would be made by the Negroes of northern Georgia. He believed they would behave like men. Every right that he had, except one, was already theirs by law. The right of suffrage they would probably get if they showed themselves qualified to exercise it. In the exercise of every other right he would certainly protect them. Exact justice should be administered, whether it took a black man or a white man to jail.

Then the Colonel spoke of education and gave good advice in reference to a great many points of conduct and character, and at the end was loudly applauded. When he told them that there were many good men in Georgia who would be their friends if they were industrious and well-behaved, who would deal justly with them and take care that the bad men of the community did not impose upon them, the Negroes cordially assented. "That's what we want," they said, when he told them that hard work and the education of their children would soon put the ballot into the hands of every Negro in the South. I noticed in the crowd several men with badges of colored ribbons. They were members of two associations, I was informed—the Union League and the Sons of Liberty— which have been formed for mutual aid and counsel. Neither of them is a secret society, and both have invited the inspection of the Freedmen's Bureau.

As the meeting broke up, I walked toward my hotel and was soon overtaken by a soldier who walked along beside me and wished me a merry Christmas. "It's Christmas Day," he said, "that's what's the matter!" Then in a minute, as we met two Negroes, he added, "And I'm goin' to punch every damned nigger I see!" With that he struck first one and then the other Negro a violent blow in the face. The men seemed too much astonished to retaliate. Afterwards quite an affray occurred between some white soldiers and Negroes, which resulted in some slight injuries to the latter, two being wounded by bullets, and in the arrest of the soldiers by the provost marshall's guard, which patrolled the streets for the rest of the day. In the course of the afternoon a colored man was shot and killed by a citizen in an altercation about the right to the sidewalk. I also met a Negro who had been severely wounded above the eyes with a knife, and was then on his way to Colonel Curkendall to make complaint.

At the office of the Freedmen's Bureau in Atlanta it was said in answer to my questions that a minority of the planters are disposed to treat their laborers kindly and justly. A majority are indisposed to give adequate wages and to recognize in practice that the Negroes are free, that the Negroes evinced an unwillingness to make contracts unless in cases where the person wishing to employ them was a Northern man. The names of three men were given me, all of whom had been officers in the Federal army who proposed planting cotton next year and who were offering as wages $12 a month, together with board, clothing and medical attendance, that no courts had as yet been established for the trial of causes in which Negroes are parties but every case is tried and all sentences are passed by the Colonel himself, that the operations of the Bureau are to a great extent crippled by the want of cavalry, cases of fraud and cruelty occurring at a distance from the town and from railroads necessarily go unpunished, that the military officers throughout the district of which Colonel Curkendall has charge could probably be depended upon to do justice between the whites and the Negroes, that very few complaints of any kind had ever been reported by the garrison officers in the country. In the Atlanta office I found recorded, as having occurred during the fortnight ending December 13, four cases of abuse and cruelty. Two complaints, one of assault with intent to kill, and one of assault and robbery, were made while I was in the office. The average number of applications for redress is twelve each day.

Major R——— of the 187th Ohio Volunteers and Captain C——— of the same regiment not long ago secured a three years' lease of two plantations situated in Stewart County and owned by a Mr. W———. They intended to cultivate cotton and, having purchased all the requiste implements and a sufficient number of mules to stock both places, they sent down forty Negroes to live on one of them, while they themselves remained in Macon and awaited the mustering out of their regiment. This event, however, not taking place so soon as was expected, Captain C——— went down into the country to perfect his arrangements for planting and, very much to his surprise, was met by his landlord with a proposal that he and his partner should withdraw from the further prosecution of their enterprise, inasmuch as persisting would bring trouble upon all concerned in it. The neighbors, he was told, had given Mr. W——— to understand that no Yankee should be suffered to live in that country, that if he rented land to those two Yankees his tenants shouldn't live to harvest their crops and his own house should be burned over his head. Out of consideration, therefore, for him and his property, if not for their own safety, he begged them not to disregard these threats, which were made by men who would carry them out, but to abandon their project. The Captain and his friend have given up all intention of planting in Georgia and propose to invest their money in some Northern state.

Another gentleman, who, during the past summer, administered a military office which brought him into contact with very many people and gave him opportunities for conferring obligations upon all of them, said that when a few months since he left the service and went North he flattered himself with the idea that he had a great many warm friends in Georgia and was exceedingly popular throughout the district in which he had been on duty. He decided to return, therefore, and establish himself in business in one of the most flourishing towns in the state. He had an intelligent partner and both members of the new firm worked hard and paid close attention to business, without, however, reaping any adequate reward for their exertions. By-and-bye he learned, through the detectives employed by the district commander, that there were several persons who entertained the intention of killing him as soon as an opportunity presented itself! He became aware, also, that it was commonly said in the town that he should not sell goods there or grow rich on Southern money. He could see nothing better to do than to sell out his share in the business to his partner, who was a Southerner, and the store is now, he tells me, quite liberally patronized. To the recital of these facts he adds the remark: "This country won't be any place for Yankees or niggers when the troops are mustered out. When the military goes, I'm going too!"

The condition of the freedmen in the country around Macon, so far as I could learn from the Sub-Assistant Commissioner of the Bureau, is exceedingly satisfactory. This officer has his headquarters in Macon, and the district over which he presides embraces thirty-four counties. In each county he has three subordinates, who were appointed from among the citizens on the recommendation of the delegates to the Constitutional Convention, and many of the delegates having been willing themselves to accept the government of the freedmen in their own neighborhood, the office was, in many instances, conferred upon them. They receive no salary, but in all cases which are tried before them they are allowed to retain such fees as are customary in justices' courts. The Bureau, I was informed, contrary to the character which it generally bears, is quite a popular institution in the Military District of Columbus.

The Negroes are quiet and well-behaved, and conducted themselves admirably during the holidays, not a single complaint having been made against them. The white people were very apprehensive of a rising of the freedmen, and in some places the militia picketed the roads and patrolled the country in all directions. During the last week of 1865 three Negroes were killed, and, of course, a great many outrages of less consequence were committed. The murderers of one Negro had not been arrested, but those of the other two were caught, and were now awaiting trial before a military commission.

From General Dawson, who is in command of the sub-district, I learned further particulars of the picketing above mentioned. The United States officers in Georgia refuse, I believe, to supply the state militia with arms, call on them for no assistance and hardly recognize that they exist. In Monroe County, contrary to the proclamation of the provisional governor, the citizens formed not one but two or three companies of volunteers. Then they requested the withdrawal of the Federal troops, and the request was compiled with, the garrison being withdrawn a fortnight before Christmas. During Christmas week the difficulties between the militiamen and the freedmen began. Negroes were stopped on the roads, which were all patrolled or picketed. Some of them were beaten, all were searched and compelled to give an account of themselves, and one was killed.

General Dawson, as well as some of the gentlemen mentioned above as having suffered from the hatred of the Southern men towards their Northern countrymen, united in saying that the persons who disgrace themselves and the community to which they belong by outrageous acts and words are but a minority of the Southern people, and that the men of wealth and social standing and, in general, the elderly men, as distinguished from the young men and the women, are well disposed towards the U.S. Government. He deprecated the complete removal of the U.S. troops from the country and thought the process of mustering out had already gone too far.

The Negroes, I was told, are very generally entering into contracts with the planters, and it is thought that almost all will have found employers before the 1st of February. All Negroes who at that time shall be unemployed and not willing to make contracts, it is the intention of the Commissioner to arrest and treat as vagrants. The demand for labor is greater than the supply, and the Commissioner has frequent calls made upon him for able-bodied men to go to other states and to other parts of Georgia. With these calls, however, he does not comply, being unwilling to drain off all the young and strong men and leave in his district a disproportionate number of women, children and aged persons. By a recent order of General Tillson, the compensation for the labor of a full hand is fixed at $12 a month [with] food and proper medical attendance. This order creates much dissatisfaction among the planters, as they had previously been hiring laborers for food, medicine and $10 a month.

All along the road from Macon to Columbus is the familiar scene of desolate-looking forest with now and then a way-station with its dozen or so of loungers and its Negro women selling cakes, and now and then a watering tank and a wood-pile, where usually the passengers walk about a little, examine the engine, look back at the long, undulating line of the track and wonder, perhaps, that such rails have been able to bear the train safely thus far. Inside the cars also the scene is familiar—here and there a uniform, gray or blue, one or two families, man, wife and children, who seem to be seeking a new home, or, more likely, returning to an old one which is safe now that the war is done and the husband is out of the army, a few Northerners and many men unmistakably Southern in manner and language.

The conversation, which may be heard by snatches, is on various topics, the chief being the war and its experiences and the Negro. The prospects of making cotton by free labor are often discussed, and one man gives details of his farming plans for the coming season and tells of the operations of the Freedmen's Bureau, an institution which commonly is severely denounced, though once in a while a man commends its action in his particular case. I hear President Johnson praised at the expense of the Radicals in Congress. While riding on this train, I noticed also one or two illustrations of the fact that the women of the South are outspoken in their dislike of the Federal soldiers. Just in front of me were two young ladies and, as the cars stopped at a little village, we saw two men on crutches. On the platform were also some of the garrison. "It makes my heart ache," murmured one of the ladies, "to see our poor wounded Confederates. And look at those creatures in blue mixing with them!" Not long afterwards these ladies left the cars and their places were occupied by three others of less pleasing appearance, whose voices could be heard even above the noise of the wheels. Two soldiers sat in a seat across the aisle, and were compelled to hear much loud talk about "the miserable Yanks" who had stolen the corn and meat of such a person or who were the probable destroyers of this or that building by the roadside. Officers on duty in Columbus tell me that some of the women still carefully gather up the folds of their dresses when they approach a man in the Federal uniform and prefer crossing the street to walking under the national flag.

Columbus is about a hundred miles from Macon, and the journey was made in nine tedious hours. The town is built on flat land and is a pretty place with many trees and like Augusta in the great width of its thoroughfares. These are not in the best order, but that is a matter of small consequence, for each driver has a broad expanse of roadway from which he may choose a path. Cows and pigs wander up and down in them without molestation. One of the pigs I praised as I was standing in a shop on Broad Street. "Yes," said the shopman, who was a small dealer in groceries and an Irishman, " 'tis a fine hog and ye may be sure it's a nigger's. One o' them would ha' knocked it on the head if 'twas a white man's was runnin' the street like that!" Then he went on to lament the changed times and customs. "The niggers is above work now and is all for living like gentlemen and ladies. Every one o' them in Columbus had seven or eight other ones living about him and stealing for him. When they was slaves they all had plenty o' money, and eating and drinking to their hearts' content and now they had nothing and wouldn't work to earn. It would be a fine day when the Yankees should be off about their business, and the people left to manage their own niggers themselves. Then they'd be brought to their senses. When one o' them runs away from his lawful work, then a man'll just take his pistol in his hand and get on his horse and, faith, if the nigger won't come back with that, he'll be welcome to stay where he's left! It was nothing but the Yankees made them so much above themselves."

Like the other large towns of Georgia, Columbus wears an appearance of more prosperity than is seen in other Southern cities and seems to be a busy place, its show of activity being perhaps partly due to the large number of idle people in the streets. The Chattahoochee, a reddish stream of considerable size, runs close by the town and adds much to its beauty. The weather during my stay has been charmingly mild and soft, many of the trees are green, the flowers are in blossom in the gardens, it is so warm, and under my open windows the children are playing barefooted.

I find that the freedmen and the farmers in this part of Georgia are now busily preparing for the work of the coming season. Since the 1st of January the officers of the Freedmen's Bureau have recorded in their books ninety-nine contracts, the great majority of which were entered into by the plantation Negroes with their employers, and each day several new ones are brought in for approval. In the month of December six contracts were put on record. The branch of the Bureau here established has charge of three counties, Chattahoochee, Muscogee and Talbot, and it is by citizens of this district that nearly all these contracts have been made. The amount of compensation given the laborer is very variable. I was told that the order issued by General Tillson, fixing the minimum rate of wages at $12 a month for a full hand, had never been enforced here and, indeed, that it had never been heard of. Most of the Negroes, therefore, have been hired for less than that, though I am informed that now $14 per month is offered. In the majority of the contracts which I examined, the planter binds himself to pay the laborer for one year's work $120 and his board. I found five instances in which Negroes had leased land. In one case a third of all the produce was to be given to the owner as rent; in another, one-fifth; in another, where forty acres of land were rented, the lessees were to pay $250 and forty-eight bushels of meal; in another, one-half of the crops was to be paid. There was one record of an indenture of apprenticeship. A boy of seven years old had been bound out by his mother for fourteen years, the master agreeing "to provide for all his temporal wants and learn him to read and write if he will take it, and at twenty-one give him a suit of clothes." The officer of the Bureau in Columbus, who is very soon to be mustered out of the service, is decidedly of opinion that a large majority of the planters will be kind and just towards their laborers, and that his successor will have but little difficulty in his dealings with those two classes of persons.

[4]

Every business block in Atlanta was burned, except one. Hundreds of inhabitants were living in wretched hovels, covered with ragged fragments of tin from burnt buildings, kept from blowing away by stones placed on the top. Everywhere were ruins and rubbish, mud and mortar and misery.

J. T. TROWBRIDGE, 1866

JOHN T. TROWBRIDGE (1827–1916) was born in New York. A teacher and writer based in Boston, he produced some forty volumes of poetry, novels and plays. He made two trips to the South following the Civil War, in the summer of 1865 and winter of 1866. These selections are drawn from Trowbridge's *The South, A Tour of its Battle-Fields and Ruined Cities* (Hartford, 1866), pp. 452–510.

I reached Atlanta at 7 o'clock in the evening. It was a foggy night. The streets were not lighted, the hotels were full, and the mud, through which I tramped from one to the other, with a dark guide and a very dark lantern, was ankle deep on the crossings. I was at length fortunate enough to find lodgings with a clergyman and a cotton speculator in an ancient tavern room, where we were visited all night by troops of rats, scampering across the floor, rattling newspapers and capering over our beds. In the morning, it was discovered that the irreverent rogues had stolen the clergyman's stockings.

Everywhere were ruins and rubbish, mud and mortar and misery. The burnt streets were rapidly rebuilding, but in the meanwhile hundreds of the inhabitants, white and black, rendered homeless by the destruction of the city, were living in wretched hovels. Some of the Negro huts were covered entirely with ragged fragments of tin roofing from the burnt government and railroad buildings. Others were constructed partly of these irregular blackened patches and partly of old boards with roofs of huge, warped, slouching shreds of tin, kept from blowing away by stones placed on the top. "In dry weather, it's good as anybody's houses. But they leaks right bad when it rains. Then we have to pile our things up to keep 'em dry," said a colored mother of six children, who

28

supported her family of little ones by washing. "Sometimes I gits along toler-able, sometimes right slim. But dat's de way wid everybody. Times is powerful hard right now."

Every business block in Atlanta was burned, except one. The railroad ma-chine shops, the foundries, the immense rolling mill, the tent, pistol, gun car-riage, shot-and-shell factories and storehouses of the late Confederacy disap-peared in flames and explosions. Half a mile of the principal street was destroyed. "When I came back in May," said a refugee, "the city was nothing but piles of brick and ruins. It didn't seem it could ever be cleared. But in six weeks new blocks began to spring up, till now you see more stores actually in operation than we ever had before."

The new business blocks were mostly one-story structures, with cheap tem-porary roofs, designed to be rebuilt and raised in more prosperous times. Nine stores of this description had just been put up by a Connecticut man, each cost-ing $3000 and renting for $2500. "He run a rolling mill for the Confederate government during the war, sold out when Sherman was coming, called him-self a good Union man—a mighty shrewd fellow!" said one who knew him.

Here and there between the new buildings were rows of shanties used as stores and gaps containing broken walls and heaps of rubbish. Rents were enormous. The destitution among both white and black refugees was very great. Many of the whites had lost everything by the war, and the Negroes that were run off by their masters in advance of Sherman's army had returned to a desolate place with nothing but the rags on their backs. The smallpox was raging at Atlanta, chiefly among the blacks and the suffering poor whites.

I stopped to talk with an old man building a fence before the lot containing the ruins of his burnt house. He said, "The Yankees didn't generally burn private dwellings. It's my opinion these were set by our own citizens that remained after Sherman's order that all women who had relatives in the Southern army should go south and all males must leave the city except them that would work for government. I put for Chattanooga. My house was plundered and, I reckon, burnt by my own neighbors, for I've found some of my furniture in their houses. Some that stayed acted more honorably. They put out fires that had been set and saved both houses and property. My family is now living in that shebang there. It was formerly my stable. The weatherboards had been ripped off, but I fixed it up the best I could to put my little 'uns in till we can do better."

Walking out one Sunday afternoon to visit the fortifications, I stopped to look at a Negro's horse which had been crippled by a nail in his foot. While I was talking with the owner, a white man and two Negroes, who had been sit-ting by a fire in an open rail cabin close by, conversing on terms of perfect equality, came out to take part in the consultation. "If ye had some tare," said the white man, meaning tar, "open his huf and bile tare and pour int'it." His lank frame and slouching dress, his sallow visage with its sickly, indolent expression, his lazy, spiritless movements and the social intimacy that appeared to exist between him and the Negroes indicated that he belonged to the class known as "crackers" in Georgia. He told me his name was Jesse Wade. "I lived down in Cobb," seating himself on the neap of the Negro's wagon and mechanically scraping the mud from it with his thumbnail. "I was a Union man, I was that, like my daddy befo'e me. Thar was no use me bein' a fule 'case my neighbors was. The Rebel army treated us a heap wus'n Sherman did. I refugeed, left everything keer o' my wife. I had four bales o' cotton, and the Rebs burnt the last bale. I had hogs and a mule and a hoss, and they tuk all. They didn't leave my wife narry bedquilt. When they'd tuk what they wanted, they put her out the house and sot fire to't. Narry one o' my boys fit agin the Union. They was conscripted with me, and one night we went out on guard together, we did, and jest put for the Yankees! All the men that had a little property went in for the wa', but the po' people was agin it. Sherman was up yer to Kenesaw Mountain then, and I left, I did, to jine him."

He was very poor. "I've got two hosses and a wagon, and I shouldn't have them if Sherman hadn't gin 'em tu me." He held up his feet and looked at his toes protruding through great gaps in his shoes. "I kain't git money enough to buy me a new pair to save my life." I asked Wade how old he was. "I'm in my fifty-one year old," he replied, "and thar's eight on us in the family and tu hosses." I inquired concerning education in his county. "Thar's a heap o' po' men in Cobb that kain't read nor write. I'm one. I never went to skule narry time, and I was alluz so tight run I never could send my chil'n, only 'tween crap time." "What do you mean by 'crap time'?" "When I'd laid by my crap," that is, stopped hoeing it. By this time a large number of Negroes had assembled on the spot, and such an animated discussion of their political rights ensued that I quietly withdrew, followed by my friend Wade, who wished to know if I could accommodate him to a "chaw of tobacker."

My last view of Atlanta was received on a foggy morning, which showed me, as I sat in the cars of the Macon train, waiting at the depot, groups of rain-drenched Negroes around outdoor fires, the dimly seen trees of the park, tall ruins looming through the mist, Masonic Hall standing alone (having escaped destruction), squat wooden buildings of recent, hasty construction, bent railroad iron by the track, piles of brick, a small mountain of old bones from the battlefields, foul and wet with the drizzle, a heavy coffin box marked "glass" on the platform, with mud and litter all around.

A tide of Negro emigration was at that time flowing westward from the comparatively barren hills of northern Georgia to the rich cotton plantations

30

of the Mississippi. Every day anxious planters from the Great Valley were to be met with, inquiring for unemployed freedmen or returning home with colonies of laborers who had been persuaded to quit their old haunts by the promise of double wages in a new country. Georgia planters, who raise but a bale of cotton on three, four or five acres, could not compete with their more wealthy Western neighbors. As it cost no more to transport able-bodied young men and women than the old and the feeble, the former were generally selected and the latter left behind. Thus it happened that an unusually large proportion of poor [black] families remained about Atlanta and other Georgia towns. Two such families, huddled that morning under the open shed of the depot, claimed that they had been hired by a planter, who had brought them thus far and abandoned them. They had been at the depot a week or more, sleeping in piles of old rags and subsisting on rations issued by the [Freedmen's] Bureau.

To me the most noticeable feature of the scene was the spirit manifested towards these poor creatures by spectators of my own color. "That baby's going to die," said one man. "Half your children will be dead before spring." "How do you like freedom?" said another. "Niggers are fated," said a third. "About one out of fifty will take care of himself. The rest are gone up." "The Southern people are the niggers' best friends," resumed the first speaker. "They feel a great deal of sympathy for them. There are many who give them a heap of good advice when they leave them." The remarks of the ladies in the car were equally edifying. "How much better they were off with somebody to take care of 'em!" "Oh, dear, yes! I declare it makes me hate an Abolitionist!" "The government ought to have given them houses!" Sneeringly, "If I had seven children to take care of, I'd go back and sell 'em to my old master." "Do see that little bit of a baby! It's a-kicking and screaming! I declare, it's white! One of the young Federals', I reckon."

From Atlanta, until within about twenty-five miles of Macon, the railroad runs upon a ridge. The doorways of the log huts and shabby framed houses we passed were crowded with black, yellow and sallow white faces, women, children and slatternly, barefoot girls, with long, uncombed hair on their shoulders, staring at the train.

Macon, at the head of steamboat navigation on the Ocmulgee River, is a place of broad, pleasant streets. It was a sort of city of refuge, where everybody was run to during the latter years of the war. Hundreds of white refugees from other parts of the country were still crowded into it, having no means of returning to their homes or having no homes to return to. Sherman's army left nothing in its track but poverty and ruin. The people raised no crops in '65, and a famine was generally anticipated. In this condition, all the better class of planters recognized the sincere efforts of the Freedmen's Bureau to aid them and to organize a labor system which should prove beneficial to both employers and employed. They generally spoke of its officers with respect. Others were bitter in their opposition to it. I often heard such remarks as this: "The idea of a *nigger* having the power of bringing a *white man* before a tribunal! The Southern people ain't going to stand that!"

Colonel Lambert, Sub-Assistant Commissioner of the Freedmen's Bureau, had on hand sixteen cases of murder and felonious shooting by white persons, Negroes being the victims. These Negro-shooters and their accomplices were no doubt a small minority of the people, but they were a very dangerous minority. Crimes of this description were more or less frequent in districts remote from the military posts. In some places the freedmen were shot down in mere wantonness and malice. In others, the very men who had been wishing them all dead or driven out of the country had become enraged at seeing them emigrate for higher wages than they were willing to pay and sworn to kill any that attempted to leave the state. Said Colonel Lambert, "To prevent these outrages, we need a much greater military force than we have. But the force we have is being reduced by the mustering out of more troops."

The Negro of middle Georgia is a creature in whom the emotions entirely predominate over the intellectual faculties. The agents of the Bureau sometimes had great difficulty in persuading him to act in accordance with his own interests. If a stranger offered him $12 a month and a former master in whom he had confidence, appealing to his gratitude and affection, offered him $1, he would exclaim impulsively, "I work for you, Mass'r Will!" Sometimes, when he had been induced by his friends to enter a complaint against his master or mistress for wrongs done him, ludicrous scenes occurred in the freedmen's courts. "Now, Thomas," says the good lady, "can you have the heart to speak a word against your old, dear, kind mistress?" "No, missus, I neber will!" blubbers Thomas, and that is all the court can get out of him. The reverence shown by the colored people toward the officers of the Bureau was often amusing. They looked to them for what they had formerly depended upon their masters for. If they had lost a pig, they seemed to think such great, all-powerful men could find it for them without any trouble. They cheered them in the streets and paid them at all times the most abject respect.

There were four freedmen's schools in Macon with eleven teachers and a thousand pupils. There was a night school of two hundred children and adults, where I saw men of my own age learning their letters and grey-haired old men and women forming, with slowness and difficulty, the first characters in the writing book. I found the freedmen's schools in Georgia supported by the New England Freedmen's Aid Society and the American Missionary Association. These were confined to a few localities, principally to large towns. There were sixty-two schools with eighty-nine teachers and 6600 pupils. The opposition to freedmen's schools on the part of the whites was generally bitter, and in several counties school houses had been burned and the teachers driven away on the withdrawal of the troops.

Travelling by private conveyance from Eatonton over to Madison on my way to Augusta, I passed a night at a planter's house of the middle class. It was a plain, one-and-a-half story, unpainted, weather-browned framed dwelling, with a porch in front and two front windows. The oaken floors were carpetless but clean swept. The rooms were not done off at all. There was not a lath nor any appearance of plastering or whitewash about them. The rafters and shingles of the roof formed the ceiling of the garret chamber, the sleepers and boards of the chamber floor the ceiling of the sitting room and the undisguised beams, studs and clapboards of the frame and its covering composed the walls. The dining room was a little detached framed box without a fireplace and with a single broken window. There was a cupboard, a wardrobe and a bed in the sitting room, a little bedroom leading off from it and two beds in the garret.

There was a glowing fire in the fireplace, beside which sat a neatly attired, fine-looking grandmother, taking snuff or smoking. The house had three other inmates, the planter and his wife and their son, who sat reading by the light of pitch pine chips thrown at intervals upon the fire. No candle was lighted except for me at bedtime. This was not the house of a small farmer but of the owner of two plantations of a thousand acres each. He had fifty-nine Negroes before the war.

The young man was far more hopeful of success than his father. The old man said, "You can't get anything out of the niggers, now they're free." After he was gone, the young man remarked emphatically, "The great trouble in this country is the people are mad at the niggers because they're free. They always believed they wouldn't do well if they were emancipated and now they maintain, and some of them even hope, they won't do well—that, too, in the face of actual facts! The old planters have no confidence in the niggers, and as a matter of course the niggers have no confidence in them. They have a heap more confidence in their young masters, and they work well for us. They have still more confidence in the Yankees. They won't steal from them like they will from us. The country is full of thieving darkies that think it's no wrong to take from a Southern white man."

The house was on the main road traversed by the left wing of Sherman's army on its way from Madison to Milledgeville. Said the young man's mother, "They commenced passing early in the morning, and there wasn't an hour in the day that they were not as thick as blue pigeons along the road. My husband was away, and I had nobody with me but our Negroes. A German soldier came into the house first of any, an ugly-looking fellow as ever I saw. Said he, 'I've orders to get a saddle from this house.' I told him my husband had done gone off with the only saddle we had. Then he said, 'A pistol will do.' I said I had no pistol. Then he told me he must have a watch of me. I told him I had none for him. He then looked all around the room and said, 'Madam, I have orders to burn this house. I'll insure it for $50.' That's the way they get a heap of money out of our people. I said, 'I've no $50 to pay for insuring it, and, if it depends upon that, burn it!' Soon as he saw he couldn't frighten me into giving him anything, he went to plundering. He had found a purse with $5 in Confederate money when he saw an officer coming into the front door and escaped through the back door. The officer said if he was caught he would be punished. The Yankee officer gave me a guard to keep soldiers from plundering the house. Some families on this road, who had no guard, were so broken up they had nothing left to keep house with. What was outdoors nothing could prevent the soldiers from taking. I had bee-gum, and they just carried it off, hives and all. A soldier would catch up a hive and march right along with it on his head and with the bees swarming all about him. I reckon they wouldn't sting Yankees!"

During the evening, I paid a visit to the freedmen's quarters. The doors of the huts were all open in a row, and I could see a dozen Negro families grouped around cheerful fires within, basking in the yellow light and looking quite happy and comfortable.

On the road to Augusta, my attention was attracted by the conversation of a Georgian. We had just passed Union Point, where there was considerable excitement about an unknown Negro found lying out in the woods sick with the small pox. "The trouble is just here," said the Georgian. "The niggers have never been used to taking care of their own sick. Formerly, their masters had them taken care of. If they've a sick baby, they let it die. They're like so many children themselves. I exercise the same care over *my* niggers I always did. Only one ever left me. He said one day he thought he ought to have wages. He went and took his family. In six weeks he came back again. 'I want to come and live with you again, master, like I always have,' he said. 'Edward,' I said, 'I am very sorry. You wanted to go, and I got another man in your place. Now I have nothing for you to do, and your cabin is occupied.' He just burst into tears. 'I've lived with you all my days, master,' he said, 'and now I have no home!' I couldn't stand that. 'Take an ax,' I said, 'go into the woods, cut some poles and build you a cabin. As long as I have a home, you shall have one.'"

Arriving in Augusta that night, I went to call on General Tillson, Assistant Commissioner [of the Freedmen's Bureau] for the state. Over $3000 had been paid in fines by the people of Georgia for cruelties to the freedmen during the past three months. "It is considered no murder to kill a Negro," said General

Tillson. "The best men in the state admit that no jury would convict a white man for killing a freedman or fail to hang a Negro who had killed a white man in self-defence." The General added, "As soon as the troops were withdrawn from Wilkes County last November, a gang of jay-hawkers went through, shooting and burning the colored people, holding their feet and hands in the fire to make them tell where their money was. It left such a stigma on the county that the more respectable class held a meeting to denounce it. This class is ashamed of such outrages but does not prevent them. And I could name a dozen cases of murder committed on the colored people by young men of these first families!"

The track of the Central Railroad, 191 miles in length, was destroyed by Sherman's army. There was still an impassable hiatus—a distance of 100 miles— of bent rails and burnt bridges. The relaid tracks were very rough, many of the old rails having been straightened and put down again. "General Grant and his staff passed over this road a short time ago," said a citizen, "and, as they went jolting along in an old boxcar on plain board seats, they seemed to think it was great fun. They said they were riding on Sherman's *hair-pins!*" Riding along the destroyed tracks, it was amusing to see the curious shapes in which the iron had been left. Hair-pins predominated. Corkscrews were also abundant. Sometimes we found four or five rails wound around the trunk of a tree. Sherman did not leave a building on the road from Macon to Savannah. For warehouses, I found boxcars stationed on the side tracks. The best rolling stock of the Central Road had been run up to Macon on Sherman's approach and could not be got down again, so I had the pleasure of riding to Savannah in an old car crowded full of wooden chairs in the place of the usual seats.

A gentleman of Jones County said, "I had a noble field of corn, not yet harvested. Old Sherman came along and turned his droves of cattle right into it, and in the morning there was no more corn there than there is on the back of my hand. His devils robbed me of all my flour and bacon and corn meal. They took all the pillow-slips, ladies' dresses, drawers, chemises, sheets and bed-quilts they could find in the house to tie up their plunder in. You couldn't hide anything but they'd find it. I sunk a cask of molasses in a hog wallow, but a nigger boy the rascals had with 'em said he 'lowed there was something hid there. They just robbed my house of every pail, cup, dish, what-not that they could carry molasses off to their camping ground in. After they'd broke open the cask and took what they wanted, they left the rest to run in a river along the ground. There was one sweet hog wallow!"

Here is the story of an old gentleman of Burke County: "It was the 14th Corps that came through my place. They looked like a blue cloud coming. They had all kinds of music—horns, cow bells, tin pans, everything they could pick up that would make a hideous noise. They burned everything but occupied dwellings. They took every knife and fork and cooking utensil we had. We wife just saved a frying pan by hanging on to it. After that they came back to get her to cook them some biscuit! They told her, if she would make them a batch of biscuit, they would bring back a sack of her own flour, and she should have the balance of it. She agreed to it, but, while the biscuit was baking, another party came along and carried the sack off again.

"The wife of one of my neighbors, a very rich family brought up to luxuries, just saved a single frying pan like we did. Their niggers and all went off with Sherman. And for a week or two they had to cook their own victuals in that frying pan, cut them with a pocket knife and eat them with their fingers. My folks had to do the same.

"General Sherman went into the house of an old woman after his men had been pillaging it. He sat down and drank a glass of water. Says she to him, 'I don't wonder people say you're a smart man, for you've been to the bad place and got scrapings the devil wouldn't have!' His soldiers heard of it, and they took her dresses and hung them up all in the highest trees and drowned the cat in the well.

"My wife took all our valuables, watches and silver spoons, and hid them in the cornfield. With a knife she would just make a slit in the ground, open it a little, put in one or two things and then let the top earth down, just like it was before. Then she'd go on and do the same thing in another place. The soldiers went all over that cornfield sticking in their bayonets, but they didn't find a thing. The joke of it was, she came very near never finding them again herself!"

Reconstruction

T HE late 1860's were years of turbulence, confusion and change that would aggravate the inevitable fears and resentments between defeated whites and long-enslaved blacks. The state government was thrice reorganized, each time with the participation of more blacks and fewer whites. Reuben S. Norton, a merchant in Rome, was denied voter registration: "An old Negro man I had owned and who could neither read nor write [or] count ten, having not sense enough to take care of himself, will be allowed to vote! I, with a number of others, was refused, because we had before the war held the office of alderman. This is a free country with a vengeance!" In November, 1865, some men were overheard talking in Americus: "Well, hell's the place for Yankees, and I want 'em all to go thar as soon's possible, and take the niggers 'long with them!" Georgia was not readmitted to the United States until July, 1870.

Stocks, bonds and Confederate money had all lost their value, and idle plantations were selling at a tenth of their price before the war. In the summer of 1865, Dr. Robert Battey, a surgeon at Rome, was obliged to go into the field with his wife and children to raise food, because his patients could not afford to pay for his services and the county had been reduced to a barter economy. He described his family's plight—old clothes and no luxuries—with sanguine good humor. "Merchants, clerks, lawyers and many doctors are upon farms in their shirt-sleeves, scratching the soil for bread." [Document Five]

During the first year or two after the war, the freedmen wandered into towns, congregating around soldiers' camps, testing their independence. A former slave was asked why she had left her old plantation. "What for? To 'joy my *freedom!*" Salathial Edgeworth, trying to resume plantation work in Fort Valley, wrote his uncle in October, 1866: "The Negroes are idle, slothful, dishonest, every way unreliable. . . . Our fields will grow nothing but weeds." The Freedmen's Bureau, created in March, 1865, tried to feed and clothe the former slaves and protect their rights. With impressive evenhandedness, the Bureau also encouraged them to return to work by supervising labor contracts and arbitrating disputes with plantation owners. [Document Six] Within the first year, the New England Freedmen's Aid Society, the American Missionary Society and the Freedmen's Bureau established sixty-two schools with eighty-nine teachers for 6600 black students in large Georgia towns. However, blacks soon discovered that the government could give them little work or land and found homelessness and starvation along with freedom.

In the spring of 1867, Louis Manigault returned to his plantations on an island in the Savannah River of Georgia. Formerly a proud planter, scion of one of South Carolina's aristocratic families, Louis was now an employee of a Charleston merchant, and his plantations were in ruins. Everything had been burned except the slaves houses, magnificent trees and ornamental gardens had been cut down for firewood, and rice fields had been damaged by flooding. Many former slaves were still on the property, but few were working. "That former mutual and pleasing feeling of master toward slave and vice versa is now a dream of the past." [Document Seven] Frances Butler Leigh and her father, the absentee owner of plantations on the Georgia coast, travelled South from Philadelphia to reclaim their property. Despite confusion over contracts, Frances felt that a mutual affection between masters and their former bondsmen survived until spoiled by political agitators—agents of the Freedmen's Bureau and demagogues like Tunis G. Campbell, a black man from New York who took control of several coastal islands. Frances wrote: "The Negroes seemed to reach the climax of lawless independence, and I never slept without a loaded pistol by my bed.

They worked just as much and when they pleased and tried speaking to me with their hats on. It was touch-and-go whether I or the Negroes got the upper hand." [Document Eight]

Protected for a time by agents of the Freedmen's Bureau and a Republican state government, freedmen had two or three years to exercise their new right to vote. In the summer of 1868, with the second reorganization of state government and approach of the presidential election, political agitation among blacks seemed particularly alarming to whites. Ella Thomas, the wife of a failed planter, later obliged to take in boarders to support her family, feared an uprising among the blacks: "The South feels instinctively that she is standing upon the mouth of a volcano. Four or five colored men said that the white folks are scared of the niggers, that things wasn't like they used to be and that they was gwine to have fine times and burn up every house along the road." [Document Nine] In late December, freedmen seized control of plantations along the Ogeechee River, armed themselves, expelled their white landlords and caused panic in nearby Savannah. The insurrection was more alarming because United States officials refused to act promptly to restore order. [Document Ten] The Negro threat seemed to be real—and growing.

[5]

The new order of things . . . merchants, clerks, lawyers and many doctors upon farms in their shirt-sleeves, scratching the soil for bread . . . ladies with the hoe in the cotton fields.

DR. ROBERT BATTEY, 1865

ROBERT BATTEY (1828–1895) was born near Augusta. Orphaned at an early age, he studied pharmacy and medicine in Philadelphia and Paris. During the Civil War, Battey was a Confederate surgeon. He was famous in his time as the originator of "Battey's operation" for the removal of ovaries. This letter was written by Dr. Battey, from Rome, Georgia, during the first grim summer after the collapse of the Confederacy, to his sister-in-law, Mary Halsey, who lived in the North. The manuscript letter is at the Emory University Library in Atlanta.

Rome

19th July 1865

Dear Mary,

Martha has written to you twice since the surrender of General Lee and sent her letters North by private hand to be mailed. You read in the newspapers glowing accounts of our sufferings in North Georgia, but, to understand these statements correctly, you must consider that the correspondents who write for your papers belong, for the most part, to two types—paid correspondents who are accustomed to travel comfortably with their umbrellas and dusters, their trunks and portmanteaus, who dine at the hotels and smoke their Havannas, or army officers, paid liberal salaries, furnished with good horses, comfortable lodgings and abundance of "sanitary stores." Such penny-a-lines estimate subsistence by the army standard and regard three-fourths pound of bacon, one pound of fresh pork or one-and-one-fourth pound of fresh beef necessary for comfortable subsistence. If such men were informed that I feed my family of twenty (white and black) on two pounds of bacon and eight, or at most ten, pounds of bread daily, they might very naturally suppose that we were suffering and so report us. When, however, I contrast my present condition and comfort with my campaign thro' the Valley of Virginia in 1862, when I subsisted for almost an entire week at a time upon an often scanty supply of roasting ears, without salt, I am loath to admit that I am suffering. And so it is with Martha, too, when she contrasts the present with her experiences last year in the lines of the enemy, during the occupation of Rome. Robbed of her entire supply of meat, flour and corn, she secreted beneath her bed the little supplies of cornmeal she was able to procure from her friends and subsisted herself and children almost solely upon bread and the milk of a cow, wrested twice from the military shambles by her indomitable energy and perseverance, as her last hope—a cow securely locked in her smokehouse by day and chained to a tree, close to the head of her bed, at night. She cannot feel that she is suffering. Undoubtedly there is some real suffering in our midst and there is vastly more imaginary suffering. But most of us have learned to endure such sufferings with fortitude and resignation. This and even greater sufferings do not [depress] us or cause us to repine.

It is a matter of pride with me that two ounces of meat and a half pound of bread, with the products of my garden and Martha's cow, all accumulated by my own labor and Martha's watchful care, are found to be sufficient for each of us, that we enjoy good health, eat our meals with relish and do not feel that we are suffering. Not long ago George spent a day in the country, gathered ten quarts of blackberries, sold them and invested the proceeds in two pounds of bacon. I feared that George was "suffering" and questioned him closely upon the subject. But he persistently denied it, and explained to me that while he had meat in plenty and did not desire an increase of his ration, he feared that our supply would not last very long, and he desired to add to it while he had the means of doing so through the blackberry crop. Grace was much mortified. George had purchased the bacon at a store upon the public street and from the nephew of Mrs. Norton. There were other customers in the store, no one knew who they were. They might have been people of influence and position who would look down upon George, making his little purchase of substantial food. She was quite sure the Nortons would hear of it, that they would draw the inference that George was not properly fed at home and that the character of the family would suffer in consequence! As for myself, I felt proud of my boy. I had allowed him a day of recreation from his house work, and he elected to spend it in making a little money and to expend his money for the general good for the article of prime necessity rather than for his own personal gratification —and this by the spontaneous exercise of his own judgement much influenced by others. I could write you a volume of these little experiences of our everyday life, many of which might interest you and all of which go to show how much and how little we suffer, and give you a more correct idea of the condition of things here than you get from the writings of the "kid glove gentry."

I practice my profession. My patrons have no money. They have no provisions to spare, and yet each one can spare me a little (unless indeed they be very poor) and many of them are willing to stint their own subsistence a little to enable me to live. Last week we had no flour. Two postage stamps footed up my cash account. I learned that a lot of condemned hard tack was to be sold at Kingston by the commissary. I borrowed from a friend $9 with which I purchased thirty boxes of the tack of fifty pounds each. Most of it was moulded and spoiled but is an excellent food for the cow and comes back to us in milk. Martha spent a day in assorting the lot and secured seven boxes of sound bread which could be eaten. It is equivalent to a barrel and a half of flour—besides oceans of milk. Martha gave one box of the tack to a friend in the country who sent her four chickens in return and often contributes to our subsistence in little presents which are of value to us. In no instance has it been necessary for me to draw subsistence stores from the government nor have I any idea that such a necessity will arise. Large numbers of our people are drawing from the A.C.S. at Kingston. Very many are forced to do so since there is not provisions enough in the country to subsist the population. But large numbers of those who draw could feed themselves had they the manliness to sacrifice their property in place of their honor.

The wheat crop in this section of country is an entire failure, but little land was sown for want of seed and labor. The corn and wheat upon the farms was ferreted out from hiding places with a skill and ingenuity truly wonderful, and the Negroes have been so demoralized that few had either the power or inclination to exact work from them. I know of but one farmer in this county who has reaped more wheat than will be necessary for his own family consumption. One farmer sowed twenty bushels and did not attempt to reap the crop at all. Another harvested eleven bushels from ten of seed, another six bushels from ten of seed. Those who have cotton can procure flour from the Northwest. The masses must subsist upon cornmeal, which is likely to be abundant enough for the white population.

The obstacles to the growth of a full crop of corn have been the same as of wheat, except that the season has been quite favorable to the growth of corn. Fortunately the fact that more than three-fourths of the tillable land in this section has been turned out by burning of fences and for want of labor has opened an abundant pasturage for what little stock is left in the country. We are thus enabled to husband our corn for family consumption and can do so for years to come until the country can again be supplied with labor. Our cows are all very fat and giving milk more abundantly than ever before. Hundreds of families are subsisting themselves wholly upon cornbread and milk with garden vegetables and are living very comfortably—by no means suffering.

The great scarcity of labor is to some degree compensated from an unexpected quarter. In former years at this season, one walking up our main street in the afternoon would encounter large numbers of merchants and their clerks, lawyers and some few doctors, lounging about, sitting upon boxes, whittling sticks and engaging in lazy amusements. Now, this is all changed. The merchants, clerks, lawyers and many doctors are upon farms in their shirt-sleeves, scratching the soil for bread, while their lounging places are daily filled with one, two and not unfrequently three hundred ablebodied Negroes from the farms. It would astonish you to see with how much grace the more sensible portion of our people submit to the new order of things. New England is having her fun now, after four years of toil and labor and sacrifice. We, as a vanquished foe, cannot complain, nor do sensible men among us feel disposed to complain. We are content to vegetate along until the frolic is over and Massachusetts is sobered and ready for work again.

It may seem strange to you that two hundred idle Negroes in the prime of vigorous manhood can be maintained in a community like Rome week after week. This fact would seem to contradict the reports you have of our starving condition. It is partly explained when I tell you that my dogs keep me awake at night running persons (supposed to be of color) out of my garden and orchard. Fortunately our supplies of meat and breadstuffs are so small usually that we are enabled to keep them securely beneath our bed, under the moral force of a small Colt repeater. The remainder of the explanation is to be found in the enormous issue of commissary rations at Kingston. The aged, the infirm, the children remain at home and render such aid as they can in the crops. There are, of course, many exceptions to this rule. Many Negroes have intelligence enough to know that they must labor to subsist and feel a desire to accumulate something more than their bare subsistence. The poor Negroes are taught that the tables are turned and accept the fact as they understand it. Time alone can teach him his error. The newspapers inform him that he cannot be maintained in idleness, but he cannot read the newspaper and has not been accustomed to look to it for his guidance. The provost marshall tells him that he must labor, but the soldier tells him it is not necessary, and his daily observation proves to him that the soldier is the wiser man of the two.

Mr. Norton's oldest son, George, raised by his father in the store, now married, and a number one businessman, has opened a blacksmith shop and, as far as he is able, strikes at the anvil himself. Yesterday I rode over the mountain to amputate an arm and spent the night in a log cabin with one of our most promising Rome lawyers who has been four years in the army and has been three times wounded in battle. He rises at daylight, musters his "hands" (three boys, eight, ten and thirteen) and goes forth to the field of his labor. I supped and breakfasted with him upon buttermilk and bread. There is not a pound of meat in the house and, he assures me, has not been for two months. Is he suffering? Probably he was never freer from care in his life. And I feel quite sure that a suggestion that he should draw rations from the government would deeply insult him. A Negro man occupying a little cabin in the woods was offered wages to assist him in repairing an out-house. The Negro demanded excessive wages and preferred to rest himself until he can get his price and "don't want to work much for white folks no how!"

Our corn crop will soon be matured. It is already in roasting ear, which can be grated and made into very sweet and nutritious bread. When mature, it can be rapidly turned into chickens and ducks for meat, while the few hogs remaining in our mountain fastnesses will by liberal feeding be forced into the largest possible amount of pork. With planty of corn we are independent. Our white population have the nerve and will feed themselves. New England will take care of the blacks.

These are our prospects for subsistence, and in the matter of clothing we are equally fortunate. For myself, I have not purchased an article of clothing in more than eighteen months and think with the sole exceptions of shoes and hat, I have on hand in the cast-off garments of former years, a supply for a year at least in the future. We don't get the New York fashion plates now as we used to do and find by experience that soap and a brush will take out dirt and grease. For years I honestly labored under the delusion that a pair of $8 French calfskin boots was actually essential to comfortable progression and that they could not last in a general way longer than three or at most four months. Now I wear a pair of English army brogans. I find them incomparably more comfortable and pleasant than the boots. And on the score of economy I must cite you to the record. I purchased them last September for $20 and have had them half-soled once. They will bear another half-sole when needed and are certainly good for another six months. I have a pair of English russet boots presented to me by General Archer in the campaign of 1862 while serving upon his staff. They are all right and [will] carry me through muddy weather for several winters yet by using proper care. Besides these, I have a pair of Confederate brogans which I am holding in store for some friend who may need them more than I do.

When I embarked in service I left at home an excellent Panama hat which would have been useful perhaps now, if Martha had not put it to better use by having it washed, dyed and pressed into a really stylish hat for Grace, which she reserves for dress occasions, having still an older and less ornamented one for everyday. As it is, I have an army cap made to my order in '62 and a very handsome thing it was then. Now it is less ornamental but turns the sun and rain as well now as when it was new. Martha does not feel altogether satisfied with herself for having appropriated my Panama to Grace and sometimes threatens

44

to send some of her wool into the country to have me a broad brim made, but I will not permit her to do so. She says the sun burns me too much with the cap, but I tell her it is a healthy color and fashionable, too, and, besides, it is quite in keeping with that of my friends who have exchanged the brief and the saddle-bags for the hoe and plough. The truth is I don't like these heavy broad brims our hatters make and greatly prefer my old cap, which is light and comfortable. I don't tell her this: it would loose me the credit I get for economy!

To pacificate the matter, I have made a compromise with her by repairing the ribs of our old umbrella, while she repaired the dry goods part of the apparatus. And this I carry under my arm when I leave the house, and she tolerates my comfortable old cap now very well. I have an excellent rubber cloth for the storm, a reminiscence of the field of Manassas, and an overcoat which was quite intolerable years ago. But it agrees well with me now. Don't fancy because I have but one cap and one pair of boots that my dress is monotonous, for my wardrobe includes certainly six, perhaps eight, pairs of pants and half the number at least of coats. I never was a man to wear one coat and pants all the time. Don't imagine me ashamed of my old clothes when I meet upon the street gentlemen freshly arrived from the emporiums of commerce and fashion. Quite the contrary! My clothes I know were bought and paid for long ago by the sweat of my own brow; theirs, I have no means of knowing whether they are paid for or not, nor where the purchase money came from. I haven't seen one of them yet that I thought was any better man than I am—unless it be in knocking me down—and I have not thus far found it necessary to make that issue. They doubtless take a private laugh at my expense—and I am sure that I do at theirs. They cannot well think my figure more comical than I find theirs when measured by my standard.

As for Martha, I don't think I ever saw her dress more becomingly or look prettier than now. The variety of her wardrobe quite equals my own, and she has the advantage of me in more recent accessions of new clothing—that is, new to her. She has several "homespuns," the result of her own industry, and has received presents of one or two very nice dresses, which, though not recently imported, are none the less pretty on that account. I must tell you a secret that we don't talk about much. Prior to the war, Martha's principal forte was in the eating line. She counted more upon crockery and glassware, &c. than she did upon dry goods. Some of her friends upon the other hand were quite "heavy" on dry goods and light upon crockery and glass. So, you see, a mutual exchange of surplus commodities has enabled the two families to live better and more comfortably than either could alone. Martha is all right every way excepting in shoes, insisting that the Confederate shoes, although cheap and very durable, are not so comfortable to wear as the imported article. Her opinion upon this point is quite at variance with my own, and I am not able by any arguments I can bring to bear to bring her to my way of thinking. Since she is all right upon other points, I cheerfully yield to her in this one. She thinks a hoop economical, because it dispenses with a multiplicity of skirts. My mind does not grasp an intricate question of this character, and although my prejudices are rather fixed against the [   ] investment, I am forced to yield to the plea of economy.

As for the children, garments go down in regular succession and with proper cleaning and patching their wants are well supplied. Will and George have recently been furnished with two blue flannel jackets from the spoils of the war. They have taken a good hearty cry over the new toggery, and for a time held a very strong position upon the point that they "would not wear them." I tendered my services as umpire and adjudicated the question in this wise: the boys are to wear the blue coats at their labor and when in the woods hunting or fishing, but that their Confederate pride must be respected by permitting them to put on their old grey on Sundays and whenever there may be company at the house. Martha and the boys all acquiesce in the decision as a fair compromise, though the former still insists that the new blue is more neat than the old grey, while the latter contend that the grey, though old and worn, is the more genteel of the two. I have a blue myself for garden and stable work and it helps to reconcile the boys to theirs, but I fancy sometimes that they are less cautious about briers and dirt in the blue uniform than they used to be in the grey. And this apparent want of care is not so satisfactory to their mother. Boys are boys and must be humored a little in their fancies.

In the matter of shoes, our children get along very well. Nature shoes them very satisfactorily and does it a great deal cheaper than I am able to do. Grace thinks she cannot go barefooted, says her feet are too tender, indeed complains that the coarse homemade shoes furnished her hurt her feet and are not comfortable. Martha upholds her in the claim for shoes, but does not endorse all her complaints of weight and coarseness. I tell Grace that I see daily in the country much older girls than she barefooted and quite often grown ladies, mothers of families. Many of these larger girls and ladies labor day by day with the hoe in the cornfields and they tell me that the wearing of shoes in the summer season is mere matter of habit which entails much discomfort upon the part of the wearer, a mere sacrifice to their pride. They assert confidentially that the feet are more comfortable and more healthy without than with shoes. While endeavoring to impress her mind with the sanitary and economic aspects of the question, I am forced to admit that the Nortons still wear shoes and her mother and myself do likewise. I indulge her in shoes such as I can get.

Little Bessie, who up to within the space of a few weeks has lived in blissful ignorance of the meaning of the word "candy," which term had become quite obsolete in the family, in an evil hour got a taste of the forbidden fruit—and now gives her mother no little trouble with her demands for the contraband indulgence. An apple or peach often effects a satisfactory compromise. Martha is nearly as heavy upon the sugar sensation as little Bessie upon candy, but unfortunately I do not always find her so easily put off with a substitute. The health of our community this season is unexampled, and I am inclined to attribute it partly to more active habits but chiefly to the scarcity of sugar and sweetmeats with our frugal fare. Martha insists upon the sanitary properties of sugar, but I cannot agree with her in her views.

There is at present a very great scarcity of money in this section of Georgia, and this scarcity seems likely to continue for twelve months or more in the future. The occupation of this country by the Federal forces destroyed a great deal of cotton, forced farmers to sell to speculators for Confederate money or to have their cotton removed to central Alabama for security. Much of this was destroyed at Selma, Montgomery and Columbus by the raid of General Wilson. With the exception of the little cotton which was carefully secreted, our people have nothing whatever but their lands out of which money can be raised. Nor have they any crop in cultivation for this purpose. I have not seen a single stalk of cotton growing in this county. I do not believe that the entire production of the county this year will reach 500 pounds, nor even 100 pounds. Our farmers have no seed which will vegetate, a striking illustration of the improvidence of our people. It is yet too early to foresee what will be the feeling of our producers in reference to cotton culture next year. There must be a radical change in the present state of affairs before a cotton crop can be "pitched" upon a large scale with any security against bankruptcy. The sentiments expressed upon this subject are anything but hopeful for cotton, but farmers are notoriously great grumblers and it cannot be foreseen now what they will do. There is one fact indisputable: no cotton crop can come into market for our relief for eighteen months to come.

During two months of my practice since my return home, I could count upon the tips of my fingers the dollars I had made. For ten days together I have not possessed the means of purchasing a single copy of a newspaper. This is a novel position for me to be placed in, but I can assure you that I do not suffer either mentally or physically. On the contrary, I laugh merrily over my empty pocket and find in it rather a fund of amusement than a source of anxious care. Last Saturday, fortune smiled upon me. I received for my service an old-fashioned $5 gold piece. I was so elated with my luck that I found it difficult to deport myself with becoming decorum in the presence of my patient—and actually played with the toy like a child with a new tin trumpet.

It would amuse you to hear Martha and myself discussing day after day the propriety of purchasing for the family a dime box of blacking and weighing carefully the various expedients which might be resorted to to render unnecessary such an expenditure of our means. Some time ago Martha practiced a commendable economy in getting up from her dyestuffs a bottle of ink. I soon found, however, that the destruction of pens was so great that I was likely to incur a more serious expenditure in that direction. After properly weighing the advantages and disadvantages, a small investment was made in ink, which proved to be judicious and satisfactory. All these little matters give us no anxiety, no suffering. We laugh heartily over them and keep cheerful and happy. I feel as much assurance of my ability to maintain my family now as I ever did and have as little, perhaps less, anxiety about the future.

In one thing, and only one, we suffer—the education of our children. This has caused and still causes me much anxiety. For two years we have had no school, for Grace and none for the boys since the commencement of the war, taught by any competent teachers. For a year past Martha has been in great degree dependent upon her children for her household and garden work. While I recognize this want of education for my children as a necessary sacrifice, still it is a sacrifice which I make more reluctantly than any other. Our old population is rapidly returning, and I think we will have schools here this winter. With my large family, I have never expected to do more for my children than to educate them well and rear them in habits of industry and economy. Prior to the war I was accumulating a property in Negroes which promised, with my own labor, abundant means for the thorough education of all my children. Now I have only a home with tillable land and my profession upon which to rely. But this I think will be ample, if my own health is maintained for all my reasonable expectations. What we have lost in ease and comfort we must make up in frugality and industry, and we will be none the worse for the change. I feel glad that I have the present opportunity of teaching my children in a practical way the value of money and what it costs to make it.

There are many reasons why I should not shrink from the labor and sacrifice required to do my part in the restoration of the country. My home is still here, my house unburned and though my fences, barn, &c. have been destroyed, time and labor will replace them eventually, so that we will be quite comfortable again. True, I realize now but very little return for my labor, but I feel that I am rendering a service to the community and look forward hopefully to a more prosperous future. To leave my people now in their extremity would be to forfeit their confidence and gratitude.

The war has developed in Martha a heroism which, though not unexpected on my part, has been to me a source of just pride and unbounded admiration. Nor is this feeling confined alone to myself. She has won for herself a similar praise from friends, and for whenever they have come within the sphere of her influence. Brave and fearless in the expression of her sentiments, she has ever been kind and generous to friends, humane and just to the foe. Generals Davis, Vandiver and Corse all respected and esteemed her, and the two former extended to her many courtesies and indulgencies. Colonel Foster of Madison, who visited Rome on business during the Federal occupation, wrote to me on his return of the condition of my family and closed with the remark, "You have reason to offer up daily a hearty thanksgiving that Providence has been pleased to direct you to such a woman." General Davis on learning that she had been robbed of her subsistence, offered her rations which she politely declined. General Vandiver called often to see her and proferred her provisions repeatedly, which were always declined—and this, too, at times when her only subsistence was bread and milk.

He was equally kind and indulgent to the children, permitting them to come freely to his quarters with all their little requests. "General, please give us a pass to go fishing today." "General, I want to go across the river to hunt rabbits. We have got no meat and Ma wants me to get her some rabbits. Can't you give me a pass?" General Vandiver always lent a willing ear to these trivial requests. One day George went up with a request for a horse. "General, I see you have got a great many horses out here in your corral, more than you need I think. Can't you give me one to carry my corn to mill? I have to toat my corn to mill on my back and it is getting to be mighty heavy." "Yes, George," replied the General, "You shall have a horse. Here is the order and tell them to give you a good one." General Vandiver afterwards rode around to see George's horse and, not approving it, sent him back to exchange for a better one. One day while the boys were waiting in the General's room for a fishing pass, several officers were discussing with the latter the policy of starving the South into submission by the destruction of crops, burning of barns, warehouses, &c. Willie rather rudely interrupted the conversation with the remark, "General, if you had seen what I saw the other day, out in the country, you wouldn't think it so easy to starve us out." "Well, what did you see, Will?" "An old, grey-headed woman out in the cornfield, ploughing a calf with a buggy harness." General Vandiver was greatly amused and admitted frankly the force of the argument.

The women of our country have played their part nobly—and are still doing so. One of Martha's intimate friends, Mrs. Hawkins, has displayed throughout the struggle an admirable endurance and spirit, her husband being in the army and she carrying on the farm without assistance. Last summer a Federal soldier was shot near her house by some Confederate scouts posted upon an adjacent mountain, and the following day a party was sent out from Rome to burn her house. Mrs. Hawkins replied to the officer, "I am an innocent, defenceless woman without protection. I have no force with which to oppose you. If your orders are to burn my house, apply the torch." And taking her chair out into the yard, she sat a quiet spectator of the scene with her four little children gathered around her. When the flames were under full headway, the Federal officer stepped up to Mrs. Hawkins and asked with surprise why she did not attempt to save some of her furniture and clothing. "Sir," she replied with a bitter smile, "I would not sacrifice the dignity of a Southern woman for a dozen such houses and all they contain." With a full heart but firm resolution, when the sad scene was over she led forth her homeless family to seek a friendly roof wherever a kind Providence might provide. And now, removed from comparative affluence to a homeless penury, while her husband is dispirited and desponding, Mrs. Hawkins still maintains her composure and dignity. While she spends much of her time in the cornfield and is earning for her little family a comfortable livelihood, she is a woman of much refinement and delicacy, while her indomitable will heeds no obstacle and her cheerful heart looks hopefully into the future. Fifty thousand soldiers, inspired with the spirit of Mrs. Hawkins and Martha, would be invincible against the world in arms. One hundred of them could never surrender to any foe.

My friend Dr. Johnson has three old maid sisters living near Cave Springs, ladies of unusual mental culture for this country who are growing this season an excellent crop of corn by their own labor—with sun bonnets and brogans and homespun dresses tucked up at the waist, they go forth at daylight to their labor. For heroic self-sacrifice and patriotic zeal, each one of them is worth a dozen Florence Nightingales! Such people as these are not suffering, cannot suffer in this land of generous soil and fruitful seasons.

Last winter, when I visited Martha and found my fences all gone, trees devoured and ground trampled by the wagon trains camped in the [yard] around my house, myself without means and unable to assist her, I despaired entirely of her making a garden for her subsistence this year. Judge of my surprise on my return in April to find the entire premises enclosed by a rather unsightly but still efficient fence, the fruit trees putting out both foliage and fruit, and the garden all planted with a promising crop of substantial vegetables. George says that Henry and himself carried the pieces of plank and rails, while Willie held the pieces and Mother nailed them on and "leaned up against the fence to blow and rest" while another load was being brought. George thinks that Will and himself with the assistance and direction of their Mother are capable of any feat of labor which the comfort and welfare of the family may demand. One thing only perplexes and troubles George. He likes to labor but "don't see what's the use of working yourself to death when there is so many idle Negroes standing around doing nothing." George accepts the new arrangement as a necessity but cannot perceive the philosophy of it. His old idea that a Negro was made for labor and not to be an idle vagrant still sticks to him and he is not yet prepared to receive the New England doctrine understandingly.

The business portion of our town including the railroad and steamboat depots, the lower hotel and cotton warehouses was chiefly destroyed by fire last fall at the evacuation. The rolling mill, foundry, engine shops and flouring mill shared the same fate. The few business houses remaining will probably be amply sufficient for all the business which can be done here for some time to come. Our own merchants are exhausted of all ready means upon which to do business. There are quite a number of Jews here with stocks of goods picking the little specie which remains in the hands of farmers and bartering for what cotton they can get. A young lady from the country came to town some weeks ago and purchased with gold a wedding dress of Swiss muslin. The transaction gave rise to much talk and no little censure. In speaking of the buildings burned, I forgot to mention that my little brick office upon the street was spared. And though much defaced by the soldiers and much of my furniture removed and destroyed, it is still habitable and answers all my business purposes.

While Martha was within the lines, she received no wanton insult from either officers or soldiers and though she was so constantly threatened with the burning of her house as to prevent her from enjoying an uninterrupted night's rest for five months, still her house and the mass of its contents was spared. Martha often begged of the soldiers that they would burn her house by daylight and quit talking and threatening so much about it. At times she did not dare to take off her clothing, but lounged the long night through with all of her children around her sleeping quietly upon the floor. For four months Mr. and Mrs. Norton kept up an alternate watch at night, while the others slept. Most of the time they dared not undress and kept always a few necessary articles of clothing and valuables in two carpet sacks at the head of their bed, ready at any moment to make their escape from the house. Three times they extinguished fire from their dwelling at night.

I have endeavored to give you as faithful a picture as I can of the condition of things here. Don't feel any uneasiness about us. There are some people in the country suffering, but the number who are *really* suffering is very small, much smaller than is supposed. We have not suffered a day and are not likely to.

⌐ 6 ⌐

The freedmen on the more important sea islands were armed and, in-fluenced by Tunis G. Campbell, a colored man from New York City, a person of remarkable cunning, would not allow any white person to land. They were mostly spending their time in hunting, fishing and destroying the cattle left on the islands by the former owners.

GENERAL DAVIS TILLSON, 1866

BRIGADIER-GENERAL DAVIS TILLSON (1830–1895) born in Maine, was Assistant Commissioner of the Freedmen's Bureau in Georgia between 1865 and 1867. Created in March, 1865, the Freedmen's Bureau was to furnish food, clothing and homesteads on public land for the former slaves, also supervising labor contracts, opening hospitals and schools and protecting civil rights. This report is among an extensive collection in the Records of the Assistant Commissioner for the State of Georgia, Bureau of Refugees, Freedmen and Abandoned Lands, in the National Archives. The report has been abridged.

Augusta, November 1st, 1866

General:

I have the honor herewith to submit a report of the operations of the Bureau in this state since September 22nd, 1865, at which time I entered upon my duties as Assistant Commissioner. Throughout the state the greatest bitterness was felt and expressed towards the Bureau and its officers, one of whom had been foully murdered a short time previous. My first efforts were directed to the organization of the Bureau and the removal from the public mind of the grave mis-apprehensions which existed as to its objects and purposes and towards securing as far as possible the countenance and support of the civil authorities.

During the latter part of last year and the beginning of this, the freedmen were impressed with the belief that the government would give them land, animals, farming implements and food to enable them to begin planting for themselves. Grave apprehensions were felt and expressed throughout the state that, enraged at the inevitable disappointment of their hopes, the freedmen would rise on Christmas or New Year's and attempt to take by force what they had been led to expect would be given them. Subsequent events proved such fears without foundation. It is difficult to ascertain the source whence they became possessed of this idea, but so far as could be learned, the charge that it had been disseminated by the officers of the Bureau is utterly groundless. By much strenuous exertions on the part of officers of the Bureau, the freedmen were finally induced to make contracts to labor this year. It was only after the most persistent efforts that employers could be persuaded to pay the freedmen reasonable wages. In some instances they compelled them by threats to contract for from $1 to $3 per month, the laborer to furnish his own clothing and medicine. Learning these facts, the parties were notified that such contracts would not be permitted and that the freedmen must receive reasonable compensation for their labors. The employers refused to annul these contracts or allow the freedmen to go to other parts of the country when they were offered better wages. Citizens going to certain counties to hire labor and offering reasonable prices were arrested and imprisoned. The freedmen were made to believe that if they left they would be sold into slavery, that the Bureau officers were paid for sending them away and were actuated by selfish and dishonest motives. Every possible expedient was resorted to for frightening and keeping them at home in order to enable employers to hire them at shamefully inadequate wages. The Bureau firmly refused to approve contracts which did not contain just and equitable terms for the freedmen, occasionally resorting to military force to secure to them the right of choice.

Generally the contracts for labor have been well observed, although in many instances they have been violated, sometimes by one party, sometimes by the other. In not a few cases the freedmen have performed their labor in a lazy, worthless manner. In others they have openly refused to abide by their contracts or leave the plantations and have actually trampled upon the rights and destroyed the property of their employers without the slightest excuse or provocation and have defied the agents and officers of the Bureau who endeavored to persuade them to do their duty, compelling a resort to military force to restore them to reason and convince them that they must obey the laws which govern other men. About the time the crops were laid by, a disposition was manifested in parts of the state to drive the freedmen off without paying for their labor. Both fraud and violence were resorted to in order to accomplish this result. In a number of counties, bands of men calling themselves "regulators" visited plantations, whipping, robbing, driving off freedmen and murdering them if any resistance was offered. These villains usually blackened their faces and took other means of avoiding identification, but it so often happened that they visited plantations and drove off the freedmen when there was a desire to get rid of them without paying for their labor that employers were suspected of being parties or consenting to these outrages. Freedmen have continued to make complaints at this office that they have been driven from planta-tions without payment. The employers usually deny the statement and assert that the laborers have been unfaithful. To settle these questions, the policy has been adopted of making these the subject of arbitration, to be enforced if neces-sary by military authority. To refer the freedmen in their present ignorance and poverty to the civil courts with their inevitable delays to collect the wages due them, which are immediately required for the support of themselves and fami-lies, is to force them to starve or steal and works a practical denial of justice.

This season has been the most unfavorable for agricultural operations known in this state for the past fifty years. Many of the freedmen have labored for a share of the crops, varying from one-fourth to one-third, the employers fur-nishing them with food and lodgings, or for one-half of the net proceeds. The failure of the crop in the northern and middle portions of the state has greatly augmented the difficulties in the way of settlement between employers and laborers. Notwithstanding the exceptions mentioned, there has been a very general and gratifying compliance with contracts by both parties. The testimony from planters is very nearly universal that, where the freedmen have been well paid and kindly treated, they have worked very well, much better under the circumstances than they expected. On the whole, the experiment with free labor has proved successful. The experience of the past year has established the fact that, when managed with tact and skill, a very large portion of the freed-men will prove most excellent and faithful laborers. My own observation im-presses me with the belief that they will work more cheerfully and with less supervision than white laborers and if treated with justice and made secure in their persons and property they will yet become an industrious, hardworking people, forming a valuable and useful part of the population, helping to develop the resources and adding increasingly to the prosperity of the state.

On the 3rd of February, I proceeded to the sea islands of the state and on investigation found them in a very unsatisfactory condition. With the exception of the Rev. W. F. Eaton, Agent of the Bureau at St. Simon's Island and whom I have found to be thoroughly honest and competent, there were no white men on the more important islands. The freedmen were armed and would not allow any white person to land. They were mostly fed on government rations and with very few exceptions were spending their time in hunting, fishing and destroying the cattle, large numbers of which had been left on the islands by the former owners. It was found that while [the] government was securing them rations, they were slaughtering the deer which abound upon the islands and selling the venison at high prices in Savannah.

Ossabaw, St. Catherine's and Sapelo islands were under the control of Tunis G. Campbell, a colored man from New York City, appointed Agent of the

Bureau by General Saxton. This man Campbell, who was afterwards dismissed, is a person of great plausibility and remarkable cunning. He was found to be cutting wood, selling it to passing steamers, appropriating the funds and otherwise managing the island where he resided for the benefit of himself and a few leaders among the freedmen. Some of the freedmen he employed and whose produce he sold have never yet received payment. Influenced by Campbell, the freedmen were unwilling to permit the white owners to return to the islands, even to occupy such portions of their property as had not been assigned to freedmen. They insisted that the government should continue to furnish them with rations in whole or in part representing that they had all the animals, implements, seed and nearly all the food required to enable them to make a crop this year. But as on the sea islands and rice fields of the state they had failed the year previous, even when they were fed and assisted by the government, to raise sufficient food for their own support and as there was a great demand for labor at high prices on the coast, I declined to accede to their request.

Procuring a small steamer from time to time, I took the former owners to the different islands, gathered the freedmen together and explained, in presence of both parties, the object and wishes of the Bureau. I was gratified to find a more reasonable disposition on the part of both than I dared to anticipate. And whereas in many cases each had threatened to shoot the others on sight, when brought together, much of their ill-feeling disappeared and very soon they were able to make arrangements for the owners to return and the freedmen to labor for them on mutually satisfactory terms. On St. Catherine's Island, 147 freedmen, in spite of the advice and influence of the Agent Campbell, went to work for Messrs. Schuyler of New York and Winchester of Boston on very liberal terms. It has been clearly demonstrated that the freedmen, if left to work for themselves and control their own labors, will not attain any considerable success. At no time during the existence of the race have the freedmen as a mass been called upon to exercise care, economy and forecast. It cannot be expected they should, without cultivation, suddenly become possessed of these qualities.

Large numbers of freedmen have from time to time made complaints, not a few of which have proved on investigation to have no real foundation, sometimes growing out of misapprehension on the part of the freedmen, sometimes from a disposition to make use of the Bureau as an instrument for private revenge. But in a majority of instances, there has been abundant cause for complaint. Bands of men styling themselves "regulators," "jayhawkers," and "black horse cavalry" have infested different parts of the state, committing the most fiendish and diabolical outrages on the freedmen. I am unaware of a single instance in which one of these villains has been arrested and brought to trial by the civil authorities. I am led to believe that in some instance the civil authorities and well-disposed citizens have been overawed by these organizations. In others, I fear the civil authorities have sympathized with them. Whenever they have neglected or refused to act, troops have been dispatched to arrest the guilty parties, but as the outlaws are usually well mounted, have the sympathy of more or less of the inhabitants, are familiar with the country and have numerous opportunities for concealment, they generally escape. In several counties where cruelties have been practiced upon the freedmen, the citizens have held public meetings, denouncing the guilty parties and pledging themselves to bring them to trial and punishment. The public press, which has maintained a studious silence on the subject, is beginning to speak out in severe condemnation of such conduct.

In some parts of the state the freedmen are organizing colonies to proceed to states in which land had been set apart for homesteads, but only those possessed of sufficient property or so situated as to make it probable they would succeed in making a livelihood were encouraged to emigrate. Unaccustomed and incompetent with few exceptions to foresee their wants or make suitable provisions for the future, there was great danger that, impelled by their almost universal desire to possess land, many, without means of support until they could clear the land and raise a crop, would attempt to enter and live upon it, thereby bringing upon themselves and families inevitable suffering, turning the intended bounty of the government into a curse.

During September of last year, upwards of 120,000 rations were issued in the city of Savannah. The absence of records before alluded to prevents my giving the numbers issued in the entire state during the same period. On the 3rd of October, orders were issued from this office directing that rations [would] not be issued to able-bodied freedmen [with] opportunities to labor for their own support. This order was rigidly enforced and a decrease in the issue of over 60,000 rations was effected in Savannah alone during the month. The issues constantly diminished until in June of this year, when it reached 19,269—in the whole state. Number of rations issued to freedmen and refugees from October 1, 1865, to date: to freedmen, 505,264, to refugees, 177,942, total, 683,206. Rations were issued to the destitute people in the northern part of the state during June, July, August and September. Issued to destitute whites, 20,975, issued to destitute colored, 9009, total issued, 29,984. Owing to the very unfavorable season, the crops have failed in the northern portion of the state, causing widespread suffering unless relieved by the government or the state. The last legislature of the state appropriated $200,000 to be expended in care for the destitute, but its distribution was confined to white citizens. Hospitals have been established and kept in operation at Atlanta, Augusta, Macon, Columbus and Savannah and dispensaries at Stone Mountain, Brunswick and St. Mary's. From September 1st,

1865, to October 1st, 1866, 143 whites and 5611 freed people have been received into these hospitals for treatment.

In the beginning great opposition was everywhere manifested against freedmen's schools, varying in intensity in proportion to the ignorance and prejudices of the community. In some places, school houses were burned and the teachers driven off. In others, the teachers were insulted and abused and the freed children stoned while on their way to and from school. And much of this brutal conduct still continues to disgrace portions of the state, but there has been a most gratifying decrease in the opposition to these schools during the past year. In most places, all interference has ceased and in some counties the freedmen are encouraged by the citizens to open and maintain schools. Quite a number of planters have voluntarily opened schools for the freedmen at their own expense. During the year there have been 113 schools, 125 teachers and 8000 scholars and attendants. Estimated number of colored people in this state [is] 400,000.

The Bureau or some similar agency has been and is still a necessity. If controlled by men, however honest, who are governed by preconceived opinions and theories who belittle or disregard facts which do not favor their convictions, the Bureau will certainly prove a source of irritation and will retard the restoration of peace and good order. But in the hands of honest, careful, discreet officers who will faithfully execute your orders, disregard opinions and be governed by the facts as they are developed and who will at all times show by their words and acts that they desire to do simple justice, the Bureau cannot fail of doing great good to both races.

[7]

About half a dozen Negroes crawled out of their houses, not knowing whether under the new regime it would be proper to meet me politely or not. I thought it best to appear but little concerned at the marked change in my situation and joked with them. One of them remarked, "Maussa, Wha mek you no come back so long?" Smiling and turning to the chimney alone standing where my former home stood, I remarked, "Lord! You tink I can lib in de chimney?"

LOUIS MANIGAULT, 1867

LOUIS MANIGAULT (1828–1899), a member of one of the great South Carolina plantation families, was born in Paris and travelled extensively in Europe, South America and Asia before returning to assume his place among the low country aristocracy in 1851 as proprietor of plantations on an island in the Savannah River of Georgia. In the spring of 1867, his fortunes sadly changed, Louis returned for the first time to survey his two plantations, Gowrie and East Hermitage, on Argyle Island. This journal and other documents are in the Manigault Papers, Southern Historical Collection, University of North Carolina, Chapel Hill. Many were published by The Beehive Press, *Life and Labor on Argyle Island*, edited by James M. Clifton, in 1978. The journal has been abridged.

I left Charleston Monday 18th [March], 1867, in a very inferior steamer called *The Pilot Boy* en route for Savannah. Permission had been granted me to absent myself from George A. Hopley & Company's Counting House, where I am a clerk, for one week. Towards the close of January, 1867, Mr. William Neyle Habersham (my father's friend and attorney and my brother-in-law) succeeded in finding a tenant [for our plantations on Argyle Island] in General George P. Harrison, a Georgian with whom I had had business transactions in former years. My object was now to make the acquaintance of General Harrison and with him if possible to visit the plantation[s].

Friday, 22d March 1867. At 6 A.M. my son Louis and I were up, my idea being to take him with me that hereafter in life he might remember it. It was exactly 7 A.M. striking by the Presbyterian Church clock that we jumpt into

Mr. Habersham's buggy at the door behind one of his fast trotting horses. Some six miles from Savannah we came in sight of the Charleston and Savannah Rail Road, which had not been touched since the advance of Sherman's army but the twisted and ruined rails remained as left by the Yankees. The vestiges of former encampments of large bodies of troops were still perceptible on either side of the road. At 9 A.M. the gradual opening in the trees ahead indicated we were not far from the once beautiful country seat of Mr. James Potter. A Negro man driving to pasture a few cows informed us that General Harrison was up at the house.

The cruel hand of war was now clearly to be seen. Most startling was the change on every side since my last visit here in December, 1864. The large rice pounding mill was burnt down. This was also the case with the fine wooden barn close at hand, the locality of these two former buildings being marked solely by a few remaining brick of the foundations. With far deeper pain, however, did I contemplate the ruins of Mr. James Potter's handsome residence, superior to any on the river. Many a time had I spent at this hospitable gentleman's house. Mr. Potter died about 1860. His only son was killed in battle near Atlanta in 1864.

General Harrison was soon pointed out to me. He was in his blacksmith shop overlooking the repair of some plantation utensil. I advanced and introduced myself. He is a man of commanding appearance, upwards of six feet in height, about fifty years of age. The General said he had not visited Argyle Island for two or three days and would be happy to accompany me. His canoe, with old Negro and paddle, was soon in readiness, and with our horse and buggy placed in charge of the servant to be taken to stable we pushed off in the river. The current was still very rapid, caused by a freshet of a few days previous. Fields in every direction were sobbed.

We very soon found ourselves at the Gowrie Red Trunk Landing on Middle River, the dividing line between the Gowrie tract and lands of the estate of James Potter on Argyle Island. The outer door of this large and important trunk [a wooden gate used to control the flow of water in canals in rice fields] was wanting, although a new one had been constructed and was on the bank near at hand. Through Negro negligence and most likely malice, it had not been replaced. As the Negro carpenter, the notorious rascal Jack Savage, well knew, the consequence of not having replaced this trunk door was that for the past ten days a constant flow of water had sobbed this entire section of the plantation, thereby annulling all work, with our friend Mr. Jack Savage sleeping in his house. When about half across the island our progress was impeded by the freshet water knee deep. The General pushed on, and Louis and I were soon soaked from knees down as we followed. The water becoming deeper still, it was determined he should send us some Negro man to take us on his back. After some delay I recognized our former cooper George approaching, delighted to meet us and calling me "Maussa" as of yore. He placed us in safety on dry land, and we walked up to the settlement. Reaching Gowrie settlement, I placed Louis in charge of George's wife, Betty, a woman I had known for many years. She made a fire for him in her house, dried his shoes and stockings and boiled several eggs for him to his great delight. We here left Louis whilst the General and I continued our survey of the place.

Not having visited the plantations since the advance of Sherman's army in December, 1864, my present visit was one of painful interest. Up to the very last moment in December, 1864, although the sound of musketry from advancing pickets grew more and more distinct from hour to hour, our Negroes behaved well and I left the entire gang unloading the flat of rice, still pleased to see me, and singing as they bore the heavy loads on their heads to the barn yard. Standing near the ruins of my former dwelling I contemplated the spot. Where once stood this country house could alone now be seen a few scattering brick and the tall chimney to denote the spot. Here the most happy period of my boyish days, together with the early years of my married life, had been spent. No remnant of my kitchen, fine stable remained, not even a brick to mark the spot, as all of these had been stolen by the Negroes and sold in Savannah. About one hundred trees—water oaks transplanted with my own hands, a most beautiful cypress tree, a handsome sycamore—a flower garden with choice roses, shrubs, fences had been used as firewood by the Negroes. Not a vestige remained, not even the stumps of the trees. The change in the appearance of Gowrie settlement is, I may say, from a village to a wilderness. With the exception of four large double Negro houses, the settlement is a barren waste and presents a most abandoned and forlorn appearance.

About half a dozen Negroes crawled out of their houses as we approached, dirty and sluggish in appearance and stupified by sleep, not knowing whether under the new regime it would be proper to meet me politely or not, but in every case I advanced and shook hands, calling each by name, which seemed to please them highly. I thought it best to appear but little concerned at the marked change in my situation and joked with them as was my former habit. Five or six were talking to me when one of the remarked, "My God, Maussa! Wha mek you trow we side so long, Wha mek you no come back?" My answer amused them highly. Smiling and turning to the tall chimney of my former happy home, alone standing to indicate the spot where stood the house, I remarked, "Lord! a Massy! You tink I can lib in de chimney?"

General Harrison and I now left the settlement and proceeded along the north and south canal bank towards the center of the plantation and the East Hermitage tract. This portion of the plantation looked as of old and in tolerably good condition. Proceeding in front of General Harrison and followed by some of his "foremen" (our former Negroes, driver John, cooper George, Big Hector, and the trunk minder Charles), I imagined myself for the moment a planter once more followed by overseer and driver. But these were only passing momentary thoughts, soon dispelled by the sad reality of affairs.

We reached East Hermitage settlement. There remain in the East Hermitage settlement seven large double Negro houses, the overseer's house and kitchen, making a total of nine buildings. We were met by twelve of our former Negroes. They all seemed pleased to see me, called me "Maussa" and the men showing respect by taking off their caps. It was singular that, after an absence of two and a half years from the plantation, I should now return to visit the place just after the death of one of the original Negroes purchased with Gowrie [in] January, 1833—a woman known by the name of Currie Binah [who] died yesterday and was buried this morning. Two of the original Negroes now remain. These are the trunk minder Charles and "Capt'n Hector," for thirty years our chief boat hand, always spoiled both by my father and myself.

Amongst the twelve Negroes who advanced to meet me was the last one I should have dreamt of—Jack Savage, the greatest villain on the plantation, the most notoriously bad character and worst Negro of the place. This Negro was purchased in 1839. He was an exceedingly lazy man, although quite smart and our best plantation carpenter. He was always giving trouble and ever appeared dissatisfied. He was the only Negro ever in our possession who I considered capable of murdering me or burning my dwelling at night. We sold this man in 1863, and I had not seen him since 1862. As we met I gave him my hand and made a few friendly remarks. Even now I felt sad in contemplating his condition—lousy, in rags, uncombed hair. That former mutual and pleasing feeling of master towards slave and vice versa is now as a dream of the past. I beheld young women to whom I had most frequently presented earrings, shoes, calicoes, kerchief, &c., &c., formerly pleased to meet me, but now, sitting idly upon the Negro house steps, dirty and sluggish, not even lifting the head as I passed.

I had to be very guarded in my inquiries of General Harrison respecting his modus operandi under the new regime for fear he would imagine I was prying into his affairs, at the same time it was difficult to divest myself of the idea that I was conversing with one of our overseers. At last I put the simple question to him: "General! Out of curiosity, could you give me an idea of how you make a contract with the Negroes and how do you work the plantation since the termination of the war?" His reply was as follows:

The portion of the Plantation rented to General Harrison contains 390 Acres. This is divided into 5 Divisions, each Division containing 78 Acres.

An intelligent Negro, & one experienced in Rice Culture is chosen, The new appellation of "Foreman" is given him, and he takes full charge of One Division (of in this case 78 Acres).

The "Foreman" is to cultivate & in every respect superintend his Division, until his Crop is threshed, and ready for Market. For this purpose He selects or procures his own Hands, which in this instance requires about 10 for each "Foreman."

A "Contract" is signed in Savannah between Gen'l Harrison and his "Foreman" as above, and for this purpose they two appear at the Government Bureau where the transaction is effected in proper form established by Law. Little or no intercourse is thus held between Gen'l Harrison and the Mass of the Negroes, & provided the Work is performed it is immaterial what Hands are employed whether the same or others.

Each Foreman is furnished one Carpenter.

One Foreman has nothing to do with another Foreman, unless as in certain cases when the Bank between them is broken, or other Work in which both of them are implicated; In such Cases their two Gangs work together.

General Harrison's five Foremen are "John," "Ishmael," "George," "Charles," and "Mac,"—the first four were our own Negroes, and most experienced Rice Planters, whilst the latter belonged to Mr. McMillan King and is looked upon by the General as a highly intelligent Man.

In the "Contract" Duly signed at the Government Bureau Savannah Ga. between Gen'l Harrison & the "Foreman," The former pledges himself to furnish: Land, Trunk-Lumber, Mules, Ploughs, Plantation Tools, and One-Half the Seed Rice. The "Foreman" furnishes: Labor, (and with the Labor is meant to Keep the Trunks in order.). ½ Seed Rice (Bought by Gen'l Harrison and deducted from the Negroes' Wages).

The Negro furnishes his own Provisions, but should he at any time be out of Provisions it is furnished by the General, & deducted from the Wages at the close of the year.

At the end of the year, After ALL PLANTATION EXPENSES ARE PAID ONE HALF THE NET PROFITS is retained by the General, and the other Half is divided amongst the Negroes.

We reached Mr. Potter's plantation at noon and [after] partaking of bread, butter and a tumbler of fresh milk our buggy was brought to the door. Thanking the General for his kindness, with Mr. Habersham's fast horse we were again in Savannah at 2 P.M. All had passed off in a most satisfactory manner, with the exception that upon reaching Savannah I found that the General's servant, who had taken charge of horse and buggy up at the place, had stolen nearly every thing I had in the buggy, but I have never thought it worth my while to mention it to the General, as I have no doubt he has annoyance enough with Negroes.

[8]

The Negroes seemed to reach the climax of lawless independence, and I never slept without a loaded pistol by my bed. They took to calling their former owners by their last name without any title before it, dropped the pleasant term of "Mistress", worked just as much and when they pleased and tried speaking to me with their hats on. It was touch-and-go whether I or the Negroes got the upper hand.

FRANCES BUTLER LEIGH, 1868

FRANCES BUTLER LEIGH (1868–1910) grew up in Philadelphia, the home of her father, Pierce Butler, the absentee owner of three plantations on the Georgia coast. In the spring of 1866, Frances and her father went to Georgia to reclaim their property and resume planting. After her father's death in 1867, Frances became mistress of the plantations and spent nine more years, off and on, in Georgia. In 1871 she married an English clergyman, James W. Leigh, and moved to England in 1877. These selections are drawn from her book *Ten Years on a Georgia Plantation Since the War* (London, 1833), a new edition of which was published by The Beehive Foundation/ Library of Georgia in 1992.

The year after the war, I went with my father to look after our property in Georgia. The whole country had, of course, undergone a complete revolution. Our slaves had been freed. The white population was conquered, ruined and disheartened, unable to see anything but ruin before as well as behind. In many families the young men had perished in the war, and the old men, if not too old for labor, were beggared and had not even money enough to buy food for themselves and their families, let alone their Negroes, to whom they now had to pay wages as well as feed them. Most of the finest plantations were lying idle for want of hands to work them, so many of the Negroes had died. Many had been taken to the Southwest and others preferred hanging about the towns, making a few dollars now and then, to working regularly on the plantations. The South was still treated as a conquered country. The white people were disfranchised, the local government in the hands of either military men or Northern adventurers.

The morning after our arrival in Savannah, my father came into my room to say he was off to the plantation at once. If he wished to do anything at all in the way of planting this season, he must not lose an hour, as it was very doubtful even now if a crop could be got in. When my father returned, he reported that he had found the Negroes all on the place, not only those who were there five years ago, but many who were sold three years before that. Seven had worked their way back from the upcountry. They received him very affectionately and made an agreement with him to work for one-half the crop, that is, one-half to be divided among them according to each man's rate of work, we letting them have in the meantime necessary food, clothing and money for their present wants, which is to be deducted from whatever is due to them at the end of the year. Only a small crop could be planted, enough to make seed for another year and clear expenses. My father also reported that the house was bare, not a bed nor chair left, and that he had been sleeping on the floor, with a piece of wood for a pillow and a few Negro blankets for his covering. So the day after, armed with 500 bushels of seed rice, corn, bacon, a straw mattress and a tub, he started off again for the plantation, leaving me to buy tables and chairs, pots and pans. I cannot give a better idea of the condition of things I found on the Island than by copying the following letter written at the time:

April 12, 1866

Dearest S——,

I have relapsed into barbarism total! I started last Saturday morning for the Island. My father was there to meet us with our own boat, and as it was bright moonlight, we got off with all our things and were rowed across to the island by four of our old Negroes.

I wish I could give you any idea of the house. The floors were bare, of course, many of the panes were out of the windows, and the plaster in many places was off the walls, while one table and two old chairs constituted the furniture. It was pretty desolate, and my father looked at me in some anxiety to see how it would affect me and seemed greatly relieved when I burst out laughing.

The next morning I went to work and made things quite comfortable, unpacked our tables and chairs, put up some curtains (made out of some white muslin I had brought down for petticoats) edged with pink calico, covered the tables with two bright-colored covers I found in the trunk of house linen, had the windows mended, hung up my picture of General Lee over the mantlepiece and put my writing things and nicknacks on the table.

I have one large pot, one frying pan, one tin saucepan and this is all. Yesterday one of the Negroes shot and gave me a magnificent wild turkey, which we roasted on one stick set up between two others before the fire, and capital it was! The broiling is done on two old pieces of iron laid over the ashes. Our food consists of corn and rice bread, rice and fish caught fresh every morning out of of the river, oysters, turtle soup and occasionally a wild turkey or duck. Other meat, as yet, is impossible to get.

I feel like Robinson Crusoe with three hundred men Fridays! The Negroes seem perfectly happy at getting back to the old place and having us there, and I have been deeply touched by many instances of devotion on their part. On Sunday morning, after their church, having nothing to do, they all came to see me, and I must have shaken hands with nearly four hundred. They were full of their troubles and suffering up the country during the war, and the variable winding up was, " 'Tank the Lord, missus, we's back and sees you and massa again." I said to about twenty strong men, "Well, you know you are free and your own masters now." When they broke out with, "No, missus, we belong to you. We be yours as long as we lib." Nearly all who have lived through the terrible suffering of these past four years have come back, as well as many of those who were sold seven years ago. One old couple came up yesterday from Saint Simon's, Uncle John and Mum Peggy, with $5 in silver half-dollars tied up in a bag, which they said a Yankee Captain had given them the second year of the war for some chickens. This money these two old people had kept through all their want and suffering for three years because it had been paid for fowls belonging to us!

One of the great difficulties of this new state of things is what is to be done with the old people who are too old and the children who are too young to work? One Northern General said to a planter, "Well, I suppose they must die," which indeed seems the only thing for them to do. My father has agreed to support the children for three years and the old people till they die, that is feed and clothe them. As we have some property at the North we are able to do this, but most of the planters are utterly ruined and have no money to buy food for their families, so on their plantations I do not see what else is to become of the Negroes who cannot work except to die.

The prospect of getting in the crop did not grow more promising as time went on. The Negroes talked a great deal about their desire and intention to work for us, but their idea of work, unaided by the stern law of necessity, is very vague, some of them working only half a day and some even less. So our properties will soon be utterly worthless, for no crop can be raised by such labor as this. No Negro will work if he can help it, and is quite satisfied just to scrape along doing an odd job here and there to earn money enough to buy a little food. They are affectionate and often trustworthy and honest, but so hopelessly lazy as to be almost worthless as laborers. My father was quite encouraged at first, the people seemed so willing to work and said so much about their intention of doing so. But not many days after they started, he came in quite disheartened, saying that half the hands had left the fields at 1 o'clock and the rest by 3 o'clock.

The rice plantation becoming unhealthy early in May, we removed to Saint Simon's, a sea island on the coast about fifteen miles from Butler's Island. The house on Saint Simon's being entirely stripped of furniture, we had to take our scanty provision of household goods down with us from Butler's Island by raft, our only means of transportation. We found the house a fair-sized, comfortable building with a wide piazza running all 'round it, but without so much as a stool or bench in it. So, hungry and tired, we sat down on the floor to await the arrival of things on the raft. Night came on, but we had no candles and so sat on in darkness till after 10 o'clock, when the raft arrived with almost everything soaked through, the result of a heavy thunder shower. This was more than I could bear, and I burst out crying. Finding the blankets had fortunately escaped the wetting, we spread these on the floor over the wet mattresses and, all dressed, slowly and sadly laid us down to sleep.

My father spent the time in talking to the Negroes, of whom there were about fifty on the place, making arrangements with them for work, more to establish his right to the place than from any good we expected to do this year. We found them in a very different frame of mind from the Negroes on Butler's Island, who, having been removed the first year of the war, had never been brought into contact with either army and remained the same noisy, childish people they had always been. Saint Simon's had been twice in possession of the Northern troops during the war, and the Negroes had consequently been brought under the influence of Northerners, some of whom had filled the poor people's minds with all sorts of vain hopes and ideas, among others that their former masters would not be allowed to return and the land was theirs, a thing many of them believed. They were perfectly respectful but quiet and evidently disappointed. Many of them had planted a considerable quantity of corn and cotton, and this my father told them they might have but that they must put in twenty acres for him, for which he would give them food and clothing. They consented without any show of either pleasure of the reverse and went to work almost immediately under the old Negro foreman or driver who had managed the place before the war.

They still showed that they had confidence in my father, for when a miserable creature, an agent of the Freedmen's Bureau, who was our ruler then and regulated all our contracts with our Negroes, told them that they would be fools to believe that my father would really let them have all the crops they had planted before he came, they replied, "No, sir, our master is a just man. He has never lied to us, and we believe him." Rather taken aback by this, he turned to an old driver who was the principal person present and said, "Why, Bram, how can you care so much for your master. He sold you a few years ago?" "Yes, sir," replied the old man, "he sold me, and I was very unhappy. But he came to me and said, 'Bram, I am in great trouble. I have no money and I have to sell some of the people, but I know where you are all going to and will buy you back again as soon as I can.' And, sir, he told me, Juba, my old wife, must go with me, for though she was not strong and the gentleman who bought me would not buy her, master said he could not let man and wife be separated. And so, sir, I said, 'Master, if you will keep me I will work for you as long as I live, but if you in trouble and it help you to sell me, sell me, master. I am willing.' And now that we free, I come back to my old home and my old master and stay here till I die." To show what perfect confidence my father had on his side in his old slaves, he returned to Butler's Island, leaving me and my maid entirely alone with no white person within eight miles of us. Neither then nor afterwards, when I was alone on the plantation with the Negroes for weeks at a time, had I the slightest feeling of fear.

I had a pretty hard time of it that first year. The country was swept, not a chicken, not an egg was left, and for weeks I lived on hominy, rice and fish with an occasional bit of venison. The Negroes said the Yankees had eaten up everything. I remained on Saint Simon's Island until the end of July, my father coming down from Butler's Island from Saturday till Monday every week for rest. I will finish my account of this year by copying a letter written at the time:

July 9, 1866

Dearest S——:

I am just learning to be an experienced cook and doctress, for the Negroes come to me with every sort of complaint to be treated, and I prescribe for all, pills and poultices being my favorite remedies. I was rather nervous about it at first, but have grown bolder since I find what good results follow my doses. The other day an old woman of over eighty came for a dose, so I prescribed a small one of caster oil, which pleased her so much she returned the next day to have it repeated and again a third time!

We are living directly on the point in the house formerly occupied by the overseer. Of course, it is all very rough and overgrown now, but with the pretty water view across which you look to the wide stretch of broad green salt marsh, which at sunset turns the most wonderful gold bronze color. The fishing is grand, and we have fresh fish for breakfast, dinner and tea. I have two little pet bears, the funniest, jolliest little beasts imaginable. They have no teeth, being only six weeks old, and have to be fed on milk, but if I make the least noise they rush off, get up on their hind legs and hiss and spit at me like cats.

Mr. James Hamilton Couper died last week and was buried at the little church on the island here yesterday. The whole thing was sad in the extreme and a fit illustration of this people and country. Three years ago he was smitten with paralysis, the result of grief at the loss of his son, loss of his property and the ruin of all his hopes and prospects, since which his life has been one of great suffering until a few days ago, when death released him. My father and I drove down in the old mule cart, our only conveyance, nine miles to the church. Here a most terrible scene of desolation met us. The steps of the church were broken down, so we had to walk up a plank to get in. The roof was fallen in, so that the sun streamed down on our heads, while the seats were all cut up and marked with the names of Northern soldiers who had been quartered there during the war. The graveyard was so overgrown with weeds and bushes and tangled with cobweb-like grey moss that we had difficulty in making our way through to the freshly dug grave. The coffin was drawn by one miserable horse and was followed by the Couper family on foot. From the cart to the grave the coffin was carried by four old family Negroes, faithful to the end.

I thought things would be better in 1867, but I found it much harder to get along. My father, finding it impossible to manage the rice plantation on Butler's Island and the cotton one [on Saint Simon's], agreed to the Misses D——'s offer to plant on shares, they undertaking the management here, which allowed him to devote all his time to the other place. The people seem to me working fairly well, but Major D——, used only to Northern labor, is in despair and says they don't do more than half a day's work and that he has often to go from house to house to drive them out to work and then has to sit under a tree in the field to see they don't run away. My father reported the Negroes on Butler's Island as working very well, although requiring constant supervision.

On both places the work is done on the old system by task. We tried working by the day (Indeed, I think we were obliged to do so by the agent of the Freedmen's Bureau, to whom all our contracts had to be submitted), but we found it did not answer at all, the Negroes themselves begging to be allowed to go back to the old task system. One man indignantly asked Major D—— what the use of being free was if he had to work harder than when he was a slave! In all other ways the work went on just as it did in the old times. The force of about three hundred was divided into gangs, each working under a head man—the old Negro drivers who are now called captains, out of compliment to the changed times. These men make a return of the work each night.

My maid telling the people that it was my birthday, they came up in the evening to "shout for me." All day they were bringing me little presents of honey, eggs, flowers, &c. and in the evening about fifty of them collected in front of the house to "shout." First they lit two huge fires of blazing pine logs, around which they began to move with a slow shuffling step, singing a hymn beginning, "I wants to climb up Jacob's ladder." After nearly an hour's performance, I went down to thank them and to stop them. I found it no easy matter to do so, they were so excited. Dear old Uncle John, the preacher, came up to me and, taking my hands in his, said, "God bless you, missus, my dear missus!" My father, who was standing near, put his arm 'round the old man's shoulders and said, "You have seen five generations of us now, John, haven't you?" "Yes, massa," said John, "Miss Sarah's little boy be de fifth, bless de Lord."

But while summer was gliding away, things were growing more and more disturbed, and my father from time to time brought me news of political disturbances and a general growing restlessness among the Negroes. A letter written at the time shows how different reports reached and affected us then and also the condition our part of the South was in:

June 23, 1867

Dearest S——:

We are, I am afraid, going to have terrible trouble by-and-by with the Negroes, and I see nothing but gloomy prospects for us ahead. The unlimited power that the war has put into the hands of the present government at Washington seems to have turned the heads of the party now in office, and they don't know where to stop. The whole South is settled and quiet, and the people too ruined and crushed to do anything against the government, even if they felt so inclined, and all are returning to their former pursuits, trying to rebuild their fortunes and thinking of nothing else.

Yet the treatment we receive from the government becomes more and more severe every day, the last act being to divide the whole South into five military districts, putting each under the command of a United States general, doing away with all civil courts and law. The true reason is the desire and intention of the government to control the elections of the South, which under the constitution of the country they could not legally do. Each commander in his separate district has issued an order declaring that unless a man can take an oath that he had not voluntarily borne arms against the United States nor in any way aided or abetted the rebellion, he cannot vote. This disqualifies every white man at the South from voting, disfranchising the whole white population, while the Negroes are allowed to vote *en masse*. Meanwhile, in order to prepare the Negroes to vote properly, stump speakers from the North are going all through the South, holding political meetings for the Negroes. Do you wonder we are frightened? The one subject that Southerners discuss whenever they meet is, "What is to become of us?"

In August of 1867 my father died, and as soon as I was able I went down to the South to carry on his work and to look after the Negroes. We reached Butler's Island in November. The people were like sheep without a shepherd. Before anything could be done, the Negroes had to be settled with for the past two years and their share of the crops divided. My father had given each Negro a little pass-book, in which had been entered from time to time the food, clothing and money which each had received from him on account. There were over three hundred of these little books. There was the large plantation ledger, in which the work each man had, or had not, done every day had been entered for nearly two years. Night after night I sat up till 2 and 3 o'clock balancing these two accounts. Not one Negro understood it a bit, but all were quite convinced they had been cheated, most of them thinking that each man was entitled to half the crop. After endless discussions, I paid them the money due them, which was always received with the same remark, "Well, well, work for massa two whole years, and only get dis much!" Notwithstanding their dissatisfaction, $6000 was paid out among them, many getting as much as $200 to $300 apiece. The result was that a number of them left me and bought land of their own.

Politics had begun working among them. The agent of the Freedmen's Bureau was our master, always ready to believe the wildest complaints from Negroes. (A Negro carpenter complained that a gentleman owned him $50 for work, so without further inquiry or any trial, the agent sent the gentleman word to pay at once or he would have him arrested, the sheriff at that time being one of his own former slaves!) Having been in quiet possession of our property for two years, we were suddenly notified one day that Saint Simon's Island came under the head of abandoned property, being occupied by former owners who had refused to make application for its restoration under the law. "Therefore," so ran the order, "such property shall be confiscated on the first day of January next, unless before that date the owners present themselves, take the required oath of allegiance and ask for its restoration." So my brother-in-law, a strong Republican who had voted for Lincoln and Grant and done all in his power to aid the Northern government, had to go and take the oath of allegiance on behalf of his wife; she also having always sympathized with the Northern cause!

My brother-in-law soon after left me and then my real troubles began. It seemed quite hopeless ever to get the Negroes to settle down to steady work, and, although they still professed the greatest affection for me, it certainly did not show itself in works. My new agent assured me that there must be a contract made and signed with the Negroes, binding them for a year, in order to have any hold upon them at all. After having two of them run off in spite of the solemnity of the contract and having to pay something like $20 to the authorities to fetch them back, we didn't trouble ourselves much about enforcing it after that. At first the Negroes flatly refused to sign any contract at all, having been advised by their Northern friends not to do so, as it would put them back to slavery. My agent told me he feared none would sign the contract, they were so dissatisfied with last year's settlement. Even old Henry, one of the captains and my chief supporter, said, "Missus, I bery sorriful, for half de people is going to leave."

I had the big mill bell rung to summon the people to sign the contract. For six hours I sat in the office, while the people poured in and poured out, each one with long explanations, objections and demonstrations. One was willing to work in the mill but not in the field. Several would not agree to sign unless I promised to give them the whole of Saturday for a holiday. At last 6 o'clock came and I closed the books with sixty-two names down. Monday morning the bell again rang. I was again in the office from 10 A.M. to 6 P.M. and found it far more unpleasant than on Saturday, as I had several troublesome, bad fellows to deal with. One positively refused to work or leave the place, so he had to be informed that if he was not gone in three days he would be put off, which had such an effect that he came the next day and signed.

Tuesday and Wednesday my stragglers came dropping in, the last man arriving under a large cotton umbrella, very defiant. "Five days I'll work, but" (with a flourish of the umbrella) "I works for no man on Saturday." "Then," said I, "I am sorry, but you can't work for me, for any man who works for me *must* work on Saturday." "Good morning, den, missus," says my man, with another flourish of the umbrella, and departs. About an hour afterwards he returned to sign. Only two men really went, one from imagined ill-health and one I dismissed for insubordination. The backbone of the opposition thus broken, the work started more or less steadily.

While we were getting things more and more settled on the place, the troubles from outside were drawing nearer and nearer as the day for voting approached and in March burst upon us in the shape of political meetings and excitement of all kinds. Two or three Northern political agents arrived in Darien and summoned all the Negroes to attend meetings, threatening them with various punishments if they stayed away. In vain I reasoned with the Negroes and did all I could to prevent strangers landing on the island. I doubled the watchmen at night but one morning found that during the night a notice had been put up on the wharf calling upon all the people to attend a political meeting on pain of being fined $500 or exiled to a foreign land! (I cared not in the least which way they voted, but I knew that if the people broke off no more work would be done for at least a week just the time one of our plantings had to be put in.) So I argued and threatened. It was useless, however, the Negroes naturally thinking that the people who freed them could do anything they liked and must be obeyed.

The election day came. My agent had me awaked at 6 o'clock in the morning to tell me that there was not a Negro in the field, all having announced their intention of going over to Darien to vote. By 10 o'clock there was not a man left on the place, even the old half-idiot who took care of the cows having gone to vote with the rest. The hands all returned to their work early in the day after voting, and all finished the entire task with the exception of two or three who promised to do double work the next day. Down on Saint Simon's, their ardor about voting was considerably cooled by the fact that they had twelve miles to walk to the polls and had not been visited by any political agents to stir them up. I think that the Negroes' voting was a wicked farce that only deserved our contempt.

I hope and believe that the Negroes will come to realize their new condition in time. But the change was too great. The fixed notion in their minds has been that liberty meant idleness. Our neighbors on Saint Simon's are discouraged with the difficulties they encounter, having to lose two or three months every year while the Negroes are making up their minds whether they will work or not. There are about a dozen on Butler's Island who do no work. They all raise a little corn and sweet potatoes and with their facilities for catching fish and oysters and shooting wild game they have as much to eat as they want.

We had a small excitement in November, 1868, owing to a report which went the round of the plantations that there was to be a general Negro insurrection on the first of the year. The Negroes this year and the following seemed to reach the climax of lawless independence, and I never slept without a loaded pistol by my bed. Their whole manner was changed. They took to calling their former owners by their last name without any title before it, dropped the pleasant term of "Mistress," took to calling me "Miss Fanny," walked about with guns upon their shoulders, worked just as much and when they pleased and tried speaking to me with their hats on and not touching them when they passed. I felt the whole time that it was touch-and-go whether I or the Negroes got the upper hand.

[9]

The South feels instinctively that she is standing upon the mouth of a volcano. Four or five colored men said that the white folks was scared of the niggers, that things wasn't like they used to be and that they was gwine to have fine times and burn up every house along the road.

ELLA GERTRUDE THOMAS, 1868

ELLA GERTRUDE THOMAS (1834–1907) was the daughter of a prosperous farmer who graduated from Wesleyan College and married a planter near Augusta, the owner of some ninety slaves. In the aftermath of the Civil War, Mr. Thomas's business failed, the plantation was sold to pay debts and Mrs. Thomas was obliged to support her family by teaching school and taking in boarders. The journal from which these selections have been drawn is at Duke University Library.

November 1st, 1868. I have not alluded to the present unsettled state of affairs among the Negroes and white people, but it has for some time been a subject of much interest. Things are rapidly approaching a crisis. Tuesday will be the day for the Presidential election, and the South feels instinctively that she is standing upon the mouth of a volcano, expecting every moment an eruption and if it takes place—what then? Tonight it is reported that all of the houses in the neighborhood are to be burnt up. When I commenced writing, I did not know this was the night. Mr. Thomas was out watching, but I did not know where. Four or five colored men came and went into Dinah's room, and Mr. Thomas went out to find out "what they were after." Ned came in a few moments after and told me, as he sat down on the floor by my side before the fire, "that the niggers out in the quarter were talking about the election, that Mr. McDonald made them a speech today at the church and that Uncle Harry said it was all some of them could do to keep from dragging him out of the pulpit and that they was all gwine to meet at the creek tomorrow night to march to town the next day with Uncle Isaiah as captain and Uncle Mac said if he had a son who was willing to be a Democrat he would cut his throat." Ned also added that these men said "that all the white folks was scared of the

73

niggers, that Dr. Eves's family was moving in town today and that he was gwine to send his things in tomorrow and that Uncle Mac said that things wasn't like they used to be, that they weren't afraid of white folks like they used to be and that they was gwine to have fine times and burn up every house along the road." Ned is a black boy about fourteen years old, boasts that he voted the Democratic ticket at McBean. Isaiah and Mac are farming with Mr. Thomas on shares.

Just then Mr. Thomas came in, his coat was covered with cobwebs. "Why, look at your coat. Where have you been?" said I. He looked warningly at me, reminding me of Ned (for we have perfect confidence in none of them) and told Ned to bring him some water, adding to me in a low tone of voice, "Under the house listening to them." "I would not allow a party of Radical Negroes to assemble here," said I. "I would send for General Harris and some of the neighbors and, if a crowd assembles, order them off." "They are all right," said Mr. Thomas, "I understand it." Putting on his overcoat, he left the room. A few moments after, two little girls, Lena and Winny, came running in the house out of breath and told me that Uncle Bob, Patsy's husband, said "please to tell Mr. Thomas to come there." This was such an unusual proceeding for him to *send* for Mr. Thomas instead of coming that I concluded to see what he wanted. Going into the room I found them in quite a state of excitement. Mr. Thomas, they said, had told them "that *they* were going to burn the house up tonight and Bob had just come from town and he wanted to understand what about it." Dinah was in the room and Warren came in. He is a very independent, impertinent hand, hired to work on the farm. I know he and Bob are both Radicals. I took a seat and talked with them awhile, told them that the white people were anxious to avoid a difficulty but that if forced to it they would fight and fight well.

Soon after Mary, who sleeps in the room and is about the age and color of Ned, came in and said, as she was fastening a window, "Miss 'Trudy, is the colored folks gwine to rise tomorrow?" I comforted her by telling her, "No." And just then Mr. Thomas came in and she went upstairs. Mr. Thomas said, "I was surprised to hear you tell the servants that I had told you nothing about the houses being fired in the neighborhood." "Told me when?" I said in the utmost surprise. "Last week, don't you remember that a Negro told a member of the 'club,' adding that he had begged for Mrs. Twiggs and Judge Allen's houses." He had told me and I had not given it one thought since.

November 2nd. After dressing and assisting the children, for Patsy is still sick, I came down to breakfast. The children greeted me, telling me there was to be no school today, as Jeff said, "Miss Maria and Mrs. Roberts had gone to town because they were afraid their house was going to be burnt up." I smiled and replied that I was not afraid, that I would expect the men on this place to keep anyone from troubling mine. As Mr. Thomas kissed me goodby he told me to have his two guns brought into this room and lock up a box of something wrapped in paper (cartridges, I believe he called them), which he brought from town for the use of the "club" or company of which he is captain. They meet at Twiggs Academy and, although they do not drill, are prepared at a moment's notice. But I do hope there will be no necessity for force. There is certainly no glory to be won in such a contest, and nothing but absolute necessity will cause the Southern men to resort to force. There the two guns are standing in the corner, and I do not know whether either of them are loaded and, if they were, I would not know how to use them.

Monday night, November 2nd. Since the weather has become so cold, I have been sleeping upstairs with the younger children and Mr. Thomas and Turner remain in the wing room to guard the place and prevent robberies. I have since tea been in the sitting room with Mr. Thomas and the children and he has been reloading his guns. The children have gone to bed and Turner taken off his military suit, which he wears today for the first time. It is the cadet dress of the academy. Mr. Thomas has two guns and two pistols, and as I came on upstairs I brought one of the latter. Mary Belle and Julian are in my bed, Jeff and Cora Lou are asleep together. Just then the dogs barked furiously and I heard Mr. Thomas call to know "who was there." He is evidently on the lookout. A little while after coming up, I thought I heard drums beating and I hear the same noise still. I went out into the piazza and listened, but could hear nothing except the distant sound of dogs barking.

Just as I closed this book I was fortunate enough to find a better pen on the mantlepiece, so I will turn the lamp up, throw an additional piece of lightwood and give Mrs. Harris's experience of yesterday. Arriving at the church, Mrs. Harris found everyone wearing an excited air. Taking a seat by Mrs. Allen, she said, "What is the meaning of all this?" "Nothing except a sensation[al] report of Mr. Ben Neely," said Mrs. Allen. "He went out of his house last night when he heard two Negroes talking. 'Is everything ready,' said one, 'ammunition and all?' 'Yes,' said the other. 'I want to begin soon in the morning.' He—Mr. Neely —was on his way to Dr. Eve's, which house he entered in a great state of excitement, creating a panic among the family."

Just here I must say that I do not in my heart wonder that the Negroes vote the Radical ticket and to have persuaded them otherwise would be against my own conscience. Think of it, the right to vote, that right which they have seen their old masters exercise with so much pride is within their very grasp! They secure a right for themselves, which it is true they may not understand, but they have children whom they expect to educate. Who can guarantee that they will ever have it extended to them again? If the women of the North once secured to me the right to vote, I think I should think twice before I voted to have it taken from me. Of course, such sentiments smack too much of Radicalism to promulgate outside of my own family and, though I do not say much, I think Grant will be elected, and I don't think, if we can have peace, that it will make much difference.

November 3rd. Today is election day. No wonder the great heart of the South throbs at the thought of how much will depend on the vote of today. Mr. Thomas has gone to vote. Turner has gone to town to have an opportunity to wear his new uniform and witness the voting—he will be fifteen in December on the 9th. All of the gentlemen in the neighborhood have gone to vote. Mr. Thomas is captain of the company organized down in this neighborhood or, as he is termed, "President of the Democratic Club." Everything is perfectly quiet with us. The servants go about their accustomed duties.

At night, Tuesday, November 3rd. Late this afternoon Mac returned from Augusta and Mary Bell inquired of him "if he voted." He replied, "Yes, the Republican ticket." "How was everything going on?" "Beautifully ma'm, beautifully," said he, throwing his arms about with much energy. Turner came in just at dark and reported that a riot took place. He was at Ma's and all of them at dinner. Cora came running in, crying "that they were fighting at the city hall and her husband was there." Holt seized his arms and all of them ran into the street to witness the scene. The men were flying in all directions. Turner did not know how it originated but thinks two men were disputing when one of them drew his pistol and this commenced it. The Negroes were uptown talking and threatening. Then they started down again. The white men formed in line to check them. The Yankees advanced, took position between the contending parties, and the police arrested several ringleaders among the Negroes. A pistol was shot and Ruffin, the deputy sheriff, a Southern Radical, fell. No one knew who fired the shot. He was taken into the hall from the yard and died soon after. When Turner left everything was quiet but a disturbance [is] expected tonight but everyone [is] prepared for it. The sight of a few dead men will calm their excited feelings more effectually than many words.

Turner asked Mac tonight "who he voted for?" Mac hesitated. He had forgotten the name. "Who did *you* vote for?" said he. (He did not know Turner could not vote.) "Grant and Colfax," said Turner. "Then I voted for the other side," said Mac and that was about all he knew! He said he voted what they told him to.

Monday night, November 29th. Old friend! Tears gather, it is only with an effort that I prevent them from rolling down upon your pages. Mr. Thomas's affairs are so complicated, and he is so depressed, "run to death" as he expresses it. For a long time I have known of his pecuniary embarrassments. Within the last two or three days a man who is the agent for a New York company has been in Augusta, and it is in his power to fall the firm into bankruptcy. I was in town last week and, walking up town, I passed by the store of Mr. Drake, above the Central States Hotel. The doors and windows were closed and upon the door was a card stating that the store had been closed and the goods levied upon by Mr. Levy, the sheriff. Mr. Thomas is afraid that tomorrow he may find his store closed with a similar card upon it.

December 30th, 1870. Tuesday and Wednesday, the 20th and 21st of December, the election took place. All the Negroes in the neighborhood marched in procession to Augusta (or most of them) to vote for Daniel Horton for the legislature. He is a respectable, well-behaved, brown-skinned man but not exactly qualified to make laws for me or mine. When the Negroes reached Augusta, they were ordered to stack their arms outside of the city. The election proceeded quietly. As Turner and Jeff went in Thursday afternoon, they found a number of Negroes on the road in a great state of excitement, Daniel Horton among them. As he would pass by a house, he would leave word, "Tell my men to meet me at the bridge tonight." Turner rode on and listened to them, as they would threaten what they intended doing. The night before, a party of young [white] men or boys had been down in this neighborhood and Thursday morning six of them took breakfast with Mr. Ben Neely. The Negroes said they were Ku Klux, that their object was to burn Daniel Horton's house up and that was the reason for his summons to them to assemble at Butler's Creek Bridge. "Color for color!" was their rallying cry and, to do them justice, I do not think they are usually the first to commence a fight.

A group of Negroes were just in front of one of their houses the other side of double branches, when, Joe Gussey Twiggs riding by, one of them told him that his brother was one of the Ku Kluxes, using menacing words and threats. A Negro woman in the crowd told him he had better ride on, that they were going to kill his brother. All along the road were eager, excited groups of colored men. Turner and Jeff met Mr. Thomas and Mr. Jones on the edge of town and they returned together. By this time the snow began to fall heavily and the air became very cold. Mr. Thomas had Turner to load up the guns, not knowing what use they would have for them. Occasionally the noise of the Negroes' shouting might be heard when we went out upon the piazza. "I don't think you need feel the slightest uneasiness," said I. "This snow will chill out all the martial glory with the Negroes." And so it proved. The snow fell thick and fast, and no more noise was heard. Mr. Thomas thought the only danger might arise from their drinking too much at the store by the bridge. Mr. Thomas proposed that they should stop and speak to them. They did so, and Mr. Thomas inquired, "Why, boys, what is the matter? You all seem to be in a great state of excitement?" They explained that the Ku Klux wished to burn Daniel Horton's house up and &c. Mr. Thomas reasoned with them, told them it was better to disperse and create no disturbance. They told him Mr. James Clanton was one of the Ku Klux. "Why," said Mr. Thomas, "Mr. Clanton is on his plantation sixteen miles above Augusta." "Well, I knows," said one of them, "it was a red-headed gentleman and if [it] wa'nt him 'twas his brother!" "Holt Clanton is in Europe, miles away from here," said Mr. Thomas. With no better evidence than this, they might have visited Augusta, reported Buddy as one of the Ku Klux and the Yankee authorities might have summoned him to prove an alibi!

The next morning, Friday, the 23rd of December, I was aroused by the glad shouts of the children at the snow. The trees were covered with the snow and the ground was carpeted several inches thick. Turner scraped up several tubs and buckets of snow and packed it away for making sherbert.

⌈ 10 ⌉

The Negroes on all the Ogeechee plantations appear to be armed and organized. They will not work and, by threats and violence, prevent those who are willing to labor from serving their employers. The Negroes have become emboldened and threaten to drive out the whites. . . . The leaders went about cursing, "The white sons of bitches were afraid to come!"

The Ogeechee Insurrection, 1868–69

IN LATE DECEMBER, 1868, freedmen living on the plantations near the Ogeechee River outside Savannah seized control of the area, running off their white landlords and farm managers and causing panic in the city of Savannah. The following narrative has been adapted from news reports in the Savannah *Morning News* between December 23rd, 1868, and January 8th, 1869.

December 23, 1868. Proof of organization and a complete league among the country Negroes come from all quarters. A citizen travelling on the Ogeechee road a day or two ago was stopped, questioned by armed pickets at every crossroad and only allowed to proceed after a great deal of palaver and pow-wow among the darkies. He concluded to get out of that country as soon as possible.

December 24, 1868. On all the Ogeechee plantations the Negroes appear to be banded together, thoroughly armed and organized. They will not work and, by threats and violence, prevent those who are willing to labor from serving their employers, their object being to prevent the rice crop from being secured by day that they may steal it at night.

To put an end to these depredations, a number of white men were employed on many of the plantations to watch the fields by night. Last Monday night a band of Negroes appeared in the fields of "Southfield" and "Prairie" plantations, owned by Captain John F. Tucker and Major J. M. Middleton. They fired a volley at the watchmen, wounding two of them. About fifty shots were fired and the watchmen driven off. The Negroes then proceeded to steal sixteen sacks of rice, about 160 bushels. Previous to that they had at frequent times stolen a greater portion of the crop made this year. At nights they picket the roads and allow no white man to travel in that section. The Negro women fear to go into the fields by reason of threats of being shot at and can only be got to work by providing them with an armed guard.

The white watchmen, owing to their having been frequently shot at, have become completely demoralized, and the planters say that they will either have to be protected by the law or abandon the country. The Negroes have become emboldened and threaten to drive out the whites. They drill regularly, are armed, equipped and organized in regular military style. They live mainly by plundering the plantations of poultry and stock, stealing the horses and selling them and ranging the woods for game. One of the ringleaders goes about at all times with an armed bodyguard and puts on as much style as an army brigadier. In that section of the country there appears to be no longer any security for life or property.

December 30, 1868. Warrants, charging some seventeen Negroes with larceny and assault with intent to murder, were issued and placed in the hands of Sheriff Dooner, who intended to execute them. Knowing the desperate character of many of these Ogeechee Negroes and feeling that they would resist being taken by any civil posse, Sheriff Dooner concluded to call upon the military for aid. Major Perkins, then commanding this post, promised to furnish the men whenever the Sheriff might call for them. Subsequently, however, the promise was revoked and the Sheriff informed that under the existing state of public affairs no action could be taken by the military until every means and all energies of the civil authorities had been exhausted and they proved powerless to act in the matter.

Thinking that perhaps it would be better to execute the warrants without show of force, as he could not have the assistance of the military, Sheriff Dooner determined to go to the Ogeechee, accompanied by two officers only and by kindness and persuasion endeavor to secure the enforcement of the laws. Accordingly he left by the Atlantic and Gulf Railroad train yesterday morning, accompanied by Deputy Sheriff Mendel and Special Officer Julius Kauffmann. They arrived at Station No. 1 at about twenty minutes to 8 o'clock, where they found horses in readiness to convey them to their place of destination.

The officers went up the Ogeechee River to Heyward's plantation, about five and a half miles from the station, where Sheriff Dooner exhibited his warrants to the overseer, who brought in five of the persons named therein. To these men the warrants were read, the matter explained to them, and they were insured of good treatment if they would go quietly, and they were left with the overseer under notice to be at the station in time to go to Savannah on the down train. The officers then went to the "New Hope" plantation, owned by Miss Elliott, to arrest other parties.

An old Negro named Solomon Farley makes his headquarters at this place. He is President of a Union League and always in some kind of mischief. Last year, when military investigating parties were sent to the Ogeechee, Solomon was frequently before them. He appears to be a great rascal. His name was upon one of the warrants, and the Sheriff proceeded to arrest him. Farley was in the Negro settlement, and when the Sheriff read the warrant, he exhibited considerable reluctance about obeying it but finally said he would go, but adding that he was not secured yet! Before going, Solomon drew something upon a slip of paper and handed it to his wife, who started off up the canal upon receiving it. He also gave similar slips to other darkies, who followed the woman's example. These actions being observed by the officers, the Sheriff ordered Solomon to stop doing so.

The officers, with Solomon in charge, then went off to the railroad station, where they arrived at half past 2 in the afternoon. While eating lunch, the Sheriff and his companions noticed a number of Negroes up the road. The number of Negroes soon increased. In about fifteen minutes, there was a great mob of the Negroes, armed with guns and other weapons. About 200, it was estimated, were present. Perceiving that the crowd designed attacking them and being almost powerless against so large a number, the officers left the station and started in the direction of Savannah. The crowd of Negroes followed, yelling like a pack of demons. About 200 yards from the station, the officers took refuge in a house belonging to Mr. Willis. The crowd at once surrounded the house. Sheriff Dooner favored barricading the doors and windows and fighting as long as they could hold out but yielded to the advice of the others who thought that the Negroes would fire the house in case such a course was pursued.

The Negroes were armed with muskets, axes, clubs, etc. They were very excited, disorderly and threatening. The Sheriff addressed them in a conciliatory manner, to which they replied that they didn't care for the Sheriff or anybody else. The three officers had come out of the house at this time, and they were immediately surrounded by the Negroes, who demanded their arms and the warrants. They levelled muskets and pistols at them and, seizing them, took their arms, the warrants, money and whatever else of value they had about them. A small pistol, which Sheriff Dooner had in a side pocket of his coat, was overlooked and was the only thing not stolen. The Negroes then went off in the direction of Station No. 1.

A boy came to the officers and advised them to leave as quickly as possible, and they started along the railroad towards Savannah, travelling as fast as they were able. About five miles from the station, the down train overtook them, stopped and took the party aboard. The Sheriff and his deputies arrived at home last evening, completely exhausted, weary and footsore.

December 31, 1868. The trouble on the Ogeechee plantations has created more excitement in the city than we have had since the election times. People gathered in the streets and read the *News* extra, talked about what ought to be done and gave their unanimous opinion that these things should be stopped and at once.

Feeling that some action was necessary to teach the blacks that they must respect the law and its officers and that the lives and property of citizens should be preserved, Sheriff Dooner and Henry S. Wetmore, Ordinary, called upon Mayor Anderson yesterday morning for consultation. It was decided that the parties guilty of the flagrant outrages committed on Tuesday night must be arrested. Mayor Anderson went in person to General Williams to ask the aid of the military, but the instructions received from General Meade prevented the granting of the request. Only after all men and means of the civil authorities had been exhausted could the military act.

Under this decision nothing was left but for the Sheriff to summon his posse. One hundred and fifty warrants against Ogeechee Negroes were issued for robbery by force upon the public highway, robbery by intimidation, assault with intent to murder and larceny. A warrant against Solomon Farley and others was also issued.

O'Donald, one of Mr. Middleton's watchmen, who was supposed to have been killed, arrived in the city yesterday evening. He states that the Negroes came and took him out of his house, struck him in the head with the butt of a musket, beat and kicked him. They marched him up and down the yard, stopping every few minutes to give him a beating and finally turned him loose, telling him that he had better leave quick and not come back there any more or they would murder him. O'Donald went off about a mile and took refuge in the house of a colored man, where he remained until morning, and then started for this city. Before starting to the city, Mr. O'Donald went back to "Southfield" plantation to hunt for his little boy who had been left there the night before. He found the child all right, and the parties of lawless vagabonds gone. They had spent the night at Mr. Middleton's house and had completely cleaned it and the other houses of their contents. He saw no Negroes on the place except the regular hands, who had come up to go to work, but there was no one to assign them their tasks, and they were lounging about the premises.

Mr. Middleton's manservant came to the city yesterday afternoon with a horse and a mule belonging to that gentleman. He reported everything quiet but said that all the houses had been plundered of everything they contained. The Gulf Railroad train brought up from No. 1 last evening a number of women and children who said that they had been driven from off plantations by the Negroes and had to flee for their lives. The summoning of the Sheriff's posse created considerable stir about town last evening. The Sheriff will go down this morning, with force sufficient to enforce the laws and arrest the bad Negroes.

January 1, 1869. The troubles on the Ogeechee plantations continue and appear to be gaining strength. The Negroes are receiving reinforcements from Bryan and Liberty counties, and trustworthy persons from that section report that they are plundering all the plantations and threatening destruction to all who dare to meddle with them. They are said to have thrown up some sort of a fortification at Peach Hill and have all the roads and approaches strongly guarded. Major Middleton has been informed that, after robbing his house of its contents, the Negroes returned on Wednesday night and burned the dwelling.

Sheriff Dooner went down to No. 1 early yesterday morning with a pretty strong force, but, on reaching there and learning that the Negroes were out in force, he concluded to return to the city to obtain a force sufficient to make the arrests. Soon after their return, Major Middleton issued a call for a public meeting to take the matter into consideration. At half past 1 o'clock a large number of young men and a few old and prominent citizens had assembled at the court house to devise measures for enforcing the law. Major Middleton said the newspapers had given a true account of the state of affairs, but it was even worse than had been represented. The Negroes were found to be in strong force and well armed by the party which went down in the morning. The Negroes had burned Mr. Habersham's house, sacked the barns and taken all his property. He said a large force was needed. General Henry R. Jackson said the Negroes were in large armed bodies and occupy a large geographical position. The mischief would not be confined to the plantations on the Ogeechee but would extend to the Savannah. And what then becomes of the city of Savannah, surrounded on all sides by an armed and brutal mob? We are warring against bandits, armed desperadoes who are ruining the city! The best moment to stop the mischief is now! Meet force by force! General Meade had refused the aid of the military, and we must prove that we are men enough to take care of ourselves.

January 2, 1869. The state of affairs on the Ogeechee continues to be the all-absorbing topic throughout the city, and people eagerly listen to all reports and rumors, however wild or improbable they may be which come from that section. We have from a gentleman who came up yesterday morning a confirmation of the report that the Negroes, in strong force and thoroughly armed, were lying near the railroad, watching the movements of and prepared to resist the Sheriff's posse which went down on Wednesday. When the train moved off, he says, some six or seven hundred Negroes came out on the railroad and the leaders went about cursing and saying, "The white sons of bitches were afraid to come and attack and have gone back for more men!" He says that there is a very large force of the Negroes at No. 1 and that they are determined to resist any attempt to arrest them.

Another gentleman confirms the report and says that soon after the return of the special train, a gravel train came along and the Negroes crowded the track and would not move off. The train then went down the road again. A countryman from Liberty County arrived here yesterday with produce to sell. He reports that the Negroes have destroyed the bridge over the Little Ogeechee River, four miles this side of Chapman's house. He was stopped by five different picket parties, each gang numbering eight or ten men. They told him to tell the white men of Savannah to come on, that they were ready for them. After questioning this man, they finally allowed him to come on to the city, telling him not to come back again or they would kill him.

The Negroes from the Augusta road were crossing to the Ogeechee in large numbers yesterday and joining the insurrectionary bands. The latest news which we have from the scene of the trouble represents it as spreading and that the Negroes, by threats and intimidation, are forcing those who are disposed to remain peaceable to join them. So far their operations are confined to the [area] west of the railroad and between the two Ogeechee rivers. But if not speedily checked, it is feared that it will extend into Bryan County. Alderman Burroughs, who was at his plantation on Wednesday, reports all quiet in that section, and his son remains there in charge of the place. A letter received from a planter in Bryan contains the following: "It is unnecessary for me to say how urgent the necessity is for immediate action, as the badly disposed Negroes are all the time increasing their force by intimidating those who would not join could they see any power to protect them. If action is delayed much longer I fear the mischief will extend."

Dave Brister, a colored man in the employ of Major Middleton, who was friendly to that gentleman, was driven away by the Negroes. Dave arrived here last evening. He says that on Wednesday the Negroes went to "Southfield" and uttered threats against his old cook and demanded to know from her where the mules were. She did not know, and they then brought up some mules and carried off the carts. They then went after Dave, who took his two children and fled. He lay out in the woods in the rain all Wednesday night and came in last evening, almost worn out. Dave confirms the statement that these disorderly Negroes are forcing the quietly disposed ones to join them.

On Wednesday the rioters took John Hogan, colored, one of Mr. Middleton's watchmen and the man who gave shelter to O'Donald and the wives and children of the white men who were beaten and driven from "Southfield" and let him off. The last seen of him he was being driven in the direction of the railroad track at the point of the bayonet by a gang of the Negroes. Nothing has been heard of him since, and it is not known whether he was murdered or driven off.

When the Gulf Railroad train arrived at No. 1 last evening, nothing unusual occurred. No Negroes appeared, but posted in a conspicuous place was a manifesto, which must have come from Solomon Farley. Planters who have seen his rude attempts at writing believe him to be the author. The paper reads as follows: "To the Publick At Large. I has been accused in the midst of 17 or 18 men's as a Capt. which cants not be approved for Stealing Tucker & Mideleton's Rice. the party Has Accused Me & Drawn me in for a Old Grudge. the Sheriff Arrested me and Brought me Some 4 or 5 Miles to Station No. 1. and their Came up a Party of the Loyal Leaguers. And Released Me in Regard that their is no Stay laws Which will Give the Republican Party no Particularity. If it was they would not Stopped my Going with the Sheriff to Savannah. If you should not See Me I will make my Appearance Just as Soon as the law Being Essued for the Right of all Classes & Color! ! ! ! Yours, Ogeechee Until Death." The Negroes appear to be strengthening themselves, continuing their plundering and awaiting a movement from this city.

January 4, 1869. Reliable news from the Ogeechee country is hard to obtain and what the insurgent Negroes are doing is not exactly known. The city is full of rumors of every kind, all of which find plenty of believers. The following report from Mr. Snyder, Master of Roadway, A. & G. R.R., may be taken as reliable and contains information of interest to the public: "Mr. Hinton, overseer on section No. 1, reported to me yesterday that on December 31st, 1868, an armed band of Negroes, numbering from two to three hundred, came to where he was at work on the track near Station No. 1 and threatened to kill him and said that no white man should live between the two Ogeechees. The hands that were at work with Mr. Hinton interfered in his favor and told the party that if they killed Mr. Hinton they must kill them also. The armed force then left, after making all kinds of threats to Mr. Hinton. He went back to his section yesterday about 1 P.M. As we passed by section 1, there was a picket of Negroes, one this side of No. 1 and one on the other side. They were quiet and made no remarks that we heard."

David Corker, with his family, came into the city on Saturday. He kept a country store on the Ogeechee Road about twelve miles from this city. He reports that on Saturday morning a large band of armed Negroes came to his store and ordered him to take himself and family off and not to come back there again or his life should pay the penalty. They then proceeded to sack the place, carrying off the goods and fixtures and destroying what they did not steal. Families residing near the canal, not far from LaRoche's mill, were also compelled to leave home and flee to the city for protection. The Negroes were also reported to be killing all the cattle and hogs and collecting the provisions in the country in readiness to convey to their strongholds, where they hope to defy the law.

On Saturday morning an Ogeechee Negro came into town and stated to a prominent gentleman that he had been sent by the insurgents to this city to make the proposition that ten or twelve colored men be sent out there by the citizens to treat with them and arrange the difficulty in a manner satisfactory to all parties. He was promptly taken into custody, being recognized as one of the fomentors of the trouble. Unquestionably there are peaceful, quiet colored people in the Ogeechee country who are anxiously looking for protection from the disturbers of the peace who are forcing all the hands on the plantations to join them under penalty of death in case of refusal. All respectable colored people in this city condemn the outbreak and can see nothing but evil consequences for their own race to follow it.

The Negroes did not visit Messrs. Tucker and Middleton's "Prairie" plantation until Saturday, when an armed body of them made their appearance at that place with wagons and carts, by means of which they carried off all the rice. Mr. William Cook, who was in charge of this plantation, made a hasty escape into Bryan County. N. J. Arnold, who had a plantation in Bryan, came up with his family on Saturday. The people in that section remained quiet at that time and expressed a determination to stand by the whites. Numbers of bad Negroes, however, had crossed the river and joined the insurgents on Ogeechee neck. Every day the trouble increases, and there is urgent necessity for speedy action.

The military commander of this port paid a visit to the Ogeechee country on Saturday. Of course everything was quiet when he reached there, and the Negroes were peaceable, quiet citizens. They offered to surrender to the military authorities but objected to being placed in custody of the civil officers. In obedience to a command from Washington, two companies of U.S. Infantry arrived from Atlanta last evening. Two other companies are expected this morning. General Sibley is in command of the whole expedition. Until a late hour last evening the civil and military authorities were in consultation. Some of the

Radical Negro apostles in this city, we understand, went down to the Ogeechee on Saturday to advise the Negroes to give up quietly.

January 5, 1869. The main body of insurrectionists continue to hold the Ogeechee plantations, undisturbed by invasion either by bluecoats or Sheriff's posse. The arrival of the military has put an end to the latter, and those who had enrolled themselves for service were yesterday notified that their services would not be needed.

The idea that this armed insurrection against the laws was preconcerted and arranged by parties whose interests would be furthered should the state be put out of the Union again is generally believed. The so-called governor, whose duty it should have been to have put down the trouble at once, was away and nothing in the world could have furthered his purpose better than a disturbance of this kind. Nothing easier than to charge it to the whites! The Negroes could not see why those rich plantations and the crop, the result of a whole year's labor, should not belong to them! It was a piece of presumption in white men, who risk all their capital in planting, to place watchmen in the field and in the Sheriff to think it his duty to arrest a thief or murderer who happened to have a black skin! We who are here, who are sufferers by the disturbed state of the country, cannot view things exactly in that light—but we do not see with Radical eyes, nor hear with Radical ears! In the course of time we may become civilized, but the Radical millennium has not yet arrived!

Fourteen [black insurrectionists] arrived in the city about 3 o'clock yesterday morning. They surrendered to the military authorities at the Oglethorpe Barracks. The prisoners were at once turned over to the civil officers of the law, and they were escorted to jail by Sheriff Dooner. They are the parties against whom warrants were first issued. In addition there are 134 others against whom charges have been made. It is expected that those persons will be arrested by the military and turned over to the civil authorities for trial. Two additional companies of the 16th Infantry arrived here yesterday morning.

January 7, 1869. About 6 o'clock yesterday morning, the civil and military expedition to the Ogeechee country left the Atlantic and Gulf Railroad depot to proceed to Station No. 1 by special train. The forces composing the expedition were Sheriff Dooner and eight deputies and Companies A and I of the 16th U.S. Infantry under command of Colonel Sweeney. The train soon arrived at No. 1, where the troops were disembarked. The expedition marched up the road towards the plantation of Messrs. Middleton and Tucker. "Wildhorn" plantation was found to be perfectly quiet. The march was continued to the Grove place, and here the operations of the Negroes were fully displayed. Everything move-

87

able about the premises was gone. The house had been ransacked from bottom to top, the mantlepieces broken and several of the sashes stove in. The door of the storeroom had been cut open, and its contents stolen. The house was filled with dirt and filth, and its whole appearance changed from a fine residence to a ruined and desolated building. One of the watch dogs lay dead under the steps, where he had been shot by the lawless Negroes.

About half-past 1 o'clock the two military companies arrived at the Grove place and formed a camp. Colonel Sweeney deemed it advisable not to make any arrests until the Negroes had been informed that any resistance to the law would be punished by the U.S. authorities and messengers were sent to the different plantations at half past 2 o'clock to summon the Negro leaders. They had not returned when our informant left the place.

Colonel Sweeney, Major Middleton and Captain Tucker paid a visit to "Southfield" plantation and found that place also desolated. The entire lot of rice in the mill, amounting to some 4000 bushels, had been stolen by the marauding Negroes. They also gained additional evidence of outrages committed by the insurgents from hands on the place, who had been threatened with death, assaulted and badly treated by the vagabonds. The military have formed a camp and will remain on the premises for some time.

The worst gang of Negroes are said to be located on Heyward's place. They work for nobody and have been engaged in stealing all during the fall and winter. The lawless blacks, after driving off the white planters, overseers and watchmen, appear to have overrun the plantations and they have stolen everything that they could lay hands on, desolated the places and destroyed the crops of Messrs. Middleton and Tucker.

January 8, 1869. Last evening Sheriff Dooner, Deputy Sheriff Russell and others arrived from the Ogeechee, having in charge sixty-eight prisoners who were captured there yesterday and from those who have accompanied the expedition we have collected a little information regarding its operations.

Yesterday morning the Negroes came up quietly and surrendered themselves. The whole number not appearing, Captain Isaac Russell, Deputy Sheriff, and two other white men went to Heyward's, "Southfield," the Elliott place and other plantations and ordered the Negroes to come up to Colonel Sweeney's headquarters. That officer also sent out several colored men to notify them to the same effect. By afternoon about sixty Negroes were present. They were formed in line and placed under guard. Several others were arrested by the officers. Some of them were quite impertinent, declaring that they would not go and that the officers could not take them. The muskets and the bayonets of the soldiers had a powerful persuasive influence, however, and the unruly parties, when that was exerted, became very quiet and went along without any trouble. Sheriff Dooner thought it best to bring the prisoners that he had secured to the city. Colonel Sweeney was applied to for a guard, and furnished a sergeant and ten men. These, with the posse of citizens, were considered sufficient. They were marched along the road to Station No. 1, none of them offering any resistance or attempting to escape.

The officers with their prisoners left Station No. 1 about half past 5 o'clock yesterday afternoon and arrived in this city a little after 6. The prisoners were then marched up to the U.S. Barracks where they were placed for the night. None of the principal ringleaders have been arrested.

On Heyward's plantation and on Alderman Burroughs's place, the Negroes have been perfectly quiet. Some of these Negroes were with the party which operated at "Southfield" and "Prairie," and these were arrested. The officers visited "Southfield" and "Prairie" plantations, which the lawless and insurrectionary Negroes had completely desolated. The house at "Southfield," one of the finest mansion[s] in the Ogeechee country, remained but a wreck of its former appearance. The furniture had been carried away, the windows broken, doors stove in and the place filled with dirt and filth, as though it had been used as a pig wallow. The overseers' and watchmen's houses had been treated in the same manner, and the whole year's crop of rice carried off. A few stacks of rice not threshed out remained, but the rest, some four or five thousand bushels, had been carried away. At the "Prairie" place, their operation had not been so extensive. They had also visited the Cheeves's place and robbed it to some extent.

The two companies of military which Colonel Sweeney took down still remain on the Ogeechee and will stay there until complete quiet is restored and all the disorderly parties arrested.

Counter-Reconstruction

AFTER a winter or two of homelessness and starvation in towns, most freedmen returned to plantations. Now they were paid monthly wages, but they were often living in the same cabins, working in the same fields under the same drivers of slavery days, again dependent on a white man's good will. Patrollers—groups of armed whites on patrol—had helped maintain order in plantation districts of the old South by keeping watch on slaves at night. By 1868 masked patrollers—"regulators," "jayhawkers," "black horse cavalry," "Ku Klux Klan"—began to scare the ignorant and superstitious freedmen into cooperation by visiting their houses, dressed in extravagant costumes, with blackened faces, blowing horns and waving guns. Uncooperative blacks who argued with whites, wanted to buy land a white wanted, courted a white woman, taught school to freedmen or voted for Republicans might be threatened, beaten or killed.

Matilda Frix, a former slave in Calhoun, complained to the Freedmen's Bureau of a typical surprise visit by the Klan in 1867: "Three men forced the door open into my house late in the night, pulled out a pistol, rubbed it over Cheany Ransom's face, said they would blow her brains out!" [Document Eleven] Charles Smith of Walton County testified before a Congressional committee about Ku Klux Klan violence in 1871: "I heard my wife hollering, 'Ku-Klux! Ku-Klux!' They knocked one door down. They beat me as long as they wanted to with rocks and pistols, and then they took a hickory and whipped me. They made my wife get down on her knees and stripped her dress down about her waist. They stripped my sister stark naked." [Document Thirteen] Though freedmen exercised their political rights in the late

1860's, the threats and floggings of the Ku Klux Klan soon eliminated an independent black vote.

Charles Stearns came to Georgia from Kansas, by way of the Colorado Territory, in 1866 and purchased a plantation in Columbia County, where he planned to establish a cooperative farm for freedmen; in 1868 a mob compelled him to resign the office of Judge of Ordinary to which he had been elected: "They raved, they called me a 'damned low-lived Yankee, a thief, a scoundrel.' They simply saw that a 'damned Yankee, elected by niggers' was placed in authority over them. A stout, red-faced man cried out, 'We own the courthouse, and it shall not be occupied by niggers or the friends of niggers!' " [Document Twelve] In the December, 1870, election, the Democrats won overwhelming control of the legislature. Governor Rufus Bullock, a Republican facing almost certain impeachment, resigned his office in October, 1871.

Though the legislature effectively curtailed black voting in 1873 by extending residency requirements for state and county elections, resentments and fears between blacks and whites became the continuing justification for a one-party system—one that would endure for almost a century. "The difficulty in Georgia is that, black and white, Republicans and Democrats, demagogues unite in maintaining the color-line in politics ... the white voters in a more and more inflexible opposition, the ignorant blacks subject to the rule of demagogues, moderate men of both sides without voice or influence," wrote Charles Nordhoff, a Prussian-born journalist who toured Georgia in 1875. [Document Fourteen]

Back at work on plantations and their vote restricted, Negroes had already lost much of their new independence. The English Parliamentarian Sir George Campbell, who came to Georgia in 1878–79, observed greater separation between the races and harsh justice for black criminals. Sir George interviewed a representative Georgian: "Colonel P—— thinks the Negro first-rate to 'shovel dirt' but no good for much else. He must be 'kept in his place,' as it is the fashion to say in Georgia." [Document Fifteen]

$\begin{bmatrix} 11 \end{bmatrix}$

Three men forced the door open into my house late in the night, pulled out a pistol, rubbed it over Cheany Ransom's face, said they would blow her brains out. The reason for their doing so was because Cheany had complained to the Bureau about Mrs. Hunt owing her $20 for services and could get nothing from her. Mrs. Hunt said if she had to pay her that Cheany should not live to enjoy it.

MATILDA FRIX, 1867

MATILDA FRIX, a former slave in the town of Calhoun, was one of many petitioners to the Freedmen's Bureau. Created in March, 1865, the Bureau was to furnish food, clothing and homestead of public land for the former slaves, also supervising labor contracts, opening hospitals and schools and protecting civil rights. The Bureau closed in 1872. These letters to the Bureau are from the Records of the Assistant Commissioner for the State of Georgia, Bureau of Refugees, Freedmen and Abandoned Lands in the National Archives.

STATEMENT OF JOHANNA GILBERT

[Washington, November 18, 1865]
I have been living at the residence of Mr. Nicholas Whiley, town of Washington, in Wilkes County, Georgia. On the morning of November 9th, Mrs. Andrew Owens took my child to put him in the smokehouse and I, being present, told her that he should not be put in the smokehouse. She did not put him in the house. She then called me a "stinking heifer." I replied that I was no more a stinking heifer than she was! She then went into the house and reported to Mrs. Martha Andrews what I had said. Mrs. Andrews then called me to her and, after hearing my statement, said she would tell Mr. Nick Whiley what I had said and done. This was on or about the 9th of November.

On the morning of the 10th November, Whiley whipped my child, then called me. I did not go to him but run away. He sent two men after me, who caught and brought me back to him. He then had me tied up and, while the two men above mentioned held my clothes up, he whipped me with a horse-whip, giving me more than fifty lashes, to the best of my knowledge and belief, before leaving me tied up. And while the men were holding me by my arms, he struck me a number of blows on my head with the butt of the whip. Before untying me from the whipping post, he had my hair cut off.

After I was untied, he ordered me back to the house to my work, first making me promise that I would not leave the place, also threatening that he would shoot me if I attempted so to do. Being unable to work, I went to my room and laid down. About 12 noon, my husband, Willis Gilbert, came home and Mr. Whiley asked now if I wanted to leave. I told him I did, when he ordered me to go and never put my foot on his place again, also saying that he had plenty of money to pay for whipping Negroes. I left his place at 2 P.M. on or about the 10th day of November, 1865.

STATEMENT OF SELA COOK

Newnan, August 18, 1866

In the latter part of July last past, Lucy Stephens and myself, colored, were on our way to church, when we met Augustus Williams and his wife, white, on the sidewalk in Newnan. Lucy, in order that Williams and wife might pass, stepped nearly off the sidewalk, pressing back her own dress to make room, &c. As Williams and wife passed, Williams struck Lucy over her left eye with his cane, laying open a gash from which blood ran down on her dress freely and nearly knocked her down, producing a kind of insensibility, so that she could not speak. No words passed between either persons present and Williams passed on in silence. I was alarmed and passed along also, leaving Lucy bleeding.

FROM J. H. CALDWELL

LaGrange, September 3, 1866

General: Although I am aware that this place is not within your department, yet I have concluded to write to you, believing that you have influence that may be exerted for the security of the freedmen in this section as well as your own.

There is, in an adjoining county (Heard), an organization of white men who, blacking their faces and riding at night, go to the homes of freedmen and, calling them to their doors, shoot them down in cold blood. Neither the Bureau nor the civil authorities seem to make an effort to ferret them out and bring these midnight assassins to punishment. There can be no doubt of the existence of such an organization, and the fact that the newspapers and the public generally are silent in reference to the atrocities committed induces me to believe that too many of the people slyly wink at these proceedings. I have been told by freedmen and also by a white Union man that six or seven Negroes have been murdered [during] the last two weeks. Is there any remedy for this? How may these assassins be arrested in their bloody career?

Today I witnessed a mournful spectacle. It was that of a man, his wife and two daughters and his grandchildren, six in all, fleeing for their lives from the pursuit of these murderous wretches. Last night they were visited, as they suppose, by the "Black Cavalry"—for so these assassins are called. They called at the house where the black people are staying, called the man by name, "Jerry!" but, receiving no answer, left. The night before they had visited a neighboring farm and cruelly murdered without provocation a poor black woman. This, with the circumstance of their visiting and calling for the man last night, alarmed and terrified them so that they fled from the place this morning. They were advised to do so by the white lady of the house where they were hired. These are the facts as narrated by the man himself. He came to me for advice and protection.

A number of circumstances induce me to suspect that the man to whom they were hired (their former owner) had a hand in this affair and that the design of the parties last night was not to murder but to frighten them off. It seems they had a verbal agreement with this man to cultivate his farm for one-third of the crop and paid themselves. They cultivated the crop, laid it by and think it will yield about twenty bags of cotton. This will give them 6⅔ bales for their share and will probably net them $600. Now it may have been an artifice of the employer to get possession of their cotton. All sorts of tricks and chicanery have been resorted to throughout this section to defraud the poor Negroes out of the fruits of their toil. It was a touching and mournful sight to see these poor creatures trudging along footsore and weary with little bundles of clothes in their hands, their earthly all, fleeing as for life. They have no money, no possessions, no shelter but are frightened away by a dishonest villain to starve.

The policy of the people in many places is to put the Negroes in a starving condition that they may cry out, "See what freedom has done!" Many, after the crops were cultivated, drove the Negroes off without any pay for the services performed by them. The Bureau is in the hands of old pro-slavery secessionists who look after the interests of the white man, not those of the freedmen. It is so, I mean, in some places and this is one of them. Will President Johnson's policy succeed? If so, I fear it may ruin this whole country. The whip and the bludgeon, cursing and abuse, are resorted to in many places just as in the days of slavery. There will be no safety for freedmen, for Union men, for missionaries, nor teachers of colored people, if Mr. Johnson succeeds in putting the old rulers of the South with power again. I felt a year ago extremely desirous to see my unfortunate section rehabilitated but with the men in power I am confident it would be the death blow to our civil and religious liberties. Our missionary operations have thus far been wonderfully successful, but I am confident that if the South is restored with her old rulers in power they will destroy every vestige of our work throughout this section. Is there any way in which you can interfere? Any authority to put a stop to these outrages committed on freedmen? Any way to protect them against brutality, oppression and fraud? I fear it can only be accomplished by the presence of troops and I am certain President Johnson will not be in favor of garrisoning any of the towns, because he has proclaimed the country at peace and would have the people of the North believe everything is looking satisfactorily. I submit this statement to you, hoping that you will be able to suggest some remedy.

STATEMENT OF RHODA ANN CHILDS

[Henry County, September 10, 1866]
Myself and husband were under contract with Mrs. Amanda Childs of Henry County and worked from January 1, 1866, until the crops were laid by, or in other words until the main work of the year was done, without difficulty. Then (the fashion being prevalent among the planters) we were called upon one night and my husband was demanded. I said he was not there. They then asked where he was. I said he had gone to the watermelon patch. They then seized me and took me some distance from the house, where they "bucked" me down across a log, stripped my clothes over my head, one of the men standing astride my neck and two holding my legs. In this position, I was beaten with a strap until they were tired. Then they turned me parallel with the log, laying my neck on a limb which projected from the log and, one man placing his foot upon my neck, beat me again on my hip and thigh. Then I was thrown upon the ground on my back. One of the men stood upon my heart, while two others took hold of my feet and stretched my limbs as far apart as they could, while the man standing upon my breast applied the strap to my private parts until fatigued into stopping, and I was more dead than alive. Then a man, I suppose a Confederate soldier as he had crutches, fell upon me and ravished me. During the whipping, one of the men ran his pistol into me and said he "had a hell of a mind to pull the trigger!" and swore they ought to shoot me, as my husband had been in the "God damned Yankee army" and swore they meant to kill every black son-of-a-bitch they could find that had ever fought against them. They then went to the house, seized my two daughters and beat them, demand-

ing their father's pistol and, upon failure to get that, they entered the house and took such articles of clothing as suited their fancy and decamped. There were eight men engaged in this affair, none of which could be recognized for certain.

H. Dodd [?] to F. W. Coleman

Macon, November 24, 1866

Lieutenant: I have the honor to report to you the following condition of affairs between the white citizens and the freedmen of Butler, Taylor County, Georgia. The population of Taylor County is in a very desolate condition, having scarcely any subsistence. There are more freedmen than are actually needed and all cannot be employed. Consequently the price for labor is low. In most cases the farmer or employer pays little or no money at all to the freedmen employed, except the cost to feed them. Some have contracts, but even in those cases in many instances the white farmer manages to extricate himself. Therefore the white citizens find it to their advantage to keep the freedmen in the country, for should one or two hundred leave there would be a demand for labor and the freedmen would soon hire themselves only to such farmers as would give them their price.

Last week two agents (Mr. Allen and Liddy) who are employed by a Mr. Abbot to hire freedmen as laborers on his plantation in Tennessee, came to Butler and, with the assistance of Mr. J. L. Harmon, Agent, Freedmen's Bureau, tried to hire freedmen. On Saturday, the 17th instant, 100 to 150 of them came to the courthouse in Butler, where Mr. Allen and Liddy tried to hire them and sign contracts in which Mr. Abbot promised to pay them $15 per month and furnish them with food, fuel, houses, bedding and clothes. The white citizens interfered, telling the freedmen these agents did not intend taking them to Tennessee but would carry them to Cuba and sell them back into slavery! This produced great excitement, and, under the influence of liquor, one of the citizens, Mr. W. L. Hall, Sheriff of the county, advised Mr. Allen and Liddy to leave Butler the first opportunity, insinuating as much that if they refused their lives would be in danger.

C. M. Caldwell to I. L. Dunning

Newnan, March 19, 1867

My dear sir:

The circumstances now surrounding me compels me to call on the military authorities for protection, as an attempt has of late been made upon my life and threats still made against it. I have just been informed by a very reliable man that they intend to kill me as soon as they can do it, so as to hide it. A few Sabbath evenings ago I was shot at while officiating in my church. I am informed twenty-five white men came to my church for mischief, but on being discovered they fled. The fact is there is no safety here for freed people nor for Union men. They may kill me, but I will never run. I will stand my ground to the last moment, but I want and must have protection. I hold a public meeting at my church on Saturday, the 30th of this month, for the purpose of making known to the colored men of this county that they are now clothed with the privilege of voting as free men at the first election that may come up, and you can see from the facts which I have give[n] you that it will be necessary to have men here on that day or riots will be provoked by the disunionists of this place. I did not intend to call on the military until the last resort, but, having been put in possession of these facts a few minutes ago, I deem it best to do so now. I cannot too strongly urge this thing, because the people are bent on mischief. Where is General Thomas? Will you please communicate these facts to him without delay? We must have a military post here or we must surrender the whole thing and go down. But, as for me, my life is laid upon the altar. I die before I surrender, and now I call upon the government I love to protect me in the discharge of my duties.

E. Yulee to C. C. Sibley

Walthourville, April 23, 1867

Colonel:

I point to my administration as Agent of the Bureau for evidence of my desire to have justice done to the colored race. Indeed a great many whites of this county have reproached me for undue partiality. Though I have ceased to be Agent for the freedmen I still retain a devotion to their interests. Hence I make known to you the proceedings of some colored itinerants who are collecting money from them under a pretense of securing their rights. A colored preacher named T. G. Campbell, a stranger, and a man named Toney Golden of this county have held several meetings here, requiring each person to pay $1. This Toney is always taking up collections among them on one pretense or another. He seems to be one of those who wish to live by their wits rather than by performing some use to the community.

There is no disposition among the whites to, in any manner, obstruct or oppose the operations of the Sherman bill. At the proper time, when the registration is to take place, all the planters will cooperate with the movement. Such

I understand is their intention. Hence, these frequent political meetings are preventing the people unnecessarily from working and will make them as destitute next year as they are this.

I was at a large mass meeting of the colored people yesterday called by this preacher Campbell and Toney Golden, and the spirit of the addresses was calculated to create a division into classes—blacks against whites. A black man calling himself "Professor" J. W. Tower presided. He is travelling about with a magic lantern to exhibit what he calls the progress of reconstruction, which together with his harangue during the exhibition tend to the arousing of antagonistic feeling toward the whites. He has a scene which he calls "Before the Proclamation," another "After the Proclamation" and then "22nd Regiment U.S.C.F. Duncan's Brigade." If the whites were to meet the issues raised disorder would result, but they are apathetic and submissive to the laws of the U.S. on which they depend for protection. I cannot see the sense of arraying the blacks against the whites under such circumstances. Such a proceeding is injurious to the peace and security of the country, now under your government.

This "Professor" Tower in his opening address told the crowd they would each have to pay $1 for voting! I felt called upon to correct this announcement and told the people the government asked no fee of the kind. Preacher Campbell rose and made an insulting comment on what I said and then confessed that the dollar was for his use. I understand $200 or $300 were collected from these half-starved people at a time when aid is wanted from abroad to enable them to hoe through the season! Toney Golden announced there were now no more Agents and it was the black man against the white man. Mr. Darlington, a Northern man, announced that the laws of Georgia were now a dead letter, that the blacks had perfect control of the county and could elect whom they pleased to all offices, that the Sherman Bill had been appealed to the Supreme Court to have it set aside but no matter what that Court decided the people of the North would rise as one man and compel its observance by force if necessary. The whole spirit evoked by this meeting leads me to dread the probable increase of crime and outrage in this county, where the blacks are ten to one of the white population, and I would advise the stationing of a military force in this locality for the protection of the whites and the repression of lawlessness.

I heard a little black doctor endeavoring to induce the crowd each to advance him fifty cents to get his medicines here, that he would put their names on his list and when they wanted medicine he would supply them to that amount. He was a perfect stranger in these parts and hailed, he says, from the North. The poor freedmen seem to require more protection from the wiley of their own race than from the whites who are now subject to the blacks!

D. Swope to F. Mosebach

Lithonia, August 21, 1867

I have been informed by several freedmen that on Tuesday, the 13th instant, three young men by name John Johnson, aged about twenty-one years, Aleck Johnson, aged about nineteen years, and John Tweedle, aged about fourteen years, armed with guns, came to a schoolhouse near Mr. Shumate, living about $1\frac{1}{2}$ miles above Lithonia on the Georgia Railroad. The schoolhouse was occupied as a school for colored people and was then in session, taught by a freed woman named Betsy Hackett. The above named white young men used threatening, menacing and insulting language such as threatening shooting through the house, driving them out and burn[ing] the same, telling them that they would not permit them to hold school there. The scholars at this time were women and children exclusively, who were very much alarmed.

On Monday following, the 19th instant, the teacher and several of her pupils repaired to the office of Squire McCarty, who lives nearby, for the purpose of obtaining protection, laying before him the facts as stated within, whereupon he flatly refused to take any notice of the case, giving as his reason that he had no right to arrest or take action against said parties for mere threats. All of this I would submit for your consideration as I know that the colored people are a quiet and peaceable class and anxious to obtain harmony.

Twenty-four Freedmen to John Pope

Calhoun, August 25, 1867

General:

We, the colored people of the town of Calhoun and County of Gordon, desire to call your attention to the state of affairs that now exist in our midst. On the 16th day of this month the Union Republican Party held a meeting in this town, at which the colored people of the county attended *en masse* and since that time we seem to have the particular hatred and spite of that class who were opposed to the principles set forth in this meeting. Their first act was to deprive us of the privilege to worship any longer in their church. Since we have procured one of our own. They threaten us if we hold meetings in it. There has been houses broken open, windows smashed and doors broken down in the dead hours of the night, men rushing in, cursing and swearing and discharging their pistols inside the house. Several times [they] came very near shooting the occupants. Men have been knocked down and unmercifully beaten, and yet the authorities do not notice it at all. We would open a school here, but are almost afraid to do so, not knowing that we have any protection for life or limb. We would humbly make this our petition to you that something be done to secure to us that protection we so much desire. We do not wish to complain, but we feel that our lives are no longer safe. Therefore, we feel compelled to ask your protection. We wish to do right, obey the laws and live in peace and quietude and will do so if we are permitted to. But when we are assailed at the midnight hour, our lives threatened and the laws fail to protect or assist us, we can but defend ourselves, let the consequences be what they may. Yet we wish to avoid all such collisions and, if possible, will do so until we hear from you. We would respectfully ask that a few soldiers be sent here, believing it is the only way we can live in peace, the only protection we can have until after the elections this fall.

STATEMENT OF MATILDA FRIX

Calhoun, August 27, 1867

On Tuesday night, on or about the 20th of August, 1867, late in the night, don't know what time, three men came into the house where myself and Cheany Ransom, colored, are living in the town of Calhoun, about fifty yards west of the railroad depot. We had the door fastened by putting a shovel under it. These three men forced the door open, came in, cursed and swore, tore around generally, came and pulled the cover from me, said they would get into bed. I complained of being sick. One of the party stood in the middle of [the] room, fired off his pistol, don't know at what he fired. Think he fired out the door. The moon was shining bright, could see them quite plain. Could not tell which one of them fired the pistol. I know that Matt Thompson and a Mr. Finchen was there. Am not positive who the third man was, think it was Mr. Pinson.

On Friday night, the 23rd of August, 1867, three men came into my house away late in the night. Had a chair behind the door. They forced the door open, came in, struck a light, walked around the room, pulled the covering from my face, went over to Cheany Ransom's bed, pulled the covering from her face. She started to holler and shout. Pulled out a pistol, rubbed it over her face, said they would blow her brains out if she made any noise. Jim Printen, a colored man, and my brother from the country, was sleeping in the house. Jim Printen started out of the door. Those men fired at him two shots in the house. Started out after him, could not catch him. Some of the party said, "Let us burn them out!" Had a light and was trying to catch Cheany's dress on fire. Think their intention was to burn us out and drive us away from town. In fact, they told Cheany Ransom to get out of here or they would kill her.

On the evening of the 24th, we got some men to come and put a fastening on our door, so that no person could come in. Went to bed. Some time in the night [we] was awakened by some party throwing large rocks in through the windows, smashing in the windows, firing pistol shots through the house, just above our bed. Do not know who they were but think it was the same party. The reason for their doing so was, I think, because Cheany Ransom had complained to the Bureau Agent about Mrs. Hunt owing her for services and could not get anything from her. They had a trial over it before Mr. Blacker, the Agent, and he ordered Mrs. Hunt to pay Cheany $20. Mrs. Hunt said that same night if she had to pay her that Cheany should not live here to enjoy it.

RICHARD EDMONDS TO GENERAL LEWIS

[Woodville,] February 11, 1868

General:

There is men at Woodville that kills all men that is not rebels. My mother's house was attacked by K. G. Chaney. He is the head one. K. R. Killson, Joe Davison, eight or ten more [came] to kill me. I want you to have me protected if you please. I had to leave home last night to save my life. If you will send down, you can find out all about it. They came in the night. They have [made] what they call [a] vigilant committee to whip Negroes and white people that don't cooperate [with] them. They say that they are going to kill me. They are sworn to keep [quiet] all they do in regard to whipping and killing. They have run off all the colored people for voting for the convention. K. G. Chaney has been accused of killing colored men. I want you to have this investigation if you please. They burnt mother's house. K. G. Chaney, I say, did it. I can't give you all the names now. I will be glad if you will stop this mob. I hope I will hear from you soon.

DENNIS COTHERN TO GENERAL MEADE

Morgan County, May 27, 1868

Sir:

It is through great distress that I attempt to approach Your Highness. I do not feel worthy to black your shoes. I have been a slave all my life, and last year I worked with Mr. Rollings Thompson, and I worked hard, and he cheated me out of everything and will not pay me one dollar. Now, General, I can prove all that I say and I want you to pay a little attention to me, a poor black man, and I want you to collect something out of Mr. Thompson for me. For I am myself and family on starvation. Mr. Thompson furnished the land and stock and was to be at all expenses, only my provisions, and we was to go halves. That was the understanding. We all made eight bales of cotton, thirty-eight wagonloads of corn, and I had four hands and he had eight. At the expiration of the year I got nothing, only what I ate, though Mr. Thompson never would have any division in the crop but said that I had nothing. I thought that he was jesting, though after I found that he was in earnest. I thought to write to you and see if you thought it lawful or not for me to be cut out of everything or not. Now there is white men who will certify to what I say.

L. LIEBERMAN TO N. S. HILL

Hawkinsville, June 29, 1868

I have the honor to inform you that serious disturbances are going on in this county on the other side of the river. Reports reach me often of these outrages and unless they are checked I fear there will be a good deal of bloodshed. I have not, nor can I, learn the real facts in these cases, as the parties on whom these outrages have been committed fear to report the parties either to the civil authorities or the Bureau. From what I have learned, it seems as if there are two or three parties who roam about at night, approach freedmen's houses who have voted the Radical ticket, take them out and beat them nearly to death and threaten to kill them should they lisp one word. These parties are using bags, sacks, &c. which they throw over their victim's head, thereby rendering him powerless, then use him at their will. All this occurs at the mid of night. It has got to be so bad that the Negroes as soon as night approaches get their guns and go out in the woods. Word has also been sent to white parties who voted the Republican ticket that they must also prepare themselves, as they will soon be visited. The consequence is that these white men who expect to become victims have loaded guns and [are] continually on the watch. These night parties are styled by some the "K.K.K.'s," "the Bag Clan." There is trouble going on and the excitement in that part of the county is intense. The civil authorities have taken no steps in this matter nor can they unless they know the parties and again it would be dangerous for one or two men to try to arrest them, should they be known. The military authorities should look into this matter at once, for, if allowed to go on, it will become hot over in this section, as they get bolder and more bolder each night. This has all occured since the election.

W. L. CARTER TO O. H. HOWARD

Baker County, September 29, 1868

Dear Sir:

There has been a most intense state of excitement existing in this and the adjoining neighborhood for the past five or six days, the white men, suspecting, on what they believe good ground, the Negroes of insurrectionary intentions and the Negroes suspecting the whites of the intention of killing them. The Negroes are said to have six leading men who are drilling companies and getting up ammunition with the intention of murdering all, and one leader is accused of having said that nothing short of a clean sweep would do, not a woman or child but must be murdered if they would succeed. The state of excitement is extreme between both parties, and the Negroes say the lives of six of them have been threatened and that they don't feel that any of their lives are safe. One of them is a man named Ralph, formerly belonging to me and who has lived on my plantation ever since he has been freed. He went out in the neighborhood this evening and as he was coming home was shot in the leg with a pistol or rifle by some person who waylaid him in the woods. I am in great distress and uneasiness and write to ask you to come and try to settle the matter for us. I think we are in a most dangerous state of inflammability and fear that this shot may be the spark which is to kindle a most dreadful conflagration. Will you not come to our relief? Come yourself if possible. You will be listened to when another would not. Ralph asked me to write for you, and I see no other way in which the excitement can be quieted than by your coming.

HOWELL C. FLOURNOY TO C. C. SIBLEY

Athens, October 5, 1868

General:

I have the honor to call your attention to very great excitement in Jackson County, Georgia. Reports have come to me that both white and colored citizens are arming themselves. The whites says the colored citizens are arming themselves to murder all the whites at a certain time not particularly specified. This, as they pretend, has caused them to arm themselves for self-defence. On the other hand, the colored citizens contend that they are desirous of living in peace with the white people and attend to their daily work, that large bodies of armed white citizens [are] roving through the district of Newtown and Harmony Grove in Jackson County, hatting and hailing every colored man they see and compelling them with threats of violence and drawn weapons upon them to make them sign certain written articles of agreement which they term as an association of peace between them. These articles are nothing more or less than that they, the colored people, solemnly pledge themselves with an oath that they will vote the Democratic ticket in November, 1868! If they sign these, they are let alone with warning. If the colored people violate their pledge, death is their doom, and, if they refuse to sign, they are driven out of the county, their lives threatened and many of them have been driven from their homes. Such are the reports that reach me.

I am daily looking for an outbreak in that section and nothing can prevent it, unless some U.S. troops are sent here. The excitement appears to be intense in these two districts. I am afraid it will extend through the whole of Jackson County and the adjoining counties and this place. These two districts were very strong [for] secession and there are a great many reckless and lawless men there from the sign of the times. No white Radicals or colored men will be allowed to vote at the next election for President unless he votes the Democratic ticket. If the government don't give us protection we will be at the mercy of a lawless band. I have lived here for nearly fifty years. I was here during the rebellion. I was more than forty times reported for arrest for my Union sentiments. But I have never seen such times in my life as a Union man's life was so insecure as at this time.

STATEMENT OF JAMES ROBERTS

Dougherty County, October 6, 1868

John Roberts, white, of Baker County, Georgia, about four months ago drove me from his plantation in Baker County, telling me that no Radical Negro could stay on his place and drawing a pistol on me with the remark to leave his place, never to come back and not to open my mouth or he would shoot me. Since that time John Roberts met me in the road four different times and told me each time not to show my head on his place again or he would kill me. Mr. John Roberts, James King, Isaac Bronson and two or three other white men whom I did not recognize came to my house on the plantation of Mr. Musgrove in Baker County about bedtime on Sunday night, the 27th of September, 1868, called my name and asked me to come out. I saw them coming through the crack of the house and recognized those above named in the moonshine. They all were armed with guns and I, fearing to get killed, jumped out of a back window of the house unperceived by them. They went into the house and, not finding me, told my wife I must leave the county or else they would kill me. They immediately after coming out of the house espied me at a distance running through a field, pursued me very closely but I escaped them in the high weeds. I have been up in Dougherty County since, and I am fearful of being killed if I go to Baker County after my family, which I have not seen since Monday morning after this occurrence.

Isom Ponder, a colored preacher who lives on Mr. James Porter's place in Baker County, was, on refusal to come out of his house on the night of Saturday, the 20th of September, 1868, forcibly dragged out of his house by three disguised men and shot through his right thigh and left laying where he was wounded. I have seen the wound and heard these statements from Isom Porter himself, and Isom Porter is considered a leading Republican amongst the people of that neighborhood.

Samuel Geder, colored, on James Porter's place in Baker County, was cruelly and severely beaten by James Porter with a large white oak stick about as thick as a man's arm and afterwards stamped so that he had to be carried away from the spot to his house and spit blood several days. Dr. Han was called in, who considered his recovery doubtful. I was an eyewitness to the scene that James Porter done the beating and stamping, while James Whipcomb, white, of Baker County and Calvin Carvey, white, of the same place held him down on the ground by his head and feet. The difficulty arose about a quarrel between Sam Geder and James Porter's children. Porter wanted to whip a child of Sam Geder, which Geder tried to prevent by trying to persuade him not to do so. Sam went to his house and was taken out of the house forcibly and whipped as described.

FROM II. C. MORRILL

Americus, November 2, 1868

Dear General:

The condition of the colored people in Schley County is most deplorable. There seems to be no protection for them at all. They are continually shot, beaten nearly to death and it seems from the testimony the most respectable citizens are engaged in it. If there can be any respectability about such people! At the recent term of the court the most notorious persons connected with this organization were on the grand jury and no presentments were made against any of the parties guilty of shooting and beating freedmen, while twenty freedmen were or had true bills brought against them for simply carrying a gun in accordance with the Constitution. Of all the cases, no colored man need look for justice unless it comes directly before the judge in points of law. They threaten with death any freedman that tries to prosecute or ever tells he has been beaten. There is a perfect reign of terror, and they swear, I am told, no freedman shall vote the Radical ticket. John T. Lumpkin, who has shot three and was recognized in a party of K.K.K.'s by Henry Davis when he was shot, was on the grand jury. Some of the freedmen have been whipped so that their intestines protruded by whipping on their stomach. It is mortifying in the extreme to have these men come down, driven from home, their year's hopes gone and say I can't do a thing. Even the notary public I recommended told me last night he would be obliged to leave as his life was in danger. Parties on horseback, dressed in white sheets, would ride 'round his house night after night.

A. Pokorny to M. Frank Gallagher

Butler, November 4, 1868

Sir:

I have the honor to report that yesterday morning at $9\frac{1}{2}$ o'clock the election polls were opened at Butler, Taylor County, Georgia. It seemed to me that the cause of this delay was that nobody here had the experience or the right knowledge in such case. The colored people appeared in strong force and even at daybreak many of them gathered before the courthouse. A few minutes after the commencement of the election, a great excitement prevailed between the freedmen on the ground that votes were refused on account that the colored voters had not paid their poll tax. I have done what I could to secure the peace and to calm those who were touched by this unjust proceedings or mode of action. Quiet was restored, although the freedmen, through the continuance of the election, bitterly complained about unjust and unfair treatment. Many of them agreed or had the promise from their employers that their poll tax shall be paid from their wages but had no receipts in their hands and many votes were refused, notwithstanding that the voters were ready to take the oath to the above facts. Confidentially, I was informed that between 175 and 200 votes of colored voters were refused. The whole crowd inside of the election room, the canvassers, challengers or what their names may be were composed [of] real Southern Democrats and their action a mere farce. In consideration that the result of this election at Butler, Georgia, is anyhow of no influence at all, I will not molest you with further particulars. The political terrorism oppressed on the people during the time between the last election to this was so far successful that only two votes were given by white Republican voters, Mr. J. Miller and John Edwards. The colored people voted all for Grant and Colfax, so I was informed by their leaders.

H. C. Morrill to M. Frank Gallagher

Americus, November 5, 1868

Captain:

I have the honor to state that on the morning of the 3rd instant there seemed to be a preconcerted action with the whites that there should be no election. No officers were present to open polls and no movement made until about 10 o'clock, when I went to the courthouse at the request of three freeholders (colored) who had in my office previously qualified and requested of the Ordinary that a place be furnished to open the polls and that three colored freeholders had taken the necessary oaths and were ready to commence the voting in accordance with law. The Ordinary replied that he had given the necessary papers to citizens who had announced their intention to open polls. At this time, Captain Thomas and one Foster, special police, wanted to know if niggers were going to open polls. I replied that was their intention, when they swore they (freedmen) should not, Foster saying that if they attempted it they would get the contents of *this* (opening his coat and touching a large cavalry pistol). At this time others came up and said it should not be done and, if I wanted trouble, that was the way to begin it. In the meantime, citizens began to crowd around and the most moderate told me they would see that polls were opened, and I desisted from any further attempt. After this there seemed to be some attempt to open a voting place and at quarter of 12 the voting commenced, the whites at one window and the freedmen at another. It would be useless for me to attempt to describe the voting. Every freedman was asked by the managers questions not pertinent to the case, such as where do you live, where did you work last year, then hold a consultation, then ask if he had paid his taxes and if not was immediately rejected and not allowed to vote. Out of 1500 freedmen that was here to vote, only 137 could vote except those they could bribe to vote the Democratic ticket, who voted without a challenge or tax paid or any other delay, so that the vote stood 967 majority for the Democrats. The whole affair was such a farce and everything connected with it so illegal I do not see how it is possible it could stand as legal vote or showing the sentiment of this county.

C. W. Chapman to John Leonard

Columbus, November 9, 1868

In regard to circumstances connected with the recent elections in my district, so far as the facts have come to my knowledge, I have the honor to report that in Muscogee County there was much unfairness and violation of law at the ballot boxes. It may not be out of place to remark here that the Ordinary of our county so arranged the managers of the election as to give almost the entire control of the polls to the Democrats. Out of eighteen managers, the Republicans had but three. Many persons who were clearly entitled to vote were refused permission to do so by the managers. A large proportion of the Republican voters were challenged and compelled to swear in their votes. At two of the polls in the city of Columbus, persons from other countries in this state were not permitted to vote for Presidential electors, but at the third poll all persons were allowed to vote provided they voted the Democratic ticket! It is believed that many persons from Alabama voted in this city. Minors were permitted to vote, and they and others repeated their votes, no questions being asked when a Democratic ticket was presented. Money was freely used for the purchase of votes. The Democratic candidate for Sheriff made open and public proclamation to the voters, inviting them to come up and get their money and their votes, at the same time he stood with the money in one hand and votes in the other. Muscogee County has about 3000 voters. The Republicans polled nineteen votes less than in April last, when they carried the county by 460 majority. About 3600 votes were polled at the election November 3rd, about 800 more than in April.

In Chattahoochee County but three Republican votes were cast. There are 700 Republican votes in that county! Persons report that they were not permitted to vote unless they had previously paid their taxes. It has been stated there were no votes sent to this county except a few from this city. Chattahoochee County has about 1400 registered voters, a majority of them being Republicans. The returns show a vote of about 600 at the late election. Many of the colored men walked from ten to twenty-five miles to vote in this place but were refused on their arrival here unless they voted the Democratic ticket.

Citizens of Marion County report that all colored persons were refused the right to vote unless they had paid their taxes. One individual states that 300 persons were excluded on that account. There are about 1100 voters in Marion County.

H. deF. Young to H. Sellers Hill

Irwinton, November 11, 1868

Captain:

The polls at this place were opened at the regular designated hour and voting progressed very rapidly until 9 o'clock, most colored men voting and they generally voting the Democratic ticket, being induced so to do by the combined influence of the fear of a discharge from their work and the plentiful supply of liquor furnished lavishly to "Democratic freedmen." One Joel D. Jones, a lawyer by profession, and Mr. Wright Carswell, teacher of the freedmen school here, were the most zealous in securing Democratic votes from the freedmen, both of them carrying bottles of liquor with them and continually treating the freedmen to it. Jones had a supply of whiskey in his office and carried many colored men there to give it out to them. In numerous instances both the men above named and many others also actually led freedmen up to the polls and compelled them to vote for Mr. Seymour. Many freedmen who voted the Grant ticket in the forenoon were led up to the polls in the P.M. and made to vote again, this time voting for Seymour. One freedman complained to me that he did this and was compelled to do so by Mr. Jones by threats. Many freedmen were refused the right to vote because they had not paid their poll tax. The vote polled here was for Grant 427, Seymour 421, majority 6. I think I am safe in saying that at least 150 freedmen voted for Mr. Seymour, either from fear of discharge or from reward given them.

STATEMENT OF GILLFORD ARRINGTON

Dougherty County, November 4, 1868

As I was entering Newton, Georgia, on Tuesday, 3rd November, I had a Grant badge pinned on my coat collar and a Grant ticket in my side pocket, which was not wholly concealed. I met Willis Williams and Bob Odum, white, who took my badge and ticket away from me, telling me that no such ticket should be voted at Newton that day. I went on into town and finding that I could not vote there without endangering my life, I walked to Albany, Georgia, a distance of twenty-two miles, where I deposited by ballot for Grant and Colfax. To my knowledge, hundreds of colored people went to Newton to vote for Grant and Colfax and, being afraid to do so, went home without voting.

STATEMENT OF JERRY GARRETT

Dougherty County, November 4, 1868

I saw on Tuesday, the 3rd of November, at the courthouse square at Albany, Georgia, James Allen, white, had a colored man, unknown to him, to poll No. 3, heard him call his name as a voter and saw him put a Democratic ticket, against the will of the colored man who protested to him against it, in the hands of Mr. Towns, who was assisting in the election.

About five minutes afterwards the same James Allen led up a colored man who followed him rather reluctantly to the same poll. I stopped the colored man and told him he had no right to let the white man pull him up to the polls in that kind of a way. Then the colored man pulled loose from the white man, and the white man stepped up to me and asked me, "Don't you like it?" And, turning his side towards him and lifting up his coat, showed him a pistol buckled to his side, saying, "You see that?" pointing at the pistol. I stepped off to the

Sheriff James Kemp, who stood about twenty steps from there, and told him. "Mr. Kemp, I thought the law was that no firearms were to be carried today?"

About 5 o'clock in the evening, George Pollard, white, went up to Poll No. 2 and voted a Democratic ticket for Abraham Cooper, who refused to come up to the polls with him. George Pollard called on Abraham Cooper, who was about twenty to thirty steps from the poll for his name and gave this ticket in for him. I think that Thomas Clark received the ticket.

STATEMENT OF ANDREW LANE

Dougherty County, November 4, 1868

I was standing, on the morning of the third day of November, during the election for President, at the right hand window in front of the courthouse at Albany, Georgia, and I saw the white man, whose name is said to be Sam Meade, receive the tickets of the voters at that window and hand them behind him to another white man, whom I saw at least one dozen times plainly drop the ticket handed to him on the floor of the room and take another one slyly out of his vest pocket, write on it and put it in the ballot box.

I saw a white man ask a colored man, who was standing at the window, what vote he was going to vote. He told him the Radical vote and showed him his ticket. The white man told him, "You are mistaken. This is not the Radical ticket!" and pulled out a Democratic ticket and gave it to Judge Wilder, the manager of the poll where this occurred. The colored man said that was not the Radical ticket but the white man told him it was all right, as did Wilder, and the colored man walked off, saying he was going to report them.

STATEMENT OF HENRY BUCHANAN

Dougherty County, November 4, 1868

On the morning of the third day of November at the courthouse square at Albany, Georgia, I was standing near the window, where Sam Meade was receiving votes. Sam Meade received the votes and handed them to Robert Zacharias, a white man, who generally put these tickets in his pocket and substituted and put other tickets, which were laying on the table in place of the ones he put in his pocket. I saw the fraud so plain that I became vexed and mad and left the place!

STATEMENT OF ISHMAEL LENON

Dougherty County, November 4, 1868

I saw young Dick Rust, receiving the tickets which voters had handed to Sam Meade out of the hands of the same. Dick Rust took those tickets behind the ballot box on the table before him, where nobody could see from the outside what he did with them. I saw Dick Rust frequently in the act of putting something in his pockets, while he was standing there behind the ballot box, doing something with the tickets. Dick Rust was a Deputy Sheriff and wore the badge marked that way all day. I soon afterwards saw Dick Rust coming out of the courthouse, saw him pull one ticket out of his pocket soon after he came out of the courthouse, saw him tear it up and picked up the pieces. [Ishmael Lenon now produced the pieces to prove them to be parts of a Grant and Colfax ticket.] Immediately after Dick Rust pulled a handful of tickets from his pants pocket, which were all pencil marked on the back and folded, started to tear them up but stopped and put them in his pocket again. I made it my business to come close enough to Dick Rust to recognize pencil marks on the back of those tickets and to recognize that they were folded. I followed Dick Rust out of the courthouse yard, hoping [he] would drop those tickets but desisted following him any further.

STATEMENT OF FOUR FREEDMEN

Dougherty County, November 4, 1868

We went in the courthouse where there were two sets of election managers. To the first we applied and offered to cast our ballots, but one of the managers told us that none but Democrats voted at that table. We then went to the other manager and officers, whereupon the clerk said they would not receive them sort of tickets (they being Republican tickets). Ely Churchill, one of our number, placed his ticket down on the table and insisted on voting. The clerk then wrote down his name and another manager pushed the ticket (which was Republican) aside, picked up a Democratic ticket and, folding, began to mark it, when Ely Churchill stopped him, saying that if he could not vote a Republican ticket he wouldn't vote.

[12]

They raved, they called me a "damned low-lived Yankee, a thief, a scoundrel." They simply saw that a "damned Yankee, elected by niggers" was placed in authority over them. A stout, red-faced man cried out, "We own the courthouse, and it shall not be occupied by niggers or the friends of niggers!"

CHARLES STEARNS, 1868

CHARLES STEARNS came to Georgia from Kansas by way of the Colorado Territory. He reached Savannah in May, 1866, and purchased a 1500-acre farm in Columbia County, where he intended to establish a cooperative farm and train the freedmen. As he describes below, Stearns was elected Judge of Ordinary in 1868 but was compelled to resign the office. This account appears in Charles Stearns, *The Black Man of the South and the Rebels* (Boston, 1872), pp. 202–227.

Bitter was the contest. The rebels gnashed their teeth. Their objections to Negro voting vanished like lightning. Barbecues were everywhere held, and the colored people were invited to sit down and eat with the whites, if they would only promise to vote the Democratic ticket. Various sums of money were also offered the Negroes on the same conditions. Prominent Democrats stationed themselves on the highway and urged their tickets upon the numerous throngs of darkies that were everywhere hastening to the polls. It was only necessary to remind a crowd of listening Negroes of the fact that the Democracy had thus enslaved them to quickly dispel the promises of windy Democrat declaimers. The election commenced April 20, 1868, and lasted four days. Our ticket was elected. I was elected to the office of Judge of Ordinary. Juries were drawn in part by him, election precincts and managers appointed, public buildings were at his disposal and the funds of the county under his control. Is it any wonder, therefore, that a howl of despair went forth from every rebel heart in our county when they learned the sad news that the control of the county had passed from their hands into that of a terrible Radical, like that "damned old Stearns," as they pleasantly

113

called me? They simply saw that a "damned Yankee, elected by niggers" was placed in authority over them.

I reached Apling about 5 P.M. and hitched my mules a few rods from the courthouse. It was court week. As I walked up to and passed by the courthouse, I was greeted with a shower of hisses from the upper windows of the building and with exclamations, "There is he, there's Stearns!" This surprised me, but I walked calmly on. I entered the post office and obtained my mail and, perceiving quite a crowd of men in the room, which was also used as a store, I bowed politely to them and said, "I am glad to see you, gentlemen," to which some of them replied, "Well, if you are, we are not glad to see you!" I remained here, perusing my letters until prudence suggested my departure, and I repaired to the office of the Ordinary on the lower floor of the courthouse.

I was followed by the motley crowd, some of whom hooted at me and others remained silent. On entering the Ordinary's office, I sat down and commenced reading. Soon the crowd increased until the hall was pretty full, and I remarked, "Come in, gentlemen, and be seated. I would like to have a talk with you." Quite a number availed themselves of my invitation, and one or two took seats at my side. The room was soon crowded, holding from fifty to seventy-five persons. One man repeatedly aimed blows at my head, but he did not actually strike me. One of them pulled my nose slightly a few times, but this was the nearest approach to physical injury I received. They stormed, they raved, they brow-beated me. They called me a "damned low-lived Yankee, a thief, a scoundrel."

To all of this terrific abuse, I replied in the mildest manner possible. While they raved, I tried to reason. They accused me of causing the blacks to commit outrages upon them and made me responsible for every act of violence lately committed by a black man in Georgia. They told me I could not live and hold the office to which I had been elected, for, as they said, "the white people of the county are determined you shall not, at all hazards, because you were elected by the niggers and we will be damned if the niggers are going to rule over us. We built this courthouse with our money, and we are going to occupy it. This is so important an office and places our property at your disposal, and we know you will steal it."

I was then invited out of doors by one of the crowd with the assurance that if I ventured out, "I will beat you into such a jelly that your own wife will not know you!" This polite invitation he repeated several times, when a bystander whispered something in his ear, and he immediately took off his hat and said, "I ask your pardon, Mr. Stearns. I did not know your wife was dead. Excuse me, sir." This affected me so much, that I burst into tears. After they had all left me, I sought the sheriff and claimed his protection for the following night, but he blandly informed me that he was leaving town very soon. Neither of the hotel keepers seemed desirous of having me for a guest on account of the danger to them, so I concluded to pass the night in the barnyard containing my carriage. A friendly black man came secretly to us and told us that the rebels intended attacking us during the night. With revolver in hand, I paced that barnyard the greater part of the night.

At about 12 o'clock the next forenoon, while sitting in the court room, the court having adjourned, I beheld a motley crowd rush upstairs and, after gazing at me with a subdued ferocity, mingled with a curious air, they took their seats around the room. At first my knees trembled a little as I beheld their fierce and besotted features, but I prayed for strength. At length a stout, red-faced and brutish looking man walked up to me and, after questioning me a little as to my intentions, cried out, "Come on, boys, let's pitch him out the window!" But he contented himself with cursing me to his heart's content. I asked him in what way I had ever injured him, that he should be so full of rage against me. His only response was that "We own the courthouse, and it shall not be occupied by niggers or the friends of niggers!"

In a few moments, a mild and pleasant-looking gentleman, a lawyer, in a polite manner said to me, "Why do you persist in holding this office against the will of the people? Why are you not willing to resign, seeing they feel so about it? I told him I would tell them all if they would give me five minutes to speak in without interruption. I spoke as follows, the kind gentleman holding the watch. "Did you not engage in war against the Northern people?" They replied affirmatively. "Were you not beaten in that war?" They nodded assent. "And after you were beaten, did you not agree to submit to the United States government?" They replied as before. "Then," said I, "the Congress of the United States gave these Negroes the right to vote and, as well-meaning and sincere men, ought you not to submit to its will?" To this proposition they quickly replied, "No, we will be damned if we will. It is only a rump Congress and had no right to let niggers vote, and we don't care a damn for it." My time was now out.

Soon a portion of the crowd left the room, replenished the stock of whiskey in their stomachs, reloaded their revolvers, doffed their coats and soon reentered the room. They rushed upon me immediately, crying out, "God damn you, get out of this courthouse. It was built with our money, and you shall not stay in it any longer." They then seized me and dragged me to the top of the stairs and hurried my departure from the hall of justice by pushing and kicking me until I had reached the bottom of the long flight of stairs, some of them crying out, "Let's push him into the creek!" As soon as I reached the door, seeing a crowd on the steps of the post office building, I was met with a fiendish shout,

"Don't come here, God damn you, we have no use for you." I cast my eyes behind me, and there was a crowd of infuriated savages maddened with whiskey. I was at a loss then what to do.

I had in my side coat-pocket a loaded revolver, which I resolved to use at the last extremity and to sell my life as dearly as possible. At length, one of the crowd cried out, "Go that way," pointing to the road leading from the town. I firmly refused, saying, "I shall not go there or anywhere else until my carriage is brought to me." They then agreed to send a man for it, and ordered me to remain standing under the hot sun until it came, which command I was forced to obey. And there I stood for an hour, at midday, with the fierce rays of the sun falling on my unsheltered head and receiving such insults as they felt disposed to heap upon me. One man threw at me a rock as big as a man's head, but two other men caught his arms quickly and the rock fell harmless at my feet, the disappointed villain boiling over with impotent rage.

The crowd continued to urge me to resign my office, and they would not molest me. Some of them said I must agree to resign the office of Ordinary, to refuse to take any other office to which I might be elected by the Negroes and never to come to Apling again. My kind defender in the court room was indefatigable in his efforts to protect me, not because he sympathized with me but because he was opposed to mob law. After a while my carriage hove in sight, the mules being driven by Frank, black. As he alighted from the carriage, a miserable ruffian asked him whether he was a Democrat or a Radical. He replied, "A Radical," when the brute attacked him, beating him on his head severely and kicking him several times. My kind defender now said, "Well, if you will not promise to resign this office, I can do nothing more for you." He left me and walked toward the crowd.

I then saw that but a step remained between me and certain death and that my colored comrade would share the same fate. It was of no use to try to hold the office unless I could have soldiers to protect me. If they would allow me to carry my arms and all of my property with me and would agree not to molest us on our return home, then I would promise not to occupy the office. The crowd immediately cried out, "That's right, bully for him!" Others said, "You have done right. You may come to Apling whenever you wish and we will protect you." I stepped into my carriage, and Frank applied the lash to the mules vigorously, and we rode off, accompanied by a deafening shout of triumph on the part of the victorious contemners of the United States Government.

[13]

I heard my wife hollering, "Ku-Klux! Ku-Klux!" They knocked one door down. They beat me as long as they wanted to with rocks and pistols, and then they took a hickory and whipped me. Eight men struck me eight licks apiece on my bare back. They made my wife get down on her knees and stripped her dress down about her waist. They stripped my sister stark naked.

CHARLES SMITH, 1871

CHARLES SMITH was one of several freedmen who testified before hearings held by the U.S. Congress between July and November, 1871, about alleged violence inflicted by the Ku-Klux Klan. These statements by witnesses were published in *Testimony taken by the Joint Select Committee to Inquire into the Condition of Affairs in the Late Insurrectionary States,* VI and VII (Washington, 1872).

JOSEPH ADDISON, 24, HARALSON COUNTY

I will tell you how they did me. They came on a neighbor of mine, a brother-in-law, who lived right close to me. They took both him and his son out and whipped them. They sent me word to leave where I was living. They said that if I did not leave they allowed to shoot me. I laid out then about three weeks. I then went into the house and laid there, I believe, two nights. The third night they came on to me and took me out and hit me some ten or twelve licks with a hickory. They then told me they would give me ten days to get away in. I begged them to let me stay until I had made my crop. They said, "You would rather go than die, wouldn't you?" I said, "Yes, I would rather do anything than die." They just went off and left me there. That was the last of March.

The next time they came on me was the last day in May, on a dark rainy evening about a half an hour by sun. One of my dogs broke out barking powerfully. I said, "What is that dog barking at?" My wife looked out and said, "Lord have mercy! Joe, it's the Ku-Klux." I jumped out of the door and ran. One of them was right in the back yard, and he jabbed the top of his six-shooter almost against my head and said, "Halt! God damn you!" They said, "We gave you

117

time once to get away, and, God damn you, you have not gone. Now, God damn you, you shall not go, for we allow to kill you." I said, "If you do not abuse me or whip me, I will go the next morning." They said they would not abuse me or whip me, but they would kill me. I turned away from the man; he jammed his pistol in my face and said, "God damn you, go on, or I will kill you." They took me about eighty or ninety yards from there into a little thicket. The tall man on my right stepped back and said to the little fellow on my left, "We have got him here now; do as you please with him." They were all standing right around me with their guns pointing at me. Just as he turned around, I wheeled and run. I must have gone seventy or eighty yards. Before I had run ten yards, I heard a half a dozen caps bursted at me. I heard a bullet hit a tree, I run on eight or ten steps further, and then I heard a bullet hit a tree just before me. Every one of them took off after me. I ran down a little bluff and ran across a branch. When I got across there, I could not run any further, for my shoes were all muddy. I cut the strings off my old shoes and left them there. That was the last I heard of them that night.

They came back Sunday night before court commenced in Haralson County. They abused my wife and cursed her powerfully and tried to make her tell where I was. They said that if she did not tell them they would shoot her God-damned brains out. They shot five or six shots in the yard; some of them said they shot into the house. They scared my wife and sister-in-law so bad that they took the children and went into the woods and stayed there all night.

CHARLES SMITH, 39, WALTON COUNTY

They came on me the 19th day of last March. Some had paper faces on, and some were just blacked and marked up. It was a rainy, cold night, and I was lying in the bed. They knocked one door open, and then they hollered for me to open the other door. My wife got up and opened it, and by that time I raised a plank to run under the house. Every time I would go to move they would say, "Hush! Hush!" One man says, "Go in and tear up the house. Turn it over, and we will have him." They raced about, raised the plank up—part of it—looked in the beds and everywhere. They said, "Look under the floor." They raised the plank and found me there. I ran out, and they shot at me ten times. But they did not hit me. I got away and ran down to where there was a house I knew. They hit my wife twelve licks, and my sister says they hit her three or four licks.

On the Thursday before the second Sunday in September, they came in on me again. They knocked one door down. My wife heard them before I did. She waked me up; she was crying. I had not got awake good then when I heard her hollering, "Ku-Klux! Ku-Klux!" I ran to the door and opened it, and they gathered [around] me. The first thing they struck me with was a rock on the head, and then they struck me over the eye. They kept striking me that way with rocks and pistols all over the yard. I said, "Men, stop if you please." And they stopped. I said, "What are you whipping me for?" They never told me, but let in to beating me again and never did tell me. While striking me they were trying to whip me. They beat me as long as they wanted to with rocks and pistols, and then they took a hickory and whipped me. Eight men struck me eight licks apiece on my bare back. They pulled up my shirt. They took my wife out and made her get down on her knees, and then they stripped her dress down about her waist. They made my sister get down in the same way in the yard, and they stripped her stark naked as she came into the world. They would come in on you and kill you if you sent your children to school. A black fellow got up a school five miles from me, and they went in on him and liked to have killed him because he was teaching school.

SCIPIO EAGER, 24, WASHINGTON COUNTY

At my own house, they came and took me and my brother out and tied my hands behind me. There were three brothers of us. The other brother was in the house. They went up to take him, and he tried to get away, and they shot him down. It was in the night. I heard some say who counted them that there were a hundred of them. Some of them had [on] white and some had black; they had all sorts of colors. They came in and got me first and tied my hands behind me and asked where was my other brother. I told them I reckon he was up to the house. One of them said, "We have come for him tonight." I said, "Gentlemen, what are you going to do with me?" He said, "Never mind, I will tell you what when I am through with you." They said that we never voted right. Mr. Alfred Harrison tried to get us not to go to the election, but we would go to the election and we voted. He said that we never voted for his interest, and he said that every man in that county that did not vote for their interest they were determined to kill him. They said, "Washington Eager is too big a man anyhow. He can write and read and put it down himself."

They carried me off into the woods about a mile from the house, while they killed my brother. I kept questioning them, "What are you going to do with me? I have not done anything at all." They said, "Never mind, we will tell you what we will do after we carry you off." They had killed a man last year over there. They carried me right through to his grave and told me they were going to kill me. I kept begging them, and when they got there they told me to halt, and I stopped. Mr. Alfred Harrison and Mr. Dudley came to me and pulled off their uniforms and asked me if I knew them. I did know them, but I was afraid to own it. They decided to whip me and my brother over there. They took off every rag of clothes I had and laid me down on the ground, and some stood on my head and some on my feet. They went out and got great long brushes, as thick as chair posts, and they whipped them all into frassels. After they quit whipping me, they told me to go home and tell that God-damned rascal that, if he was not prepared to die, he had better be prepared to die.

I thought it was all right better to be whipped than to be killed like my brother. In my brother's back I counted some hundred and odd shots, bullets and buckshot holes. He was shot clear through, and he breathed out of the bullet holes that were through him. He lived from Saturday night clean to Sunday about dinnertime.

ABRAM COLBY 52, GREENE COUNTY

After the war was over, I took the Republican part. I was elected to the legislature in 1868. On the 29th of October, 1869, they came to my house and broke my door open, took me out of my bed and took me to the woods and whipped me three hours or more and left me in the woods for dead. They had on white gowns that came down below their knees, masks on their faces, and their heads were covered up with white caps, or something of the kind; a mask and a cap on, too, I think. They said I had voted for Grant, Bullock and Blodgett. They said I had influence with the Negroes of other counties and had carried the Negroes against them. They said to me, "Do you think you will ever vote another damned Radical ticket?" I said, "If there was an election tomorrow, I would vote the Radical ticket." They gave me 400 or 500 licks before they commenced counting. My drawers fell down about my feet, and they took hold of them and pulled them down and tripped me up. They then pulled my shirt up over my head.

MARIA CARTER, 28, HARALSON COUNTY

They came hollering and knocking at the door, and they scared my husband so bad he could not speak when they first came. I answered them. They hollered, "Open the door!" I said, "Yes, sir." They said, "Kindle a light." My husband went to kindle a light, and they busted both doors open, two in one door and two in the other. One put his gun down to him and said, "Is this John Walthall?" They had been hunting him a long time. They said they were going to kill him when they got hold of him. They asked my husband if he was John Walthall. He was so scared he could not say anything. I said, "No." They asked where he was, and we told them he was up to the next house.

I heard them up there hollering, "Open the door!" And I heard them break the door down. A parcel of them ran and broke the door down and jerked his wife out of the bed. She commenced hollering, and I heard some of them say, "God damn her, shoot her!" They struck her over the head with a pistol. The house looked next morning as if somebody had been killing hogs there.

At that time four [more] men came in my house and drew a gun on me. They asked me, "Where is John Walthall?" I said, "Up yonder." They said, "Who lives here?" I said, "Jasper Carter." They said, "Where is John Walthall?" I said, "Them folks have got him." They came in and out all the time. One of them had a sort of gown on, and he put his gun in my face. The other said, "Don't you shoot her."

I heard John holler when they commenced whipping him. I undertook to try and count, but they scared me so bad that I stopped counting. But I think they hit him about three hundred licks after they shot him. I heard them clear down to our house ask him if he felt like sleeping with some more white women. We all knew he had been charged with sleeping with white women. He was warned to leave them long before he was married. His wife did not know anything about it. And they said, "You steal, too, God damn you." John said, "No, sir." They said, "Hush your mouth, God damn your eyes, you do steal." They beat him powerfully. She said they made her put her arms around his neck and then they whipped them both together.

LETTY MILLS, 29, WALTON COUNTY

On the 19th of March, they broke in on us one night when we were abed. I heard them and waked Gus, my husband, and told him that I knew there were Ku-Klux coming. There had been so much talk of Ku-Klux about there that I had been expecting them. I heard of their shaking hands with people and then leaving their hands in folks' hands. I heard of their going in and telling about their bursting out of tombs and rising from the dead. He said they were not, but someone going turkey-hunting. I said they were Ku-Klux. After awhile, they knocked at the door and told us twice to open the door. Felker came in and he made Gus get up and pull off his clothes. Then he told me to strip off. He made us get down on our knees and he gave us a good beating. He made Gus stretch out on the floor, and he gave him a good beating.

JASPER CARTER, 25, CARROLL COUNTY

It was done on a Monday night, along in corn-planting time. They all came to my house first, and knocked the doors down and came in and hollered to me

121

to kindle up a light. They knocked both doors down and came in with pistols and guns and drawed them on each side of me. One had one right at my head. They struck me above the eyes with a pistol. The scar is here yet. They asked me if I was John Walthall. I said, "No, sir." They said, "Where is he?" I said, "Up to the other house," which was about fifty yards off. They said I had to go with them up there. One had hold of my arm, another had hold of my shirt. We went up there. John Walthall, when he heard them knocking the doors down at my house, raised up a plank, went under the house, aiming to get out at the back end of the house. They ran around the house and knocked his doors down, went in there, jerked his wife out of bed, and beat, and knocked, and stamped her about on the floor, and beat her over the head with guns and pistols. There is a great scar on the back of her head half as big as the palm of my hand. She was scared. They had a great big light. They jerked up a plank and happened to get a glimpse of his shirt. One of them had a little rifle, and ran it down close to him and shot him through the small part of the back. After they shot him, they pulled him out and hit him three hundred licks and made her hug him and and then they beat them both. They beat their heads together. They beat them with a great big stick and with their fists. They said he was always running after women, and asked him when he thought he would sleep with another white woman. He told them that he never slept with any. They said, "God damn you, you are a liar." And then they just knocked him plumb over nearly, and then the man on the other side would knock him back again. His head was beat all to pieces nearly. After they beat him and shot him, and beat her and him as much as they wanted to, they took me about a quarter [of a mile] from the house and whipped me. One stood on my head, and the others beat me. They just took and pulled the shirt out from under my pants and then pulled my pants down and beat me.

COLUMBUS JETER, 41, DOUGLAS COUNTY

I and my wife generally taught school at home. The neighbors would come into the school, and I would give them lessons as far as I knew how. I did not charge them for it. On the night of the 4th of April, after school was over, I and my wife went to bed. I had just laid my head on the pillow, when I heard a terrible howling around there. I thought it was dogs. They kept howling to such an extent that I said, "Wife, what does that mean?" Just then my dog broke out, and I heard them say, "Shoot him, kill him." I knew then it was the Ku-Klux, and I broke right to the chimney in my drawers and shirt and went right up the chimney. They hollered, "Open the door." They broke the door open and in they came. My child in the bed, twelve years old, was jerked out of bed, and she knew the young man and called his name. He said, "Hush, Emily, I will not hurt you." They wanted to make them tell where I was, but they said I was not at home. I was up in the chimney. My wife hollered so that I was excited, and I looked out of the chimney. One hollered, "God damn him, here he is in the chimney! Fire up the chimney." I hollered to them not to fire, and I would come down. I thought that would be better then to allow them to kill my wife and children.

The first man who took hold of me that I swear to was Mr. McWhorter. He had a piece of cloth on his face. They jerked me down on the floor. Mr. Mc-Whorter held me by the hair of my head. I patted him on the leg as I was lying on the ground and said, "Master, don't let them kill me." I kept getting up by degrees until I had my hands on his shoulders. At that time they hollered for another man, who said he would kill me or run me off. Herbert Morris was the man. They tied an apron over my face, so that I could see nothing. I kept falling down as they carried me along. They carried me to a tree. Mr. Morris wanted to sell me a horse and charge me twenty percent on the money. Mr. Farmer sold me one and charged me no percentage, and they were mad at me for that. One of them said, "Now, Columbus, do you think a colored man is as good as a white man?" Mr. Morris tried to kill me once, and I drew a stick on him. He said, "This is for saying that a nigger is as good as a white man, and for drawing a stick on a white man." They carried me to a tree and made me hold my head down to the tree. I raised up my head and as I raised it, he said, "God damn you, if you raise again I will burst your head open." I said, "Lord, save me!" and jumped and run, and as I got eight or ten steps off they fired a gun and the load struck me. I have forty-four shot in my left shoulder now.

ALFRED RICHARDSON, 34, CLARKE COUNTY

On the 18th of January, a very wealthy white man by the name of John O. Thrasher came to me. This man told me, "There are some men about here that have something against you, and they intend to kill you or break you up. They say you are making too much money, that they do not allow any nigger to rise that way, that you can control all the colored votes, and they intend to break you up and then they can rule the balance of the niggers when they get you off." He said they said they wanted me to join their party, but I told them I did not want to do it. These are a parcel of low-down men, and I don't want to join any such business.

I went to bed about 9 o'clock. Between 12 and 1 o'clock, these men came. There were about twenty or twenty-five of them, I reckon. Some had on the regular old-fashioned doeface. Some had on black cambric, with eye-holes, and tied around the face. Some wore cambric caps. I have one of their little horns that they blow when they are gathering. I have, too, a long white gown. When they ran against the door, I asked who was there. They said, "Never mind, God damn you, we'll show you who it is! We'll have you tonight!" About eight or ten of them got abreast and ran against my door. One fellow had a new patent axe with him, and he commenced cutting down the door. I thought I would stand at the head of the stair-steps and shoot them as they came up. But they came upstairs firing in every direction. I had some small arms in the garret. There was a door up there about large enough for one man to creep in. I thought I had better go in there, and maybe they would not find me.

They all came upstairs. My wife opened the window to call out for help. When they saw that window open, they said, "He has stepped out of the window!" And they hallooed to the fellows on the ground to shoot on top of the house. Thinking I had gone out the window, they all went downstairs except one man. He went in and looked in the cuddy-hole where I was and saw me there. He hallooed to the rest of the fellows that he had found me. Then he commenced firing and shot me three times. He lodged two balls in my side and one in the right arm. They came upstairs with their pistols in their hands. I shot one of them as he got on the top step. They gathered him up by the legs, and then they all ran and left me. I never saw any more of them that night, and I have not seen them since.

THOMAS M. ALLEN, 38, JASPER COUNTY

I ran for the legislature and was elected. After we were expelled from the legislature, I went home to Jasper County. I was carrying on a farm there. Two men came to the field where I was working. They told me that I ought to take part with the Democrats now and take the stump for Seymour and Blair. They then went off. I called a political meeting in town to organize a Grant club. Captain Bartlett told some colored people a day or two before the meeting that they had better stay away from town, that he did not think I would live to see the meeting.

I went home. I felt very curious. About 2 o'clock, my wife woke me up and said there were persons all around the house, that they had been there for half an hour and were calling for me. I asked them what they wanted and who they were. One said, "Andy Minter." That was a friend of mine. My wife said that was not his voice. I asked what they wanted. They said they wanted a light, that they had been hunting and the dogs had treed something and they wanted a light. They asked me to come out. At this time my brother-in-law woke up. He said, "I will get up and give them a light." He put on his shoes and vest and hat. That was all he was found with after he was killed. He opened the door and hollered, "Where are you?" He hollered twice, and then two guns were fired. He seemed to fall, and I and my wife hollered, and his wife hollered. We made up a light, and then I saw my brother-in-law laying on his back as he fell. There were four or five number one buck-shot in his breast. He seemed to be dying very fast. Next day I got up and went out and counted 180 shot in the house, and they will be there until Judgement.

MITCHELL REED, 22, JACKSON COUNTY

They had on masks over their heads and faces, most of them. Some of them just blacked up the biggest part of the face. They came to my house. I was lying in bed, but was not asleep. I was sort of expecting them. I had heard that they had put out threats that they were coming there. I and a white man had a falling out at a corn-shucking, and I had been expecting them for some time. They called to me to come out, and I told them I did not want to. They said, "Come out, we want to talk with you a while, and the quicker you come out the better it will be for you." I opened the door and came out. Two of them took me and carried me down the road about fifty yards from the house. One of them told me to take off my shirt. I did so, and they whipped me. I caught the staff end of a big whip at the time they were whipping me. They jerked it out of my hands and said, "God damn you, if you catch hold of it again, we will kill you." They said they were Ku-Klux and came out of the ground, that they were dead men. They said they had heard I had been sassing some white man, and they came there to make me a good boy.

REUBEN SHEETS, 53, WALTON COUNTY

There were five of them came into my house this last March. My wife and children got scared, and waked me up and said that the Ku-Klux were there. They kicked the door two or three times, and I jumped up and asked who it was. They kept hollering, "Open the door." I did not open it for some time, until they called my name. After awhile, they asked, "Is this Uncle Reuben?" I said, "Yes." They said, "Open the door and we will not hurt you." I opened the door then, and they all came in. I gave them seats, and they all sat down and said that they wanted to advise me a little. One man I never saw much; his head was covered up with something that looked like a meal sack, with red around his mouth and eyes.

They told me that they had heard I was a good man, that they had heard my name a hundred miles. They said there were colored people up there in Ogle-

125

thorpe County that cursed right smart and some talked sassy to white people, and they did not intend to have them run over the county. I said to them that I always behaved myself and that the man who raised me and the man who owned me last could tell them so. They said they had nothing against me, but they thought they would come in and see if I would like to have anybody visit me. They asked me if I liked to have such company as they were. I said nothing. Of course, I was scared nearly to death. The same night they came to my house, they whipped Augustus Mills and his wife mighty bad.

SIMON ELDER, 56, CLARKE COUNTY

I was compelled to leave [Clarke County] by the Ku-Klux, or what they call the Ku-Klux, anyhow. They came to my house on Saturday night about 11 o'clock in the night. There was no one there but me and my wife, and we were sitting down laughing and talking just before they came in. The fire was very warm, and I was lying down before the fire, for I was tired. I dropped off into a little doze of sleep. When I waked up they were knocking at the door. It was just like a whole gang of rocks coming against the door. I jumped up and said, "Halloo!" By that time they flung the door down, and fell against me. They had their faces in disguise, and all had uniforms on. Four of them jumped on me at once and commenced beating me over the head with clubs that they had. One of them said, "You damned Radical son-of-a-bitch, we intend to put an end to you." Said I, "Lord, have mercy!" They told me I was getting too much for them. I rented land, and I and my wife and son and daughter paid taxes. They said I was a damned old Radical. I voted the Republican ticket, that is what they meant.

They then dragged me out of the house and carried me off. When they did that, I asked them if they pleased to let me put on my shoes. It was mighty cold. Said he, "No, God damn you, you need not put your shoes on. We are Yankees from the Federal city, and we will have you in hell before tomorrow night this time." They took me out and dragged me over the fence. They asked me if I could run. They had been beating me, so they wanted to see if I could run or not. I went blundering along making out that I could not run. They made me go into the thicket of woods, and there it looked almost like Judgement to me. When they got me out there they got around me and ordered me to strip myself as naked as ever I came into the world. I made a spring and ran off. They shot one bullet through an old pair of breeches but I got away from them clear.

[14]

The difficulty in Georgia is that, black and white, Republicans and Democratic, demagogues unite in maintaining the color-line in politics . . . the white voters in a more and more inflexible opposition, the ignorant blacks subject to the rule of demagogues, moderate men of both sides without voice or influence.

CHARLES NORDHOFF, 1875

CHARLES NORDHOFF (1830–1901) was born in Prussia and immigrated to the United States as a child. He was educated in Cincinnati, apprenticed to a printer and worked as a compositor at a Philadelphia newspaper. After serving in the U.S. Navy, Nordhoff became a writer and journalist. In 1860 he became managing editor of the New York *Evening News*; he was Washington correspondent for the New York *Herald* between 1873 and 1890. These pages are drawn from *The Cotton States in the Spring and Summer of 1875* (New York, 1876), pp. 101–112.

"Georgia," said a Federal officer-holder, a Republican and long resident in the state, to me, "is still a rude community. In the country districts the people are what you would call careless of law and apt to take revenge into their own hands. If a man offends or wrongs another, this other takes the law into his own hands." Another Federal officeholder said to me, "Rude men in the country districts are too apt to take the law into their own hands. Negroes are generally more openly attacked than white men when they become the subjects of dislike by others, but otherwise there is no difference. The Negro usually will not defend himself and thus encourages attack." He gave me as an example the case of a Negro who complained to a United States officer that a white man had beaten him over the head with a stick. The Negro's hog had got into his white neighbor's garden, whereupon the beating.

On the day I came to Atlanta news came that a United States deputy-marshal had been shot through both legs and had had his horse shot in a northern county. This looked a good deal like Ku-Klux, but the marshal told me his deputy was engaged in ferreting out illicit distilleries. He had just captured and destroyed two or three, and the enraged owners took their revenge on him. This business of illegal distilling is followed to a great extent in the mountain region of Georgia; these people hate the sight of a deputy-marshal and do not hesitate to shoot at him.

Petit larceny is here the principal and the most vexatious offense of the plantation Negro. "They are an excellent working force," said more than one planter to me, "but they will steal cattle, hogs and many other things." This crime is very severely punished in Georgia—they are relentless toward it—and it results that Negroes are sent to the penitentiary and the chain-gang for very long periods. The severity of the sentences would be with us inhuman, but the crime is so serious and frequent I am satisfied that it must be checked with a strong hand.

There are only very few counties in Georgia in which colored men are drawn for jury duty. But there are certainly in the large towns a few colored men who answer to the definition of "upright and intelligent," and these ought to be included in the jury-lists. In Atlanta the other day, the colored people made up a list of 150 names of men of color whom they regarded as fit jurymen and presented it to the Ordinary. They now assert that no attention was paid to their request.

You hear a good deal of complaint, both among planters and in the cities, about the unsteadiness of the Negro as laborer or house servant, but a number of planters and citizens later explained to me the cause. "Whoever pays his black laborers regularly and honestly can get as many as he wants at all times, and they will work faithfully," said a south Georgian planter to me—a rough man, whose conversation in some respects impressed me unfavorably. "Come down into my county," he added," and I'll show you plantations standing idle, whose owners will tell you that the nigger won't work: and I'll show you plantations right along side of them where one hundred hands work faithfully year after year and don't think of moving away. All you've got to do is to pay them honestly and sell them nothing and you won't complain. I don't keep a store. I make the niggers go off to the village. I can get one hundred extra hands whenever I like, and I'm not an easygoing man either."

The same story I heard from citizens. "Where a man complains that his servants leave him, you'll find that his wife has paid them in driblets—a dollar now and half a dollar another time. They don't understand accounts, they are spendthrifts, and, at the end of the month when they have but little due them, they think they have been cheated and go off dissatisfied. Now I pay them their whole month's wages punctually at noon on the day their month is out, and they never leave me. Punctual and honest pay is all that is needed to make them faithful and steady servants."

A poll-tax of one dollar deprives a man of his vote at an election who has not paid his taxes for the year previous. A Republican said to me, "The Negroes evade its payment or are careless about it or lose their tax receipts, and then their vote is rigorously challenged and they lose it." "Half the Negroes in Georgia are disfranchised for non-payment of their poll-tax," was the assertion of another zealous Republican. "Many whites do not pay either," he added, "but the Republicans do not challenge as rigorously as the Democrats."

I am persuaded that in Georgia other means have been used to overcome the colored vote—means not at all justifiable. In some cities, Atlanta and Savannah, insufficient voting boxes are provided, and the Negro voters are crowded out and prevented from casting their full vote. A candid planter, living in a county which had a black majority, said, "We had white Republican officers. We discovered they were corrupt. They kept the county offices for themselves but were ready enough to let a Negro go to the legislature, where the Democratic majority left no chance for stealing. As we could get no county reform by arguments or appeals to the Negroes, who were as three and a half to one white voter, we made up our minds to buy the black leaders, who fooled their people with imitation Republican tickets. Later we bought over also some of the white leaders, and others we put in jail when we could prove corruption against them. We have had a struggle for it, but we have managed to maintain a pretty good government."

In another case I was told, "In my county and others, I do not doubt there has been ballot-box stuffing. I don't justify it, and I very deeply regret it, but where the blacks are in a large majority, men are apt to think that any thing is justifiable to save themselves from such gross misgovernment." The whites have been determined to keep the local governments in their own hands. The Negro voter has been the prey of demagogues and scoundrels. His ignorant attachment to the Republican name and his readiness to follow black leaders who are easily corruptible and low whites who flatter him have made him the tool of robbers. That the whites should protect themselves even by counter-frauds is lamentable but natural.

It may seem to you that the condition of the Negro in Georgia is not happy under all these circumstances, but in general the colored people are safe in their lives and property. An official report of the property and taxes returned by colored tax-payers for that year: 83,318 colored polls returned taxable property amounting to $6,157,798, they owned 338,769 acres of agricultural land, and they paid $30,788 in taxes. Remembering that when they obtained their freedom only nine years before they owned absolutely nothing except what they stood in and acquired all this property, I think it clearly establishes that they have labored with creditable industry and perseverance and that they have been fairly protected in their rights of life and property by the Democratic rulers of the state.

Georgia had no free schools before the war, and the system makes but slow headway. The schools are open, in general, less than three months in the year. In 1874 there were 93,167 white and 42,374 colored children attending school; this was out of a total of 218,733 white and 175,304 colored children within the school ages. There is still in many counties some prejudice against colored schools. Atlanta has a colored university, but there is some ignorant prejudice against the [white] teachers on the ground of their sitting at table with the colored students, which is thought to promote "social equality."

One cannot help feeling a little contempt for the people here who make themselves needlessly unhappy about "social equality." A sensible planter—a Democrat and a native Georgian—said to me, "It is absurd in us to make such a fuss. There is scarcely a man of us whose children are not suckled by Negro nurses. Our playmates were Negro boys. All our relations in the old times were of the most intimate. For my own part, I would as soon ride in a car with a cleanly dressed Negro as with a white man. It is all stupid nonsense and makes us absurd in the eyes of sensible people." In Atlanta and Augusta, colored people are allowed to ride in street-cars; in Savannah, they are forbidden. Why the difference?

In the cotton country the planter usually pays his hands ten dollars a month by the year, with a house and ration of three pounds of bacon, a peck of meal and a pint of molasses per week. The laborer has also a patch of land for a garden and Saturday afternoon for himself, with the use of the planter's mules and tools, to work the garden. They work from sunrise to sunset and in the summer have two and a half hours for dinner. The cotton-pickers receive fifty cents per one hundred pounds in the seed and are fed (The ration costs about fifteen cents a day) or sixty-five cents per one hundred pounds if they feed themselves. Most planters keep a small store and sell their laborers meat, bread and tobacco on credit, the general settlement being made once a year. The women receive for field work six dollars a month and a ration. One of the most intelligent planters I met told me that his laborers cost him about fifteen dollars a month—wages and ration. Where the Negroes plant on shares, the planter furnishes the land and mules and feeds the mules. The Negro furnishes labor and feeds it and gets one-third the crop.

A planter from one of the "black counties" where the Negroes are most numerous, amused me with some stories of how the blacks were deceived by white rascals after the war. These fellows brought red and blue sticks, which they sold for one dollar each to the Negroes, wherewith to "stake off" the land which the government was to give them. When they went to the polls to vote, the blacks used to bring halters with them for the mule which General Grant was to give them. The planter told me that the young Negroes who had grown up since the war worked less steadily than the old hands. He kept a colored school on his own plantation.

The chief difficulty is that Georgia is an old state with worn lands. One evidence of a general lack of prosperity I came upon even before I entered Georgia —the considerable number of emigrants of both colors leaving the state for Arkansas, Texas and Mississippi, where they need no manures and can get greater returns for their labor. Georgia has lost in this way since the conclusion of the war, I have been told by good authorities, Democratic citizens, at least fifty thousand people—half of each color. In Atlanta I had some conversation with a Negro who showed me pamphlets recommending parts of Mississippi, which he was distributing among his people. He told me that emigration agents come into Georgia from the three states I have named in search of laborers. These agents make known the fact that rich lands lie open and, not unfrequently, they are ready to pay the expense of a family's removal.

There is no Republican party worthy of the name in the state. One of the most zealous Republicans in the state said to me, "The Republican party, so far as its white members are concerned, consists mainly of Federal office-holders and men seeking office. There are not more than a hundred active white Republicans in Georgia who are honest and out of office." Another zealous Republican said to me, "The white Republicans of Georgia are made up almost entirely of Federal office-holders whose aim is to keep their places and of men who are trying to get these places. There is substantially nobody else, white, in the party." One of the most prominent Federal officers in the state, a bitter opponent of the Democratic party, said to me, "I don't know that there is any Republican party in the state. The blacks are almost totally disfranchised by their neglect to pay their taxes. At least two-thirds of the colored voters are thus disfranchised." Since the winter of 1871 the state government has been entirely in Democratic hands.

The difficulty in Georgia is that black and white, Republican and Democratic, demagogues unite in maintaining the color-line in politics. The bad Democrat does not object, for it enables him to control the state. The bad Republican likes it, for it makes him a martyr and gives him what he longs for—a Federal office— or at least the excuse for demanding one. Governor Smith said to me that only when the color-line was broken could the politics of the state be settled, and this would bring absolute security to the Negro. The efforts made to maintain a spurious Republican party in the South have only tended to band the white voters together in a more and more inflexible opposition to the Federal administration and to band the ignorant blacks together and subject them to the rule of demagogues, leaving the moderate men of both sides without voice or influence.

Colonel P——— thinks the Negro first-rate to "shovel dirt" but no good for much else. He must be "kept in his place," as it is the fashion to say in Georgia. They would be all right but for the interference of carpet-baggers and "New Engand school marms." These they declare to be the pest of the world, putting false ideas of equality into the heads of the blacks.

SIR GEORGE CAMPBELL, 1878–79

THE ENGLISHMAN Sir George Campbell (1824–1892) was a colonial administrator in India, off and on, between 1842 and 1874. He was a member of Parliament from 1875 until his death. In the fall of 1878 Sir George journeyed to America to study "the Negro question." These selections are drawn from *White and Black* (London, 1879), pp. 362–395.

At daylight in the morning we were passing through a flattish country with much cotton cultivation, and soon afterwards we reached Augusta in Georgia. Augusta is handsomely laid out with broad boulevards and houses surrounded by beautiful shrubs and trees. It must be charming in fine weather, but today it is raining heavily. This is a great cotton mart—the center of a large cotton-growing country. The only complaint is that the farmers grow cotton too exclusively and do not rotate enough or grow food enough for themselves. Augusta is on the River Savannah, which gives an immense water power, the fall being rapid, the stream strong and the supply constant and unfailing. Advantage has been taken of this to establish great cotton mills, which are doing a large and prosperous business. At a very large mill which I visited, they make only coarse unbleached goods, using only very low numbers of yarn, but at another mill close by they make finer goods. The labor employed is entirely white and is upon what they call the "family system." Here they have workmen's houses near the mills, much like what one sees in England. The manager says that the people work quite as well as Northern mill workers of whom he has had experience. There are good schools in the town and most of the people are now fairly educated, but there is no compulsory school law and no restriction as regards the work of children. The women earn from $3 to $5 a week, fifty cents a day being the wages for common hands. They are very regular and well-behaved. Some men work well, too, but they are not so good as the women. They work eleven hours a day. No blacks are employed in the mills here. The manager says they are not "responsible." He has not tried them. Before the war there were, I understand, several small mills successfully worked by slaves. It would not be possible to work black and white women together. The white women would not submit to it.

I was introduced to Mr. N——, a Charleston man, settled here as a cotton buyer. He seems to think that the Negroes have hardly so good a chance in Georgia as in South Carolina. They are the majority of the population about here, and most of the cotton is raised by their labor—principally on shares and cotton rents—but it is not a very satisfactory system. The farming is poorly done, and the Negroes are apt to change about a good deal. There are a good many Irish in these parts, especially in the upper parts of the country, but they are mostly rather a low type. They are employed on the streets and ditches of the town and to a considerable extent on the railways.

From Augusta I travelled to Atlanta, the capital of Georgia. All the way on to Atlanta the country was a good deal undulated and varied, with a good deal of wood. A large proportion of the cottages we passed seemed to be inhabited by whites. These cottages generally are very miserable-looking dwellings, according to our ideas, but they seemed to be full of healthy children. I understand that in the country we have been passing through the population is about equally divided between blacks and whites. To the south of this line are the great cotton-producing districts, where the black population prevails, but to the north, again, where the country rises considerably, there is a portion of Georgia which is quite a white man's country and now contains a large white population.

I made the acquaintance in the train of Mr. Stephens, a senator of this state, going to the legislature, which is now in session, and had a deal of talk with him. He repeats and emphasizes the complaint about scarcity of money I have before heard. He says that comparatively few blacks own land. They do not save money to buy it. On the contrary, they are generally obliged to get advances to carry them through the season in the cultivation of their small farms. By law the proprietor has a lien on the crops for his rent and advances, and when the accounts are settled at the end of the season the black farmers are often behind and have nothing to get, and then next year they either go on in the same way or go off somewhere else. I have since, however, met men who declare that they have kept their old slaves on their land except, perhaps, that just at first most of them may have gone off for a year or two to prove their independence, and then returned and settled down. The common rent is two bales of cotton— that is about 900 pounds—for as much land as a mule can work.

I asked Mr. Stephens about Georgian politics. (He is a nephew of the well-known Alexander Stephens, the Vice-President and brains of the Confederacy.) He says that after the war for a time they were allowed to manage their own affairs. Then the Constitution of 1868 was forced upon them by the Federal government and for a short period the Republicans were in power in the state, but apparently by no means an irreconcilable Republican party. The Governor of those days was a Northern man who had been settled in Georgia before the war, was "a good rebel" during the war and generally liked. In 1870 the Democrats again got the majority and kept it—so much so that they have now almost everything throughout the state. There are now only two blacks and five or six Republicans in the legislature, but there are many Independent Democrats. He talks as if the blacks are not politically irreconcilable but amenable to influence and money. They can be managed well enough, if only a little money is available.

Atlanta is in an elevated region about 1100 feet above the sea. It is now a great railway center and a prosperous place, but I am disappointed to find that it is not at all a pretty or nice town, very inferior in amenities to all the other Southern towns I have seen. It is, in fact, a new, brick-built town with no trees in the streets but abundant mud, for there is now a good deal of rain. The principal hotel, the Kimball, is crammed full, and I had difficulty in getting in. It is a fine large establishment with a great hall in the center which is immensely crowded. I have here realized for the first time what American spitting is. It really requires some nerve to walk across the hall. This is about the busiest season of the year for the cotton traffic and mercantile business generally, besides that the legislature is in session. Atlanta is a new place, and there are a great many self-man men in it.

At the hotel I met a planter of extreme Democratic views, strongly opposed to Independents and all other defectors from the party. He thinks niggers are only made to be slaves. They work well when compelled, but will do nothing without compulsion. He has himself a farm of 500 acres, and no man has worked harder than he has, but he cannot make a living—with the price of cotton so much down and wages not down, the cultivation is a dead loss, and he is disgusted with the world. Between us, however, we made out the moral to be that a farm so large as his does not pay, especially when the owner does not like niggers. He is now dividing it up. Part he has given to his sons, and part he is selling. He admits that men with small farms, who work themselves and can look well after two or three nigger servants, may live.

In the evening I walked out into the country and saw some of the country people. I interviewed a small black farmer who has a farm of twelve acres, in the midst of the woods. He was a slave. After emancipation the owners of this land, who were relations of his former mistress, allowed him to squat and clear this patch, on the understanding that he was to pay rent when he could. Presently the land was sold, and the new owner makes him pay $4 an acre—a heavy rent. But he does not seem to complain, as the land is near the town. He has eight acres in cotton, and expected to have got three or four bales or more. But there has been much drought this year, and he has little more than two bales. One bale I saw screwed up and ready for market, but he is keeping it back for a better price.

Next day I made the acquaintance of Mr. O——, the superintendent of state schools, a thorough old Southerner, who literally "never set foot on free soil" till his own state was made free, and to this day he has never been in the Northern states. He is now, however, very zealous in favor of progress and education. The state has behaved very handsomely in maintaining a black college, where 200 young Negroes receive what he thinks only rather too high an education. The educated blacks look to be politicians, preachers and teachers. He says, with hosts of other Southerners, he considers the war is ended, and they do not want to renew it, but want to make the best of the existing situation.

I was introduced to an ex-member of Congress, Mr. P——. He comes from the extreme northeast of this state, the hilly country where the gold mines are worked. Some of the mines are now to a considerable extent worked by convict labor. It seems that a very large number of blacks are sent to prison and that they are generally hired out. In slave times little was thought of petty pickings—such as taking a turnip from a field—but now such things are very severely punished.

I visited Colonel P——, a gentleman to whom I had an introduction, and who is a very old institution here. He came up here a long time ago and acquired land which had been bought from the Indians. He was, in fact, one of the first settlers in Atlanta. He is evidently now a thorough Southerner in feeling. He thinks the Negro first-rate to "shovel dirt," a function for which he was made but no good for much else. He must be "kept in his place," as it is the fashion to say in Georgia. In accordance with the common opinion here, he says that the cultivation of cotton has been overdone and the soil exhausted by over-cropping. Many people are now emigrating to Texas, and, besides the white people who go there, a good many unattached blacks have been carried off to the Southwestern states by people who have embarked in enterprises in that direction. He, like others, says that the attempt to carry on large farms in this part of the country has not been successful. They are now being divided up. He talks with horror of the immorality of the Negroes and is altogether pessimist upon this subject. He and others are strong on the badness of the free and independent young Negroes who have grown up since the war. The old ones have some virtues, but you cannot strike them now.

Colonel P—— took me to see some great ironworks. All seemed to be agreed that for manual labor, in this climate at any rate, the blacks are better than the whites, and in the works here the ordinary labor is exclusively done by black men. They would not have white men if they could get them. If the Negro is kept in his place and is made to work he does very well, but he is not fit to rise higher. He has no "judgement" and does not make a skilled mechanic. The Georgian who is head of the office at these works takes entirely the same view as Colonel P——, or goes even farther. According to him, the Negro is unthrifty to the last degree, drinks and dances, is dishonest and immoral.

On the other hand, an Ohio man, who superintends the iron manufacture, tells quite a different story. He says that there are instances here of Negroes developing much mechanical skill and conducting themselves very well. He doubts if the Negroes will be allowed to rise. There is a general view that the Negro must be kept in his place. No doubt most of them are somewhat wanting in judgement. According to the Georgian the Negroes cannot see straight! As carpenters they always will fit their work crooked. The Ohio man, however, says that a good many are not only quite good workmen, but also thrifty and disposed to save and have by saving come to own their own houses and a little land. But he says that they are frequently ousted on questions of title. There are many pettifogging lawyers about always ready to get up a case, civil or criminal, against a Negro. The blacks are sent to the chain gang very readily. When men are wanted for the chain gang they are always got. He concurs, however, to some extent with what I had been told about the indiscipline of the younger Negroes. He has some who have been to prison, and the chain gang discipline certainly improves them. He prefers to take a young man who has served for a time in the chain gang.

In the evening at the hotel I had some talk with Georgians of the upper class. Their opinions are unfavorable to the Negroes, who are, they say, of an extremely migratory disposition. They wander about too much. If a man is discharged, he does not care. He steals till he gets another job. A farmer sitting by, however, interposed to say that in the last three or four years they have much improved. Judge C——, a sensible man who has a considerable estate, seems from what he says to get on pretty well with the Negroes upon it. He likes the share plan, provided that he keeps the management and direction entirely in his own hands and pays the cultivators their share of the crops instead of their paying him. Some of them do very well. They have a house and small enclosure of land for vegetables and provisions for themselves and then, with a mule supplied by him, a man will cultivate perhaps forty acres, half in corn and half in cotton. He gives them half of the corn and one-third of the cotton for themselves or the value of it.

I had again a good deal of talk with several men. They all stoutly maintain that Georgia deserves credit as having set an example to other states in the treatment of the Negro. They say the blacks are now quite content and willingly go with the whites. They would be all right but for the interference of carpetbaggers and, above all, of the "New England school marms." These they declare to be the pest of the world, putting false ideas of equality into the heads of the blacks, especially the black women, whom all agree in describing as the most troublesome of the race. They say that the blacks like society, their wives like dress and dances and shows, and being free to do as they liked they sought to obtain these advantages of freedom in the towns. Now many have gone back to the country. I could not obtain any explanation of the fact that there has been scarcely any increase in the Negro ownership of land in the last two or three years. I had been told that in one county there was a Granger's League, a combination not to sell land to Negroes, and that the Negroes thereupon checkmated the landowners by themselves making a league to leave that county. My friends admit that very many whites have disgraced themselves by failing to pay wages earned by the black laborers.

I confess I am more and more suspicious about the criminal justice of these Southern states. In Georgia there is no regular penitentiary at all, but an organized system of letting out the prisoners for profit! Some people here have got up a company for the purpose of hiring convicts. They pay $25,000 a year besides all expenses of food and keep, so that the money is clear profit to the state. The lessees work the prisoners both on estates and in mines and apparently maintain severe discipline in their own way and make a good thing of it. Colonel P——, who is not very mealy-mouthed, admits that he left the concern because he could not stand the inhumanity of it. Another partner in the concern talked with great glee of the money he had made out of the convicts. This does seem simply a return to another form of slavery.

Here, too, I am told that there is a greater separation of the white and black castes than there was before the war. Now there is complete separation in churches and schools. The blacks are always ready to vote for any man who goes against the regular Democratic ticket. There is still a little bulldozing and a good deal of influence bribery and whiskey used to back the regular Democratic candidates. The editor of the small weekly Independent paper joins, however, in the general statement that Georgia treats the blacks fairly well. Fair justice is given to them in the courts; there is a disposition to treat them as not very responsible children. In the last sessions one white man was convicted of murder when two blacks were acquitted. In lower Georgia there is still some unfairness in the settlement of their accounts at the end of the year. Mr. W, a Scotch-Irishman, had mills here before the war. Before the war he employed Negroes and Negresses in his mills along with some free whites; that was not an uncommon practice and they did very well. But since emancipation the blacks have not been employed in the mills.

Today I noticed a very large number of small farmers bringing cotton to market in their wagons. Most of them were whites, driving themselves, and evidently quite laboring men. They had one or two blacks with them, but not very many. There were also a few black farmers. The blacks whom I questioned were mostly tenants upon the share system. They appeared to me rather a low class, and their answers to my questions quite tallied with the accounts I had had of their migratory habits. They generally had not remained very long in one place. The white farmers seemed good-looking men, but poorly clad. They looked like poor Irish farmers. They came in covered wagons, in which they live and sleep, and some of them had their wives and children with them in the wagons. I am told a good many people from these parts have gone to Texas, both white and black. Some of them have come back again.

I drove out a good way into the country. There is a great deal of game about here. I saw many of the small American partridges, sometimes called quails. They rise in regular coveys. There are also rabbits, running with cocked tails, showing the white. There are many wild turkeys, very shy birds, seldom seen. Much poultry is kept by small farmers. Most of the work in the upper country is done by the whites themselves. I saw some good specimens of people of this class. Many of them have Scotch names—Campbell, McIntyre, Macinroy and so on—but they did not know their origin. They came up from the Carolinas and Virginia. Most of them live in miserable houses, but some of the houses are quite good. Even some considerable proprietors live in poor log houses. Some of the smaller tenants live in places unfit for an Irishman with no windows and showing much daylight between the logs. I never saw such poor places, except Irish turf huts. I asked one man about it. "Yes," he said, laughing, "you cannot call it a house, but as we have so much air inside we do not catch cold when we go out!" This man was a poor laborer, and he had half-a-dozen nice-looking children in his wretched one-room hut. These people seemed altogether a fair-spoken and quiet, laborious population. We met many farmers with bullock-wagons coming down from the upper country. They do not grow cotton there and scarcely ever had any Negroes.

At Dalton I had a beautiful day and utilized it by taking a long walk into the country, where I saw much of the Southern white people, visiting a good many of their farms. I also came across some blacks. The whites seemed to be a pleasant-looking people, though they had still the appearance of being poor. Most of them owned land, but some rent, and some go out as laborers. A few of them hire one or two blacks as laborers. They say the blacks are not so good workers as the whites, and they will only take them at cheaper rates. These blacks work very well when they are sharply looked after, but they will waste time whenever they get the chance. I looked over the log cabin of a small white farmer, and it was about the lowest thing of the kind I have seen. On account of the want of water power and the scarcity of sawmills, most of the cabins here are built of very rough logs and very imperfectly boarded within. This one had no windows, but very many casual openings in the wall and even in the roof. It consisted of one room with a light shed attached to it behind, which was used for cooking, etc. The farmer was away, but I found his wife, a very nice-looking young woman with a baby and a boy of twelve, an orphan whom they seem to have adopted. He could read print, she said, but not write. The woman did not seem to realize that the house was particularly bad. Her husband is only a renter, but he built this hut himself two years ago. She had a loom and was weaving. She says she makes her husband's and her own everyday clothes, but they have to buy Sunday clothes and some other things. There was also a spinning-wheel, as is generally the case here. She says she spins some thread when it is wanted, but they buy most of the thread. I was inclined to pity her primitive innocence and ignorance and tried to draw her out by asking her questions on subjects in respect to which I was not very much at home. At last she burst out with a smile, "Whoy, it seem that you do'ant know nothink!"

The New South

A real economic and political revolution had taken place in Georgia during the Civil War and Reconstruction. The industrial revolution at last came to Georgia, which was compelled to manufacture rather than import many goods. Power had shifted from the aristocratic planters of middle and coastal Georgia, whose property in bonds, cash and plantations was destroyed by the war and who were specifically excluded from the Reconstruction governments, to the common people of north Georgia, who benefitted from rapid inflation and depreciation of the currency.

Henry Grady, the energetic and optimistic editor of the Atlanta *Constitution* in the 1880's, may not have invented the phrase, but he became the most acclaimed Southerner of his day to proclaim a "New South" of reconciliation and reform. Grady preached political harmony to a generation of Georgians who had suffered conquest and occupation, economic achievement in a poverty-stricken land and justice for blacks where slavery had been ended only recently and, for most whites, reluctantly. Grady prophesied: "A vision of surpassing beauty unfolds before my eyes . . . a South, the home of fifty millions of people, who rise up every day from blessed cities, vast hives of industry and of thrift, her streams vocal with whirring spindles, her valleys tranquil in the white and gold of the harvest, her rulers honest and her people loving, her homes happy, her wealth diffused and poor-houses empty, her two races walking together in peace and contentment!" [Document Sixteen]

Atlanta, a city created and destroyed by the war, was a scene of amazing recovery, fast rebuilding amidst crumbling walls, solitary chimneys and charred timbers. The Scottish-born writer Robert Somers visited Atlanta in 1870: "The city is gathering in thick and hot haste about the railways. Like everything else in Atlanta, a general depot is unfinished. Passengers are put down in the mud to be screamed at by steam engines, barricaded on every side by trains of cars, bales of cotton, boxes of merchandise, gable-ends of houses and building materials. Atlanta is expected to grow into a great city." [Document Seventeen] Atlanta's population increased from 37,000 in 1880 to 90,000 in 1900.

No matter how well intentioned, Grady's words were not the reality of life in New South Georgia. Georgia's post-war leaders were pragmatic, opportunistic men who represented the concerns of businessmen and cities and monopolized the power of the redeemer Democrats between 1870 and 1906. Unhappy farmers, represented by Dr. William H. Felton's Independents, were easily defeated in the 1870's by appeals for unity against the threat of black domination. The Doctor's widow, Rebecca Latimer Felton, recalled: "A button, pushed in Atlanta, headquarters of the ring masters, moved another smaller wheel in nearly every courthouse in Georgia. A few prominent politicians, calling themselves the Democratic party, managed to control political power in Georgia, not to benefit the people but the great corporations." [Document Eighteen]

Despite the New South's promotion of economic diversification, most Southerners remained farmers, producing cotton and too much of it. In 1900 eighty-five per cent of Georgia's population still lived on farms or in small villages and sixty per cent worked in agriculture. David Barrow described plantation life in 1881–82—primitive labor, unrelenting except for holiday frolics—a system reminiscent of slavery days. "The man does the plowing, his wife and children do the hoeing. The usual quantity of land planted is between twenty-five and thirty acres, about half of which is cotton and the rest corn and patches. The dwelling house is an ordinary log cabin." [Document Nineteen]

Despite the New South's promotion of industrial development,

Northern cotton mills did not come to Georgia in significant numbers until after 1900, and industrial diversification did not materialize until after 1945. The "industries" that came to Georgia before 1945 were cotton, lumber and paper mills, which exploited the region's low wages and natural resources. Blacks were excluded from employment in factories, but it was employment without much opportunity for whites. Clare de Graffenried described the poor whites employed in mills in 1891: "In complete isolation, dead monotony and dense, undisturbed ignorance, their toilsome lives run out. Like so many machines, the creatures drudge on . . . demoralized by a lifetime of travail amid unsanitary conditions, underfed and badly housed, without education, incentives or ideals." [Document Twenty]

Meanwhile, in the twilight of the South's agrarian empire, white farmers, as well as blacks, were sinking under the failure of one-crop cotton, sterile and eroded soil, overproduction, declining prices, low cash incomes and cumulative debts. Despite the growth of cities, the South's per capita wealth and income remained virtually unchanged between 1880 and 1900—about one-half of the national average—and Georgia's per capita income showed no increase at all during the period. In 1903 Clifton Johnson, a writer from Massachusetts, visited a poor white family in the northern part of Georgia. The women wore old-fashioned sun bonnets, cooked over an open fire and dipped snuff. [Document Twenty-one] The poor whites of the factories and farms viewed the relative progress of blacks as a threat to their own precarious social and economic position.

$\left[\,16\,\right]$

I see a South, the home of fifty millions of people... blessed cities, hives of industry, her countryside the treasures from which their resources are drawn, her streams vocal with whirring spindles, her rulers honest, her wealth diffused. Almighty God shall not look down on a happier land!

HENRY GRADY

HENRY GRADY (1851–1889) was born at Athens, attended the University of Georgia and the University of Virginia. He commenced his career as a newspaperman at the Rome *Commercial* and was later employed by the Atlanta *Herald*. In 1880 he became editor and a part-owner of the Atlanta *Constitution*. He became the most acclaimed Southerner of his day to plead for sectional reconciliation, industrialization and agricultural reform and fair treatment of the Negro. These selections from his writings and speeches are adapted from *The New South Writings and Speeches of Henry Grady*, published by The Beehive Press in 1972.

Let me picture to you the footsore Confederate soldier, as buttoning up in his faded gray jacket his parole, he turned his face southward from Appomattox in April, 1865. Think of him as ragged, half-starved, heavy-hearted, enfeebled by want and wounds, having fought to exhaustion, he surrenders his gun, wrings the hands of his comrades in silence and, lifting his tear-stained and pallid face for the last time to the graves that dot old Virginia hills, pulls his gray cap over his brow and begins the slow and painful journey home. What does he find when he reaches the home he left so prosperous and beautiful? He finds his house in ruins, his farm devastated, his slaves free, his stock killed, his barns empty, his trade destroyed, his money worthless, his social system swept away, his people without law or legal status, his comrades slain and the burdens of others heavy on his shoulders. Crushed by defeat, his very traditions are gone. Without money, credit, employment, material or training and confronted with the gravest problem that ever met human intelligence—the establishing of a status for the vast body of his liberated slaves! What chance had our soldier-farmer of '65 for the future as he wandered amid his empty barns, his stocks, labor and implements gone, his crop mortgaged before it was planted, his children in want, his neighborhood in chaos, plodding all day down the furrow, hopeless and adrift?

What does he do—this hero in gray with a heart of gold? The soldiers stepped from the trenches into the furrow. Horses that had charged Federal guns marched before the plow, and fields that ran red with human blood in April were green with the harvest in June. Women reared in luxury cut up their dresses and made breeches for their husbands. The soldier returning home after defeat and roasting some corn on the roadside, made the remark to his comrade, "You may leave the South if you want to, but I am going to Sandersville, kiss my wife and raise a crop, and if the Yankees fool with me any more, I'll whip 'em again!" The people of this section, reduced to poverty by war, began that march of restoration and development that has challenged univeral admiration.

Cotton makes the Southern farmer king, as it unfurls its banners in our fields. It is gold from the instant it puts forth its first tiny shoot. The dominance of our king is established for all time. But the old South rested everything on slavery and agriculture, unconscious that these could neither give nor maintain healthy growth. Agriculture alone, nomatter how rich or varied its resources, cannot establish or maintain a people's prosperity. From chaos and desolation, the currents of trade trickled and swelled. Rivers were spanned and the wilderness pierced with iron rails. Having ores and coal stored in exhaustless quantity, iron can be made and manufacturing done cheaper than elsewhere. Our coal supply is exhaustless. In marble and granite we have no rivals as to quantity or quality. In lumber our riches are even vaster, more than fifty percent of our entire area in forests. By furnishing work for the artisan and mechanic you meet the demand of your population for cheaper and essential manufactured articles.

The industrial growth of the South in the past ten years has been without precedent or parallel. It has been a great revolution. The iron furnaces have opened the way to collateral industries. The cost of shipping so heavy a thing as iron to the North to be made into gins, plows, stoves and like heavy goods and the cost of shipping them back tempted capital into shops and factories. Many factories have found the freight saving the profit they needed. Rolling mills were the first industries that followed the furnaces. Gins and cotton presses were close to these. Plows and cotton planters followed. Then came stoves, hollow-ware, nails, piping, and sash stuff. After these came bridge-works, engine and boiler factories, chain works, car works and locomotive works. Excellent saws are now made in the South. In Atlanta the best gold watches are now made, the finest pianos, double concave razors and sewing machines.

When my business partner came home from the war, in which he had commanded a battery, he had neither breeches, home nor money. His wife cut up a woolen dress she had worn for years and made him a pair of breeches. Gathering odds and ends from the ruins of Atlanta, he built a shanty. His father gave him a $5 gold piece. In three years he had built a $1500 home, in eight years a $6000 home. He has now a $60,000 suburban home and is worth well over a quarter of a million dollars. His life is an epitome of the South—its swift energy, its cheerful heroism, its shrewd knack of turning something from nothing, its growth and its present prosperity.

From the ashes General Sherman left us in 1864 we have raised a brave and beautiful city. The people of Atlanta in 1864 crept out of the diagonal holes cut, like swallows' nests, in the hillsides, in which they had abided the siege, to find their city in ruins. Old citizens could scarcely thread the course of familiar streets through ashes and debris. As the refugees straggled back and the soldiers, afoot from Virginia, found once more their dismantled homes, the ruined city trembled with the energy of a camp. From defeat and utter poverty were to be wrought victory and plenty. Atlanta worked for all that was in her. Five hundred shanties were made of the iron roofing of destroyed buildings. Four posts were driven up, iron sheeting tacked about them, a cover laid, a door cut. In 1866 there were but four men in Atlanta worth $10,000. In 1889, there are six millionaires whose wealth aggregates $10,000,000, nine others assessed at more than $750,000 each, fourteen others worth over $500,000 each, and twenty-one worth from $250,000 to $500,000 each. These fifty citizens, now worth over $30,000,000, were not worth $250,000 in 1865. Back of them is a prosperous city filled with well-to-do people and capital of a prosperous state.

A few years ago I told of a burial in Pickens County, Georgia. The grave was dug through solid marble, but the marble headstone came from Vermont. It was in a pine wilderness, but the pine coffin came from Cincinnati. An iron mountain overshadowed it, but the coffin nails and screws and the shovels came from Pittsburgh. With hard woods and metals abounding, the corpse was hauled on a wagon from South Bend, Indiana. A hickory grove grew nearby, but the pick and shovel handles came from New York. The cotton shirt on the dead man came from Cincinnati, the coat and breeches from Chicago, the shoes from Boston, the folded hands were encased in white gloves from New York and 'round the poor neck, that had worn all its living days the bondage of lost opportunity, was twisted a cheap cravat from Philadelphia. That country, so rich in undeveloped resources, furnished nothing for the funeral except the corpse and the hole in the ground!

There are now more than $3,000,000 invested in marble quarries and machinery around that grave. Its pitiful loneliness is broken with the rumble of ponderous machines. Twenty miles away, the largest marble-cutting works in the world! Forty miles away, four coffin factories! The iron hills are gashed and swarm with workmen! Forty cotton mills in a near radius weave infinite cloth that neighboring shops make into countless shirts. There are shoe factories, nail factories, shovel and pick factories and carriage factories, to supply the other wants.

The South, under the rapid diversification of crops and diversification of industries, is thrilling with new life. In her industrial growth the South is daily making new friends. Every dollar of Northern money invested in the South gives us a new friend in that section. Every settler among us raises up new witnesses to our fairness, sincerity and loyalty. We shall secure from the North more friendliness and sympathy, more champions and friends, through the influence of our industrial growth than through political aspiration or achievement. Companies of immigrants sent down from the North will solve the Southern problem and bring this section into full and harmonious relations with the North quicker than all the battalions that could be armed and martialed could do. The tide of immigration is already springing this way. Let us encourage it.

But what is the sum of our work? We have sowed towns and cities in the place of theories and put business above politics. We have challenged your spinners in Massachusetts and your iron-makers in Pennsylvania. We have learned that our cotton crop will make us rich when the supplies that make it are home-raised. We have learned that one Northern immigrant is worth fifty foreigners and have smoothed the path to southward, wiped out the place where Mason and Dixon's line used to be. We have fallen in love with work! We know that we have achieved in peace a fuller independence for the South than that which our fathers sought to win by their swords.

The race problem casts the only shadow that rests on the South. The New South rejoices that slavery has been swept forever from American soil. It rejoices that the American Union was saved. The problem is to carry in peace and honor and prosperity two dissimilar races nearly equal in number on the same soil. Let us impress upon the Negro that his best friends are the people among whom he lives, whose interests are one with his, whose prosperity depends on his perfect contentment. Let us give him his rights and measure out justice in that fullness that the strong should always give to the weak. Let us educate him that he may be a better, broader and more enlightened man. Let us lead him in steadfast ways of citizenship that he may no longer be the prey of the unscrupulous.

It must not be imagined that the Negro is outlawed in the South. White and black carpenters and masons work together on the same buildings, white and black shoemakers and mechanics in the same shops. White and black hackmen drive on the same streets. White and black farmers work in the same field. But the white and black carpenters, working together on the same building, go to separate homes at night, to separate churches on Sunday. White and black

147

mechanics in the same shop send their children to separate schools. White and black farmers in the same field ride to market in separate cars.

The whites and blacks must walk in separate paths in the South. As near as may be, these paths should be made equal—but separate they must be now and always. This means separate schools, separate churches, separate accommodations everywhere—but equal accommodation where the same money is charged or where the state provides for the citizen. Railroads in Georgia provide separate but equal cars for whites and blacks, and a white man is not permitted to occupy a colored car. This separation is not offensive but is accepted by both races as the best conducive to the common peace and prosperity. There are fanatics and doctrinaires who hold that separation is discrimination and that discrimination is offensive.

No section shows a more prosperous laboring population than the Negroes of the South, none in fuller sympathy with the employing and landowning class. He shares our school fund, has the fullest protection of our laws and the friendship of our people. The relations of the Southern people with the Negro are close and cordial. The South protests against injustice to this simple and sincere people. To liberty and enfranchisement is as far as law can carry the Negro. The rest must be left to conscience and common sense. It must be left to those among whom his lot is cast, with whom he is indissolubly connected and whose prosperity depends upon their possessing his intelligent sympathy and confidence.

The whites own the property. They have the intelligence. Theirs is the responsibility. They are the superior race and will have clear and unmistakable control of public affairs. They will not and cannot submit to the domination of an inferior race. Let this resolution be cast on the lines of equity and justice, giving the Negro every right, civil and political, measured in that fullness the strong should always accord the weak. Standing in the presence of this multitude, sobered with the responsibility of the message I deliver to the young men of the South, I declare that the truth above all others to be worn unsullied and sacred in your hearts, to be surrendered to no force, sold for no price, compromised in no necessity, but cherished and defended as the covenant of your prosperity and the pledge of peace to your children, is that the white race must dominate forever in the South. It is a race issue. Let us come to that point and stand here.

Many wise men hold that the white vote of the South should divide, the color line be beaten down and the Southern states ranged on economic or moral questions as interest or belief demands. I am compelled to dissent from this view. The worst thing in my opinion that could happen is that the white people of the South should stand in opposing factions, with the vast mass of ignorant and purchasable Negro votes between. The blacks are ignorant and therefore easily deluded, impulsive and therefore easily led, passionate and therefore easily excited, poor, irresponsible and easily bought. The fear is that this vast swarm of ignorant, purchasable and credulous voters will be controlled by desperate and unscrupulous white men and made to hold the balance of power wherever the whites are divided. It would invite the debauching bid of factions. This fear will keep the whites "solid."

A vision of surpassing beauty unfolds before my eyes. I see a South, the home of fifty millions of people, who rise up every day to call from blessed cities, vast hives of industry and of thrift, her countryside the treasures from which their resources are drawn, her streams vocal with whirring spindles, her valleys tranquil in the white and gold of the harvest, her mountains showering down the music of bells as her slow-moving flocks and herds go forth from their folds, her rulers honest and her people loving, and her home happy and their hearthstones bright and their waters still and their pastures green and her conscience clear, her wealth diffused and poor houses empty, her churches earnest in the gospel, peace and sobreity walking hand in hand through her borders. Almighty God shall not look down on a better people or a happier land!

The town is gathering in thick and hot haste about the railways. Like everything else in Atlanta, a general depot is unfinished. Passengers are put down in the mud to be screamed at by steam engines, barricaded on every side by trains of cars, bales of cotton, boxes of merchandise, gable-ends of houses and building materials. Atlanta is expected to grow into a great city.

ROBERT SOMERS, 1870–71

SCOTTISH-BORN Robert Somers (1822–1891) was a lecturer on political subjects, a newspaper editor and a writer in Edinburgh and Glasgow. In 1870–71, Somers travelled in America for six months, studying the effects of the Civil War on the South. These pages are drawn from his *The Southern States Since the War* (London, 1871), pp. 62–102.

The thriving and busy town of Augusta at once establishes in the mind of a stranger a favorable prepossession of the state of Georgia. It is lively, well built, well organized and as amply furnished with merchandise as any small inland town of the most flourishing province could be expected to be. During the war, Augusta shared the general impoverishment which blighted every portion of the Southern states. It is surprising, therefore, to see already so much spirit and abundance as prevail in Augusta. The town has a "Broadway," three times as broad as that of New York, and has a neatly constructed marketplace at either end. Nearly the whole ground space is occupied with well-stocked stores, in which everything from a needle to an anchor, from the humble fabrics woven on the spot to the finest clothes of Europe and all the products of the soil from cranberries to cotton may be bought. And how substantial the houses are and how many fine buildings meet the eye!

Augusta is an extensive cotton market. The telegraph works all day betwixt Augusta and Savannah and betwixt Augusta and towns farther inland, telling what cotton can be bought or is selling for, while prices at New York and Liverpool are eagerly scanned. The local factors and merchants deal freely in cotton, though the former operate chiefly on order from Savannah, Charleston and New York. Seldom has cotton been brought more rapidly to market than this season, which is to be ascribed to the necessity, rather than the interest, of the planters. The growers of cotton, though restoring rapidly their plantations and their stock of implements, are for the most part still poor in purse and have to draw heavy advances on the growing crop. The planter finds that to hold back the crop in expectation of better prices is a costly business, and that it is better to sell at once than to extend his borrowings and storage and insurance charges.

A great revolution in agriculture is going forward in this district and throughout the whole of Georgia. The most lively discussion is kept up on such points as the preparation of land for crops, the selection of cotton seed, the use of fertilizers, the improvement and increase of livestock and a more careful and varied cultivation than has hitherto been followed. There appears to be a strong feeling of the necessity of bringing intelligence and an active spirit of improvement to bear on the management of plantations, which, in ante-war times, were allowed to drag along with slave labor and overseers as they had done for generations. Agricultural societies have been formed in all parts of the state and have been consolidated into a general institution which holds two conventions every year for the discussion of agricultural questions and for making arrangements for the holding of annual fairs or exhibitions of industry. Numerous periodicals are published here and throughout the state which are chiefly devoted to the land interest and discuss practical farming in all its branches with much vigor and intelligence.

In middle Georgia much cotton is now grown by white labor. This occurs chiefly on small farms, the proprietors of which were formerly unable to compete with the large combinations of slave labor but are now raising a considerable amount of cotton. There are now also many small patches of cotton in the neighborhood of towns and villages, where fruits and vegetables cannot be so well preserved from depredation by vagrant or destitute Negroes as in former times. The large planters who cannot command labor or capital to cultivate more than a section of their former cotton area, endeavor to sell or to farm out portions of their plantations. Some land is farmed out at a crop-rent of one-fourth the produce, while a good many strangers come into this part of the state, buy land and settle down to its cultivation. The field Negroes command from $8 to $12½ a month, with rations, houses and fire, women from $5 to $8. But the share system of paying labor prevails more than that of wages, at the rate of one-third of the crop with rations or one-half without rations. "The Negroes," says a very competent authority to me, "are working better and stealing less every year and would be well enough if the political agitators would only let them alone." The agitators complained of are "the carpetbaggers" who come into the South with very light equipment for the sole purpose of getting themselves elected representatives by the Negro vote and of working themselves into some office in which they may make rich at the public expense. The tactics of these trading politicians are declared to be sometimes of the most wild and desperate description. It is said the Negroes have been told from the stump that their former masters owe them wages from the date of Mr. Lincoln's proclamation and that anything stolen from them now is but in fair liquidation of the account!

There is a prosperous cotton factory in Augusta, which produces sheetings and shirtings and other plain domestic fabrics. The hands are all white people, male and female. The factory has both steam and water power and has established a basis of skilled labor that is not likely in a town of such considerable population to fail in the future. In such considerable towns as Augusta a large amount of labor, otherwise idle and unprofitable, may be utilized without impairing in any degree the main interest of agriculture and this cotton factory proves with what advantage various manufactures may be prosecuted in the Southern states.

The distance from Augusta to Savannah, the great seaport of Georgia, is 132 miles by rail and is travelled with frequent stoppages for freight in eight to nine hours. I do not think the railway from Augusta to Savannah, while stopping often at depots and little stations in the woods, touches a single place of such considerable size as to form a small town or village. The landholders and farmers enjoy much sport when so inclined. The field for poachers is boundless. One party stepped out from the train, rough and unkempt, with guns and dogs and blankets rolled in sailcloth for nightly bivouac, who appeared to me marvellously like persons of this class. I have observed trains of bullock wagons carrying farmers and their families from Georgia and South Carolina westward to Texas and Arkansas, and this movement is said to be much more extensive than could be supposed from cursory observation. The few cattle that do appear are generally in poor condition with rough coats covering an anatomy of bones. The hogs roaming through the woods are mostly lean and seem to have to go through a heavy day's work for their necessary repast of acorns. The Southern states have not yet surmounted the indifference to livestock that prevailed under the slave system. It is also to be remembered that nearly all the livestock on the plantations was consumed by the war, that many of the planters were left without a cow or an ox, with scarce a hog or even a chicken, and that since the war they have had to buy, breed and recover every useful animal on their lands. The planters had to resume operations with their farms in ruin, with fences to rebuild, with labor scarce, scattered and disorganized with everything to buy at prices three times higher than before the war and no money to buy with.

The business of the port of Savannah has made a remarkable advance since the close of the war, and the increase of shipments this year has exceeded all former precedent. When the cotton season opens, the great demand for tonnage then known to arise brings a forest of masts to the river and shipmasters crowd the brokers' offices seeking cargo. The liberation of the Negroes, while thinning the number of field hands on the plantations, has thrown an ampler supply of labor into thriving towns and cities in the South than could have been obtained under the slave system. It is generally admitted that the Negroes have worked more steadily this year than in any previous year of free labor and planters have declared to me that they could not do without the "darkies" in the field, so superior are they to any white labor that has yet been tried. Public opinion is well reconciled to free Negro labor, and the main cause of dissatisfaction with the colored population is the too ready ear they lend to political agitators and the blind persistency with which they are said to enable such persons to acquire predominance in the state government against the will of the white citizens. The Negroes in the Southern cities and towns, I fear, are falling into the habit of drinking inordinate quantities of bad whiskey.

I can vouch for the picturesque effect of the town's sylvan character, buried among trees that give a novel and striking beauty to the city. It is very pleasant to saunter along Bull Street from end to end, passing from shops and stores to squares, churches, theaters and elegant private mansions, the forest shadows deepening as the architecture becomes more choice, to look on either side down the long wooded streets, two, three, four rows deep in trees, according to their importance in the general intersection, to dwell for a little in admiration of a fine monument, glistening white as snow amidst the many colors of the autumn forest, to stand with curiosity before tropical plants that adorn the fronts of the houses, prominent among them the banana, covering the windows to the second floor with its great leaves, and again to pass on, with new sources of attraction at every step, till the avenue debouches on a small Bois de Boulogne, where an elaborate fountain plays, pointing the way to shady walks in which the ladies promenade with their babies and nurses and lovers meet to exchange vows. The street-ways betwixt the trees are several inches deep in a blackish sand that muffles every sound of hoof or wheel. Savannah looks as if 30,000 people had gone out from town into a bowery forest glade and, without disturbing its silence or its beauty, made summer houses amidst its flowers and plants and under the shade of its spreading trees.

In my progress from Savannah I met four great cotton trains, twenty trucks at least in each, passing down to the seaport. The passenger trains seldom contain many people, except when some public gatherings are being held or when immigrants and other through-passengers happen to be numerous. Smoking is prohibited in all but the front car, to which the smokers go as it suits them. By this subtle arrangement the railway companies have arrived at a practical dividing line, betwixt first and second class passengers—Negroes and others desiring to travel cheap and smokers who must smoke all the time being required to take their passage in the smoking car and not allowed to leave it during the journey. The "ladies car" is the choice part of the train and is strictly guarded from male intruders at the passenger depots.

Cotton is brought down over twenty and thirty miles of country to some of the railway stations on drays, with four mules to each and almost as many Negroes, a few bales at a time. While Negroes and mules are toiling along the country roads with cotton, the backwardness of picking is everywhere observable. Whole fields along this route, even at this date, are white as snow with cotton wool. Since the war, picking has seldom been finished till February, and, besides causing much deterioration of cotton, has cut largely into the time and labor required to prepare the ensuing crop. Planters fret and worry under this state of things more, of course, than anybody else, but it is an evil that injures all. The Negroes get up difficulties of wages and fall into difficulties of debt and liens on their share of the crop. The fall of price is even a difficulty to the Negro for, when cotton is cheap, it is not worthwhile picking it. The Negroes have some very peculiar traits of character and are more like children than grown people. Served with the stipulated rations for a week, they will sometimes eat them up in three days and fall into debt to their employers and their merchants for more than enough. Yet the prevailing remark is that they are improving. The courts in Georgia punish them for stealing and as the resources of theft and idleness are closed against them, they begin to feel they must work to live.

The position of Macon in the heart of middle Georgia, where all the railways —north, south, east and west—converge as to a common center, renders it probably the most important and most promising inland town of this state. It receives from 90,000 to 100,000 bales of cotton annually and the drafts of planters in the surrounding country are honored eagerly by merchants and warehousemen to the extent of their resources, with the view of fostering and increasing the importance of the town as a mart for cotton. The railway lines which meet and radiate from Macon would alone be sufficient to give a powerful and permanent impulse to its trade and industry. Extensive railway workshops have been established, and have gathered 'round them a numerous body of mechanics. Macon, like Augusta, has a cotton factory that has long been a successful element in the industry of the town. The goods manufactured are shirtings. This factory has only 5240 spindles and works at less advantage than the Augusta factory, which has more extensive and newer machinery. The number of hands employed in the Macon factory is 120. They are all whites. The wages paid to women are $24 to $25 a month and to boys $13 a month. Another cotton factory is about to be opened in an extensive building that was erected during the war for a Confederate arsenal. A very general desire is evinced for the establishment of cotton factories, but the Southern people seem to fall into a series of mistakes on this point. Their ideas of manufacturing run in too narrow a groove. There are many branches of manufacture which, both in the towns and country parts of the South, might be prosecuted with probably greater advantage than simple cotton fabrics. Variety of enterprise is desirable. It is the North which the South has always in view when it sighs for more and more cotton factories.

I arrived in Atlanta under a shower of rain. It is now rising up a more ambitious town than before. But an architectural chaos reigns in the meanwhile over all its center and circumference. The railway from Macon, after gliding through a suburb of cabins and passing a military barracks, begins to toll its bell and perform a sort of funereal procession amidst the debris of newly-built houses and the ruins of old ones, pieces of streets to which there is no visible entrance and deepening files of cars and trucks from which there is no imaginable exit, finally drawing up more apparently from the impossibility of moving backward or forward than from the fact of having arrived anywhere. The various railroads which meet at this crowded point do not go to the town; the town is gathering in thick and hot haste about the railways. A general depot is being built, but, like everything else in Atlanta, it is unfinished, and on the arrival of a train under rain the passengers are put down in the mud to be screamed at by steam engines and high-pressure Negroes, scared by the tolling of bells and barricaded on every side by trains of cars, bales of cotton, boxes of merchandise, gable-ends of houses and all sorts of building materials. "Is there any hotel in this city of Babel?" I cried out and was immediately told Atlanta had the biggest thing of the kind in creation. "Where is it?" "There, sare, I take you," said a darkey, who had already marked me for his own. "There it is," pointing to a really magnificent edifice, which on the side next us seemed to have everything but windows, an edifice forming nearly two streets of Atlanta, so large, indeed, that it seemed impossible to judge where the entrance might be. "The H. I. Kimball House, sir. Have you nary heerd of the H.I.?" said a short, thick man, all beard and no whiskers. Whereupon he put into my hand a printed paper, which, as I was now scaling a heavy intrenchment of brick and mortar, flanked by wet ditches of no mean account. I put into my pocket to cull some particulars from by and by. The hall of the Kimball House is as big as a church. This hall is open almost to the roof of the building, with tier upon tier of galleries communicating with the various floors of the hotel and affording the guests an opportunity of looking down on all that passes below. A gaselier drops from the higher stories over the hall, of such magnitude and brightness as might grace any opera house in the largest cities of the world. The whole hotel is brilliantly lighted with gas. I was hoisted to my room in a steam-powered elevator.

Atlanta has several great business houses in the dry goods, hardware, grocery and confectionary lines with fine shops on the street for retail business and upper floors for wholesale trade. One receives at every step a lively impression of the great power residing somewhere in the United States of filling the most distant and unpromising places with wares and traffickers of all kinds. Stores full of "Northern notions," New York oyster saloons and "drummers" of the latest patents out at Washington are seen on the streets of Atlanta. One man showed me a more perfect kerosene oil or spirit lamp than I had seen or imagined. He lighted three or four of them and, flinging them heedlessly on the floor to burn at leisure in various corners of the store, instantly pulled out a patent washing-machine which is to drive everything else out of the market. He was about to show me a marvellous pot-hook with cradle appendages for weighing babies, when, notwithstanding my deeply awakened interest, I was obliged to come away. The streets of Atlanta are not yet lighted with gas, but the patentee came with me to the door and sprung an immense spirit torch which threw a blaze of light into the gloom revealing, in the distance, of course, a wing of the great hotel. (I found myself, in various attempts, always going away from it and always coming back to the Kimball House! It is difficult for a guest of the H.I. to lose himself in Atlanta!)

But it is easy for any one to be abruptly stopped by some impassable barrier or dangerously inveigled in the network of railway tracks. The railways cut Atlanta for the present in two. I found myself standing on one occasion beside a grave, elderly man who was waiting like myself for an opening betwixt the long trains that blocked the way. As one moved on, another close behind was sure to give a snort and jolt along, too, and when the down track was a little clear the tolling bell of a train on the up track gave note of warning to adventurous citizens. I ventured to remark to my patient friend that it was strange the people of Atlanta could bear such an obstruction in the heart of the town. "Friend, you are a stranger. I guess the railways were here before the people of Atlanta," was his reply, and what he told me I recognized at once to be true. The railways were the beginning and the end of Atlanta in the old times, and the new city rising up around the place where it was erewhile convenient for the railway engine to be fed with wood and water has not yet had time to adjust all its relations. One of the difficulties of the present chaotic stage of Atlanta is that few people in it know anybody else. I had an introduction to a gentleman of some fame, whom I casually met in Macon just as he was going to the train for Atlanta. He had only time to say, "Be sure to *hunt me up* when you come to Atlanta." I did not take up the whole meaning of the phrase at the time, but

I learned it afterwards! Yet when all ordinary means of hunting up people in Atlanta fail, there is one resource which, if you are a guest of the "H.I.", may be reverted to with some confidence. Begin and end your inquiries at the hotel and ten to one you find that you have been breakfasting, dining and supping with the people you want all the time!

Atlanta is already quite a large place. Its population is given in the usual round numbers of the census enumerators at 28,000 to 29,000. But how is it possible to state with precision the population of a city to which a hundred is added today and probably half a thousand may be added tomorrow? I am informed on the best authority that of the 28,000 to 29,000 souls in Atlanta, the whites are in the proportion of 15 to 13 colored. That the colored people should be so numerous in a practically new town proves the large flux of Negroes from country to town since the war. The marvel is how so large a population, white or black, has been gathered here in so short a time. "Northern capital" is the general explanation given, and the great hotel is constantly referred to as a sample of the grand effects which "Northern capital" is destined to achieve in the Southern states. The number of Northern firms established in Atlanta and the commercial prospecters flocking down from as far as Boston and New York attest the mark which Atlanta and the "H.I." together have already made in Northern imagination. But the town is mainly indebted for all the progress yet made to political influences. The capital of Georgia has been removed from Milledgeville, situated as nearly as possible in the center of the state, to this northern town, and give[s] Atlanta both traffic and *éclat* and may render it more and more a place of general concourse from all other parts of the state. Poor Milledgeville has been left in widowhood and desolation, and the state buildings, as well as much private property, been rendered of no account, while Atlanta is expected to grow into a great city. Two brothers Kimball came down from Boston at the close of the war in a humble and unassuming character, but probably with ulterior ideas in their heads. They are types of a class of aspiring Northern men who have rushed to the South since the war, some to run plantations, some to open mines of coal and iron, some to build railroads, others to establish great hotels and all to give a grand impulse to Southern progress and show the "old fogies" in the South how to do it. The brothers Kimball appear to have seen the tide in the affairs of Atlanta sooner than almost anybody else and seized it with remarkable success. They saw that Atlanta had an opera house which was never likely to be finished, and could yield no return to anybody even though it were. They bought this building, it is said, for $85,000, and they sold it immediately to the "reconstructed" state at $350,000 for a state house!

After this, Mr. H. I. Kimball conceived the design of a grand hotel "to beat all creation" and in eight or nine months has reared a splendid structure at an estimated cost of $600,000. The main front is 210 feet and the sides 163 feet each. The dining room is 75 by 40 feet, and the grand hall or ballroom is 103 by 46 feet and 23 feet high. Besides the hotel proper, there are twenty-one stores and warehouses in the building. Two thousand laborers and mechanics have been thumping away in this mammoth caravansera since March last and are still thumping. There is a French cook at $250 a month. The gas bill alone would open half a dozen coal mines. Mr. Kimball has naturally become a man of great influence in Atlanta. He is a munificent patron of state fairs, horse races and every good work. His political influence is even thought, with probably a little dash of popular superstition, to be supreme in the state. A common saying in Georgia is that Blodgett, senator, controls the Governor, but that Mr. H. I. Kimball controls Blodgett! The old native citizens look with some distrust on the general briskness of trade and speculation in Atlanta. While willing to see "progress" in it all, they doubt whether robbery may not be going on. The narrow base on which the universal Negro suffrage, "carpetbag" qualification and white proscription under the Reconstruction Act of Congress have placed political power, tends everywhere to destroy confidence in the financial operations of the state authorities.

The Atlantian who is fond of field sport and chooses to keep a dog and gun has abundant liberty of pastime. Partridges, turkeys and sometimes deer are shot freely in the wilds and woods 'round the town. One gentleman, on whom I called, had just returned from a day's hunting and was able to show me his spoils, among which was a bottle of homemade peach brandy that had been presented to him at a farmhouse. Peaches are abundant in Georgia. The people scarcely know what to do with them. They dry them, pickle them, preserve them and distil them, and, after all, the hogs, I daresay, eat a great many!

⌐ 18 ⌐

A button, pushed in Atlanta, headquarters of the ring masters, moved another smaller wheel in nearly every courthouse in Georgia. A few prominent politicians, calling themselves the Democratic party, managed to control political power in Georgia, not to benefit the people but the great corporations.

REBECCA LATIMER FELTON

REBECCA LATIMER FELTON (1835–1930) was born outside Decatur, graduated from Madison Female College in 1852 and married Dr. William H. Felton in 1853. As writer, speaker and helper, Mrs. Felton's assisted her husband's campaign for political reform as leader of the Independent movement in the 1870's. She was an advocate of women's rights, temperance and penal reform. Mrs. Felton served briefly as the first U.S. Senator in 1922. These extracts are adapted from her long and rambling book, *My Memoirs of Georgia Politics* (Atlanta, 1911).

For more than fifty years I walked side by side with a reformer—a native-born, independent son of Georgia. My husband often said to me, "Don't forget to tell the people of Georgia what you know. I have been badgered, abused and persecuted beyond the limit!" The full story of his protest and what followed should be given to the public—this story of political heroism and political desperadoes. I am here to trace the difficulties, the dangers, the persecutions, the unreasoning partisanship of those who made fortunes out of politics in Georgia —and especially of the prejudice and cowardice of the Democrats who followed the fife and drum against the prosperity of our common country. I am old now —with the snow of seventy-five winters resting on my head. I lived through these perils.

William H. Felton was born in Oglethorpe County, June 19, 1823, reared on a farm and received his preparatory education in the "old field" schools. He matriculated in Franklin College in 1838 and graduated from the state university in 1842. He was a member of the Demosthenian Literary Society and became known as a speaker in the society debates. After leaving college, Dr. Felton took up the study of medicine under Dr. Richard D. Moore of Athens. He graduated from the Medical College of Georgia at Augusta in 1844, the valedictorian of a large class of students.

Moving to Bartow County, Dr. Felton entered upon the practice of medicine, but the strain of the work was too much for his nervous system, and he was forced to give it up. He pursued his literary studies, however, and entered upon an agricultural life. In 1848 he was licensed as a local preacher by the Methodist church. For more than forty years he filled preaching appointments in this and other counties. He served one term in the state legislature, 1851–52. In our plain country home, we were busy people trying to make an honest living.

The war swept off a number of slaves from us. Our buildings were badly abused, where they were not destroyed, and we had nothing to look to but the land, and it was robbed of the fencing and otherwise dilapidated. We had to be very busy, very economical and thrifty to live in any sort of comfort. In September, 1854, while my precious Willie, a lovely child nearly six years old, was slowly dying with typhoid dysentery, Sherman's troops were destroying Atlanta preparatory to the march to the sea. We were too honest with the Confederate government to buy up greenbacks, and the surrender caught us without a dollar.

We started home to northwest Georgia with a few dollars in pocket, the remainder that was left from the sale of our handsome panelled carriage that cost us just before the war over $600 in gold. We sold it at auction in the city of Macon for a little over $100 paid in greenbacks, then $2½ for $1 [in gold]. We reached Cartersville with only enough cash to pay drayage on our stuff out to the old dilapidated home that had not one pane of glass left in the entire building. Such were our beginnings after the war. For a considerable time after the war, I had too much to do, school teaching, making a living and restoring our war-swept plantation and home, to bother very much about the doings of our Georgia politicians.

For forty years the South has been crippled by the Civil War issues, and the politicians on both sides have worked these war issues, ad infinitum, to keep the offices of the country in their own grasp. They could rise up in their various canvasses and hurl epithets at Yanks or Rebs, as the case might be, and then, as soon as they met in Washington or even at home, the politicians would get together on the back stairs and enjoy the situation immensely. Both the great national parties had swollen to immense proportions by covering up graft and condoning the vices and immoralities which disgraced free government. We could not obtain a clear vision on either side of Mason and Dixon's line. The Northern politicians worked in a similar way to produce the same political effect. Demagogues in both the great parties discovered a rare opportunity and snatched it.

There came a time in Georgia, soon after the war, when even well-informed men and honest politicians seemed to be impervious to the dictates of reason and prudence in their political efforts. The "rebel yell" was tremendous, and the party lash cracked incessantly. So it is not strange that the timid and especially the ignorant were carried by this flood of slush and vituperation to the polls. Corrupt politicians would raise the "rebel yell" to cover their schemes of public plunder. Sectional prejudices completely blinded their political judgement. War experiences were too recent, perhaps, for the complete exercise of sound judgement or even common sense. The people despised carpetbaggers. Down at the bottom of their unrest was the ever-present dread of Negro domination. The Negro and his future in politics became a bugbear, a scarecrow used by crafty office-seekers to infuriate the minds of Southern men and women. It was the clamp that held thousands of good men to the Democratic party after it was known to be dominated by industrious grafters who worked the party for personal ends with selfish motives. A great many patriots in the South, especially among the old Whig element, held on to what they could not approve, because of the Republican party and its alliance with the Negro. At the North they professed false friendship for him. In the South they perpetually lambasted him, because it was popular to do so. Tens of thousands of Southern men had no other political platform except "I'm a Democrat, because my daddy was a Democrat, and I'm a'gwin to vote agin the nigger!" The hullaballo was deafening. The "solid South" really meant antagonism to Negroism. It was skillfully worked to perpetuate in office many of the men who urged on the war and who now fanned this war prejudice into fury for political success. So it happened that ring rule in Georgia expanded into full flower!

The times which followed the war and reconstruction were full of excitement. Scores of our ever-ready politicians hung around Republican Governor Rufus B. Bullock, getting all they could out of him in jobs and positions. They used their offices to make money and too many of them were not particular as to how they made it. They backed this Republican governor in all his schemes for public plunder and then posed as Simon-pure Democrats, immaculate and truly patriotic. There were two acts of Governor Bullock's administration that were absolutely vicious—the illegal signing of fraudulent railroad bonds and the illegal methods used in buying the state capitol from Hannibal I. Kimball. The same men who were prominent in Governor Bullock's time were in the forefront of legislation in the early '70's, calling themselves Democrats. Of all the inexplicable things in my entire political experience, it was the insensate fury of the Georgia people against Republicans in the abstract and their asinine and actual support of the former ring-leaders of Radicalism in Georgia!

A "Bullock Democrat" was a name won and worn by a horde of corrupt Georgia politicians who fattened under Governor Bullock's administration and who held their sway under the leadership of Joseph E. Brown, who had been the most extreme Republican just after the war. In 1868 his Radicalism was oozing out in every pore. Brown sought in 1868 to be a Republican official in these words: "I am a Republican. I expect to give Grant and Colfax a cordial support." Brown was a delegate to the National Convention that nominated General Grant in 1868 and is reported to have introduced a resolution in behalf of Negro suffrage. Somewhere between 1868 and 1874 Governor Brown turned over in his politics and emerged as a rampant Democrat. In 1874 his Democracy was burning him up with its fire and fury! Was this a Janus face to be turned only to patronage? "Now you pay your money and take your choice." The extremes are before you. Governor Brown was always a master-hand in managing his men. His life was stormy but successful, because he knew that money made power and both money and power were necessary to run politics.

From Bullock's time no oligarchy was ever more absolute or more formidable than Bullockism in Georgia under its new name of "organized Democracy." Atlanta was the headquarters of the ring masters. It was a great big wheel that turned any number of smaller wheels! After Bullockities joined their hands with "drums and fifes" and used the "rebel yell" to get what was wanted, this machine became all powerful. It worked like it was well greased and so it was! A button, when pushed in Atlanta, moved another smaller wheel in nearly every courthouse in Georgia, and in every courthouse was a miniature Tammany Hall! I do not believe any state in the Union ever before witnessed such a political combination, which I call a triumvirate. It was evident that Colquitt, Brown and Gordon were in active alliance with Republicans in Georgia and had filled all the Federal offices in the state with their own henchmen—the actual coalition of Democrats and Republicans in Georgia! One of the triumvirate was in the chief office, while the other two occupied seats in the United States Senate and controlled federal patronage in Georgia. When they saw a close contest coming, they either placed one of their own number in the executive seat or named the man who was to do their bidding and the triumvirate filled their pockets always. Calling themselves the Democratic party, they made the Democratic temple a hiding place for money changers, and the capitol in Atlanta was controlled by men who made private fortunes for themselves and also political reputation abroad by keeping in their own grasp these opportunities for graft and thus entrenched in power they cracked the party lash over the heads of the people of Georgia. A few prominent politicians, generally interested in corporations, managed to control political power in Georgia, their purpose not to benefit the people but the great corporations. At the head of this great combine were a few men who ruled and dictated. They also absorbed the revenues of the state's great properties. This gave them ready money!

The moral salt of character could not be rescued inside the party controlled by such machinery. Only a few dared fight them! A real demand for higher standards of political duty was obliged to come from outside. These men in the saddle were full, fat and saucy! No genuine Republican candidate had the ghost of a chance. Bullockism, carpet-baggism, Loyal Leagues and Negroism put them out of the running. A rescue party was obliged to be either insurgent or independent. It was only an independent who could raise a banner and cry out for reform.

In June, 1874, a friend came to tell us that lobbyists were making ready to remove Bartow County from its regular Cherokee judicial circuit and shift it into the Rome judicial circuit. The Superior Court judge had made a prominent and wealthy citizen angry by some of his decisions, and thus Bartow County must be lifted over to the Rome circuit, where a Bullock judge had authority and where things would be different! The citizen was to pay the most noted lobbyist in Cherokee County $500 for securing this legislation. A great many citizens in the Seventh Congressional District look[ed] around for someone to lead a revolt against the tyranny of the unscrupulous politicians. Accustomed to public speaking, Dr. Felton was well known in several counties outside of his own, Bartow, and he was deluged with letters imploring him to announce his candidacy as soon as the people were convinced that ring rule would prevail in the nominations of that year in the Seventh District. Their entreaties prevailed when he finally consented to lead the Independents in the race for Congress during the year 1874.

His campaign lasted over a period of more than six months. From June, 1874, to election day, November 2nd, the fire on Dr. Felton never abated. The fight was so picturesque and stirring that it gave the cognomen "The Bloody Seventh" to this district. The newspapers of Georgia were dependent on the office-holding element in the matter of advertising, etc., so they raised a howl against Independentism all along the line. The fire of the ring organs was concentrated on Dr. Felton and they were frantic with their abuse and imploring entreaty to hold the Democratic organization intact. As these double-faced Democratic politicians had run Governor Bullock out of the state and covered Radicalism with obliquy, it was easy enough for these self-seeking, so-called Democratic politicians to open fire on an Independent Democrat, to revile him as a "Radical disorganizer." Every newspaper in the Seventh District except two little weeklies—one in Cartersville, the other in Cedartown—began to yelp as soon as general orders to howl and defame were issued from the capital city. But Dr. Felton was elected to the 44th Congress by 82 votes. Dr. Felton's reelection in 1878 was positive gall and wormwood to the ring. It could be easily foretold that they were resolved to wipe off all political opposition and rule the state of Georgia!

The politics of Georgia seemed as soft as a lump of putty in the hands of designing men, backed by floods of money of mysterious origin and indefinite ownership. Nothing was certain save its ubiquitous presence and its absolute authority in every election. C. P. Huntington bought and sold Congressmen and Senators with the bribe money of the Pacific Railroad lobby. Pacific lobby money had more to do with Georgia politics than was understood at that time. It has never been a question in my mind as to the employment of Huntington's money in more than one Georgia political campaign to defeat some candidates for Congress and to set "back fires" on those who could not be bought or would not sell their votes. Dr. Felton was reliably informed that Huntington's money was paying for published articles in a Georgia newspaper in the year 1878. General Gordon's connection with C. P. Huntington was not openly known in Georgia until his name appeared in 1884 in Huntington's correspondence. The Huntington letters elicited much comment and criticism. The New York *World* said: "A careful examination of the letters shows that Senator Gordon of Georgia, who posed as the representative of everything that was respectable in the South, was a servant of the corporations!" That General Gordon was Huntington's man is proven beyond the shadow of a doubt.

The year 1880 witnessed the most perfect whirligig in Georgia politics. Dr. Felton was there in the corridors of the state capitol and convinced that the Pacific lobby had been instrumental in shaping Georgia politics for a number of years. Huntington was seeking to find a Southern outlet through Georgia in the direction of New Orleans. About this time the papers were filled with reports about the organization of certain railroads entering Georgia from the North, and we were told that president Victor Newcomb of the Louisville & Nashville had said that an independent line into Atlanta might [become] a necessity. Huntington's money was the motive power with greedy Southern men in high offices. Henry Grady told twenty members of the Pioneer and Ladder Company on May 10, 1880, on their way to Rome on the train that ex-Governor Brown would succeed Gordon in the Senate and Gordon would get a position with Victor Newcomb at $14,000 a year. The next thing we saw was the notice of the resignation of Senator Gordon from the United States Senate and the appointment of Joseph E. Brown in his stead on May 19. The surprise was universal and astounding. When the smoke lifted, Senator Brown was seated in the Senate and an active supporter for Governor Colquitt for reelection, and General Gordon was sloshing around in a score of enterprises. Character seemed to have gone out of Georgia politics. There was nothing in sight except a sort of Puss-in-the-corner game, where Governor Brown slid into the Senate, General Gordon slid into a lot of money from somewhere, and Grady slid into a fourth interest in the Atlanta *Constitution*!

Georgia politics were dominated by parties who used the convict lease of Georgia to fill their own coffers. The convict lease ring defied the law, made swollen fortunes out of the illegal leasing of convicts and continued to occupy the highest offices in the state. The lease under which General Gordon and his associates acquired possession of these miserable slaves was made on June 21, 1876, by an executive order signed by Governor J. M. Smith. Three companies were to pay a total of $25,000 per year, with all expenses of guarding, delivering, chaplains, etc. to be paid by the state. Governor Brown had 300 able-bodied, long-term slaves guaranteed to him for twenty years; Governor Colquitt was a silent partner with General Gordon. The convict lessees—Brown, Gordon, Colquitt! This leasing of convicts by private parties was atrocious and abominable— to provide these men in high political office with valuable slaves to fill their pockets! They were coining large wealth out of these poor convicts—ninety-nine one-hundredths of whom were Negroes. There were about 1500 of these slaves divided into three lease companies and from the year 1876 to the end of the lease of twenty years, it kept two senators in the United States Senate and elected two governors besides A. H. Stephens to the executive chair. This crime poured in millions of profit to the bank accounts of these men entrenched in the highest offices in the state of Georgia, and they were so full and saucy that they named the successful politicians all over the state. Their convict lease property was worth anywhere from a quarter to a half million of dollars annual income. Every few years these convict lessees were compelled to pay out big money when legislative investigations were ordered, and, despite the fact that the atrocities were proven, the worst things complained of were found to be mildly presented. These all-powerful convict lessees paid their kept organs, their corrupt legislators, their subservient judges and obedient solicitors with either political positions or plain cash until the evil was well nigh impregnable.

In December, 1878, Bob Alston lost his life, because he prepared a report in which some of the prison camp atrocities were set down, after the penitentiary committee had examined these places of torture and indecency, and because his committee reported twenty-five little bastard children, under three years of age, born of prisoned convict women and lustful guards in the winter of 1878–79. (The killing of Alston in the state capitol convinced me that Dr. Felton would be unwise to attempt a Congressional canvas in 1880 with little money and confronted by the famous trio—Brown, Colquitt, Gordon—in control of the politics of the state. But we thought somebody out to stand up for right and truth!) It was necessary to name a governor who would pardon Edward Cox. Cox had killed Bob Alston, [was] sentenced to life to Senator Brown's coal mines and knew a great deal about the inside workings of the convict lease. He could tell a great deal if he chose.

Senator Brown and Governor Colquitt worked on Alexander Stephens until the aged man became a lump of clay in the hands of the potters. Stephens was past seventy and beset with the usual infirmities of old age. It was a cruel thing to use this aged man, over seventy years old, as cruel as murder. This aged statesman, under the influence of continual hypodermics aided by stimulants which were constantly kept up, was led along. There is no question that he was under the influence of sedatives most of the time. He constantly stimulated himself with whiskey. Mr. Stephens might have been unduly doped at times. He became infatuated with an ambition to be governor. Mr. Stephens proved to be nothing but a tool in the hands of his captors. He was deceived and cajoled by crafty and designing men. There is no knowing what sort of tales were poured into his ears. Mr. Stephens was elected Governor in October and Edward Cox was pardoned in less than two months afterward! This frail old man was literally hastened to the grave by the unusual worries of a new and untried position. He died early in March, 1883. There will be disappointment evermore that he did not pass away at "Liberty Hall," surrounded by his peaceful household and mourned by those who loved and honored him.

I submit there was no earthly chance to win any election in Georgia against the Colquitt administration and Huntington's "man," and the money of the convict lease and every judge and solicitor in Georgia of one political party— and that party led by these powerful forces against all who opposed them. The whole state of Georgia was run over by tricksters, and it was only occasionally that an honest election was held, in my opinion. There were said to be grips, signs and pass-words, like they had in Loyal Leagues and Ku Klux days. A candidate who expected to get in without the "hall mark" had a rocky road to travel. Dr. Felton's election was a miracle in Georgia politics.

A citizen of Houston County told me how they elected their candidates. The Negroes outnumbered the whites anywhere from three to five to each white man. At one election, when Grant was a candidate on one side and maybe Greeley on the other, the citizens agreed among themselves to place a Radical manager at one ballot box for Negroes and a Democrat at the other. Before the polls opened a squad of men had an interview with the Radical manager. They said, "Here's $200. You must sign your resignation right here. But here's another $100 if you hold the election at the black box today." He held the election, and it was published far and wide that Houston's election was as quiet as you could ask. That night they threw out the box where the Radical took in the votes with every vote in it, because he had resigned!

Another party has given me a description of the way that Crawford County was counted and a large majority secured in the Congressional race between Colonel Reuben Arnold and Colonel Nat Hammond. There was an abandoned precinct that hadn't been opened in a year, maybe more. The Hammond men had a box fixed with enough majority to defeat Mr. Arnold, ready made, and they used it for that purpose with the abandoned precinct!

An eye-witness to the election scenes told us that the front entrance to the polls in Savannah was thronged with men who stayed there. Crowds of men were kept back, particularly poor men. They had but a short time to leave their work, and many were never allowed to reach the ballot box at all. In Rome the same plan was put in force on November 2, 1880. There was a side entrance in Rome where Clements voters could hand over their ballots and they were shoved in to reach the box. That back way was kept open, and the front way was kept crowded—packed by men put there to keep voters away. The county officials were the ring masters! Floyd County was dominated by these men, who secured their own elections in the same manner.

In 1880 Dr. Felton was defeated for Congress. In 1884 he was elected as representative from Bartow County in the General Assembly. In 1894, on account of his belief in free coinage of silver, he joined the Peoples' Party and led the Populist forces through a heated campaign. In the election of 1894, wagonloads of Negroes were driven from poll to poll by white men, time and again voted as they were driven around and paid ten cents a vote. They finally beat Dr. Felton down with stuffed ballot boxes and bogus tickets!

⌐ 19 ⌐

The last census showed three white and 162 colored people on this plan-
tation. The labor is performed by the man, who usually does the plowing,
and his wife and children, who do the hoeing under his direction. The
usual quantity of land planted is between twenty-five and thirty acres,
about half of which is cotton and the rest in corn and patches. The
dwelling house is an ordinary log cabin.

D A V I D   C.   B A R R O W,   J R.,   1881–82

D A V I D   C.   B A R R O W,   J R.   (1852–1929) was born in Oglethorpe County and graduated from
the University of Georgia in 1874. After teaching mathematics and engineering, he was chan-
cellor of the University of Georgia between 1906 and 1925. The following scenes of post-
bellum plantation life appeared in two articles written by Barrow, "A Georgia Plantation" in
Scribner's Magazine, XXI (April, 1881), pp. 830–836, and "A Georgia Corn-shucking" in *Century
Magazine*, XXIV (October, 1882), pp. 873–878.

One of the first planters in Middle Georgia to divide his plantation into farms
was Mr. Barrow of Oglethorpe. The plantation upon which he now lives is a
fair exponent of Negro tenant life in Georgia. This place contains about 2000
acres of land and, with the exception of a single acre which Mr. Barrow has
given to his tenants for church and school purposes, is the same size it was before
the war. Here, however, the similarity ceases. Before the war everything on the
place was under the absolute rule of an overseer. He it was who directed the
laborers each day and to him the owner looked for the well-being of everything
on the place. Under him and subject to his direction, the most intelligent and
authoritative Negroes were selected, whose duty it was to see that the overseer's
orders were carried into effect. These head men were called foremen.

For several years after the war, the force on the plantation was divided into
two squads, the arrangement and method of working of each being about the
same as they had always been used to. Each of these squads was under the control
of a foreman, who was in the nature of a general of volunteers. The plantation

was divided into two equal parts and by offering a reward for the most successful planting and thus exciting a spirit of emulation good work was done and the yield was about as great as it had ever been. Then, too, the laborers were paid a portion of the crop as their wages, which did much toward making them feel interested in it. There was no overseer in the old sense of the word, and in his place a young man lived on the plantation who kept the accounts and exercised a protecting influence over his employer's property but was not expected to direct the hands in their work. The Negroes used to call him "supertender," in order to express their sense of the change.

After a while, however, even the liberal control of the foreman grew irksome, each man feeling the very natural desire to be his own boss and to farm to himself. As a consequence of this feeling, the two squads split up into smaller and then still smaller squads, still working for part of the crop and using the owner's teams, until this method of farming came to involve great trouble and loss. The mules were ill-treated, the crop was frequently badly worked and in many cases was divided in a way that did not accord with the contract. I have been told an amusing incident which occurred on a neighboring plantation: A tenant worked a piece of land, for which he was to pay one-fourth of the corn produced. When he gathered his crop, he hauled three loads to his own house, thereby exhausting the supply in the field. When, soon after, he came to return his landlord's wagon, which he had used in the hauling, the latter asked, suggestively, "Well, William, where's my share of the corn?" "You ain't got none, sah," said William. "Haven't got any! Why, wasn't I to have the fourth of all you made?" "Yes, sah, but hit never made no fourth. Dere wasn't but dess my three loads made."

These and other troubles led to the present arrangement. Under it our colored farmers are tenants, who are responsible only for damage to the farm they work and for the prompt payment of their rent. All of the tenants are colored men, who farm on a small scale, only two of them having more than one mule. When the hands all worked together, it was desirable to have all of the houses in a central location, but after the division into farms, some of them had to walk more than a mile to reach their work. Then, too, they began to "want more elbow room," and so, one by one, they moved their houses on to their farms. Wherever there is a spring, there they settle, generally two or three near together, who have farms hard by. When no spring is convenient, they dig wells, though they greatly prefer the spring.

The dwelling house is an ordinary log cabin, twenty feet square, the chimney built of sticks and dabbed over with mud. Then there is a separate kitchen. Off to one side are the out-houses, consisting of a diminutive stable, barely large enough to pack a small mule in, and a corn crib and fodder house. Every tenant has a cow, most of them several. An open pen in this mild climate serves in place of cow stables. On the opposite side from the lot, the house is flanked by the garden, surrounded by what is known as a "wattle fence." This fence is made of split pine boards, "wattled" around three horizontal rails, fastened to posts, the first at the ground and the others respectively two and four feet above. Inseparable from this garden is a patch of "collord greens." The only other noteworthy feature in connection with this home is the 'possum dog, who is the first to greet your approach. You will know him by the leanness of his body, the fierceness of his bark and the rapidity of his retreat.

The labor of the farm is performed by the man, who usually does the plowing, and his wife and children, who do the hoeing under his direction. Their crops are principally corn and cotton, but they have patches of such things as potatoes, melons and sorghum cane, from which they make their syrup. They plant whatever they please, and their landlord interferes only far enough to see that sufficient cotton is made to pay the rent, which is 750 pounds of lint cotton to each one-horse farm. The usual quantity of land planted is between 25 and 30 acres, about half of which is in cotton and the rest in corn and patches. An industrious man will raise three times the amount of his rent cotton, besides making a full supply of corn, syrup and other provisions. Whenever they get into trouble, they remind their landlord in pathetic terms that he is their old master and generally get off with the payment of half the rent.

Mr. Barrow lives on his plantation, yet there are some of his tenants' farms which he does not visit as often as once a month. All of these Negroes raise hogs and these, with chickens, constitute a large portion of their meat food. The last census showed three white and 162 colored people on this plantation. Very soon after they were freed, these hands manifested a desire to establish a school, and Mr. Barrow gave them a site upon which they promptly built a school house, and they have employed a teacher ever since. Free schools in Georgia last only about three months, but the Negroes cheerfully pay their teacher the remainder of the year themselves. Quite a number who were grown when freed have since learned to read and write, and they all send their children. That they have improved and continue to improve seems beyond controversy. The one man on this plantation who, as a slave gave most trouble, so much, in fact, that he was almost beyond control of the overseer, was Lem Bryant. Since he has been freed, he has grown honest, quiet and industrious. He educates his children and pays his debts. Mr. Barrow asked him one day what had changed him so. "Ah, master!" he replied, "I'm free now. I *have* to do right."

The first work toward gathering the corn crop in Georgia is to strip the stalks of their blades, "pull the fodder," which is done in August or September. The corn is left on the naked stalk until some time in October or November. If Georgians had nothing to gather in the fall but the corn, we might spend the whole fall gathering it, but on any farm where cotton is cultivated to any considerable extent most of this season of the year must be devoted to gathering and preparing it for market. It will appear then that the corn must be disposed of in the quickest possible manner. Now, if the corn were thrown in the crib with the shuck on it, it would probably be eaten by vermin, and, besides, the farmer would be deprived of the use of his shucks, which form the chief item of food for his cattle during the winter. Out of these conditions has sprung the corn-shucking, more a social than an economic feature among our farming people.

The farmer who proposes to give a corn-shucking selects a level spot in his lot, conveniently near the crib, rakes away all trash and sweeps the place clean with a brush broom. The corn is then pulled off the stalks, thrown into wagons, hauled to the lot and thrown out on the spot selected, all in one pile. If it has been previously "norated" through the neighborhood that there is to be plenty to eat and drink at the corn-shucking, there will certainly be a crowd. Soon after dark the Negroes begin to come in, and before long the place will be alive with them, men, women and children. After the crowd has gathered and been moderately warmed up, two "gin'r'ls" are chosen from among the most famous corn-shuckers on the ground, and these proceed to divide the shuckers into two parties, later comers reporting alternately to one side or the other, so as to keep the forces equally divided. The next step, which is one of great importance, is to divide the corn pile. This is done by laying a fence-rail across the top of the corn pile, so that the vertical plane, passing through the rail, will divide the pile into two equal portions. Laying the rail is of great importance, since upon this depends the accuracy of the division. It is accompanied with much argument, not to say wrangling. The position of the rail being determined, the two generals mount the corn pile and the work begins. The necessity for the "gin'r'ls" to occupy the most conspicuous position accessible, from which to cheer their followers, is one reason why they get up on top of the corn. If it is possible, imagine a Negro man standing up on a pile of corn, holding in his hand an ear of corn and shouting and you will have pictured the "corn gin'r'l." It is a prime requisite that he should be ready in his improvisations and have good voice, so that he may lead in the corn song. These songs are kept up continuously during the entire time the work is going on, and though extremely simple, yet, when sung by fifty pairs of lusty lungs, there are few things more stirring. The most common form is for the generals to improvise words which they half sing, half recite, all joining in the chorus. In this the generals frequently recount their adventures, travels and experiences.

An amount of work which would astonish the shuckers themselves, and which if demanded of them in the day time would be declared impossible, is accomplished under the excitement of the corn song. They shuck the corn by hand, sometimes using a sharp stick to split open the shuck, but most commonly tearing them open with the fingers. As the feeling of rivalry grows more and more intense, they work faster and faster, stripping the shuck from the ears so fast that they seem to fly almost constantly from their hands.

It is no rare occurrence for a corn-shucking to terminate in a row instead of a frolic. If one side is badly beaten, there is almost sure to be some charge of fraud, either that the rail has been moved or part of the corn of the successful party thrown over on the other side or some such charge. These offenses are common occurrences and are aided by the dimness of the light. It is most often the case, however, that the race has been about an equal one and that good humor prevails amid the great excitement. The first thing is to express thanks for the entertainment, which is done by taking the host, putting him on the shoulders of two strong men and then marching around, while all hands split their throats to a tune, the chorus of which is "Walk away, walk away!" The fun usually begins by someone who is a famous wrestler offering to throw down anybody on the ground, accompanying the boast by throwing aside his coat and swaggering 'round.

A corn-shucking should end with a dance. These dances take place either in one of the houses or else out of doors on the ground. Endurance is a strong point in the list of accomplishments of the dancer, and, other things being equal, that dancer who can hold out the longest is considered the best. The music is commonly made by a fiddler and a straw-beater, the fiddle being far more common than the banjo. The fiddler always comes late, must have an extra share of whiskey, is the best-dressed man in the crowd and, unless every honor is shown him, he will not play. The straw-beater is a musician [without] preliminary training. The performer provides himself with a pair of straws about eighteen inches in length and stout enough to stand a good smart blow. These straws are used after the manner of drum-sticks, that portion of the fiddle strings between the fiddler's bow and his left hand serving as a drum. The "caller-out" not only calls out the figures but explains them at length.

The corn-shucking is one of the institutions of the old plantations which has flourished and expanded since the Negroes were freed. The larger liberty they enjoy has tended to encourage social gatherings of all kinds. The great number of small farmers who have sprung up since the war necessitates mutual aid in larger undertakings, so that at this time the corn-shucking as an institution is most flourishing.

[20]

The pathos and tragedy of the cracker of the factories. . . . In complete isolation, dead monotony and dense, undisturbed ignorance, their toilsome lives run out. Like so many machines, the creatures drudge on . . . demoralized by a lifetime of travail amid unsanitary conditions, under fed and badly housed, without education, incentives or ideals.

CLARE DE GRAFFENRIED, 1891

MARY CLARE DE GRAFFENRIED (1849–1921) was a graduate of Wesleyan College. She became a teacher in Washington, D.C., and later a collector of statistics for the U.S. Bureau of Labor. She spent an active career collecting industrial and sociological data in the United States, France and Belgium. The following selections are from her article, "The Georgia Cracker in the Cotton Mills," *Century Magazine*, XLI (February, 1891), pp. 483–498.

Flung as if by chance beside a red clay road that winds between snake fences, a settlement appears. Rows of loosely built, weather-stained frame houses, all of the same ugly pattern and buttressed by clumsy chimneys, are set close to the highway. Over the scene broods the stillness of virgin woods. It is a deserted village. The homes are but the shells of human presence. The wood fire is half burned out, the embers dead. A simple breakfast has been partly consumed. Great hollows formed by recent occupation punctuate the unmade feather beds. A steady, throbbing pulsation, a persistent whir not caused by bird or beast or wind, unnoticed at first, frets the ear. A turn in the road, and around a farther bend comes into view a low, straggling brick mill [which] gives forth the sound of flying spindles and the measured jar of many looms. Here are gathered the missing grandmas, mothers, sons and daughters of the settlement.

The race that tends the spindles of the cotton-growing states is altogether unique. A name must be coined to specify this strange, homely, ungainly, native folk that delve in tobacco, cotton and corn, distil whiskey in the mountains and spin or weave in villages and towns. "Crackers" they are in dialect, feature, coloring, dress, manner, doings and characteristics, hundreds of thousands of non-slaveholding whites in antebellum days and their present descendants. The crackers of our time are an impressive example of race degeneration caused partly by climate, partly by caste prejudices due to the institution of slavery. "Fo' the war, honey, them 'ristocrats had all the plantations, en houses, en fine doin's. Po' white folks wasn't nowhar. We was glad ter run er loom, en buy er pint uv 'lasses en live offen rich man's corn. Now, ev'ry cuss with er yaller steer is er' gittin' rich. Even them niggers, bless yer soul, is er-buyin' uv er house. White folks cain't let them niggers be er lead mule. We's bleeged ter get up en git."

They have lapsed into laziness, ignorance and oddity. The Georgians in the wiregrass region choose as dainties chalk, starch and the gum from the pines whose turpentine they collect for barter. They use snuff and tobacco and subsist on scanty, innutritious diet. The overshadowing political importance of the Negro and, in some localities, his numerical superiority help on the deterioration of the poor whites. They form a large fourth of the white population of each cotton state. Alien to the educated classes because of ancient yet vital caste prejudice, the crackers are at the same time hated by the colored man. Thus, crushed between the upper and the nether millstones of popular scorn, their condition in the New South is often deplorable. Breeding in for generations, the crackers grow more sharply defined and are now the butt of ridicule, shiftless and inconsequential, always poor though always working.

Located in the cotton-producing region, where in the absence of prohibitive legislation, the working hours are longer, Southern mills have a distinct advantage. No colored people are employed in textile industries. The operatives are lodged to some extent in houses belonging to the corporations and which are conducted less as a source of revenue than to allure workers. Whole families huddle together irrespective of sex or relationship. They have land but no gardens, pasturage but no stock. Wasting their earning on gewgaws, drink and indigestible foods, they are unhealthy and inefficient. Despite a favorable climate, a bountiful earth, the mortality among the poor whites is shockingly high. The mothers being immured in the factories, family life is a travesty. Early marriages are frequent. Desertion often ensues. The mill operatives display a propensity for roving. Improvident and imperturbable, the easy-going philosophy of the lazy is "Cain't wuk for two days' victuals in one" or the rather skulking faith of the pious, "The Lord will provide."

One clever, original manufacturer for five years devoted head, heart and purse to ameliorate the condition of his operatives. They had no homes: he bought and built houses, which fell to pieces through neglect or were burned up in drunken orgies. When their dwellings were again repaired, the crackers felt out of place in a setting of order and neatness and "jes ter make things sorter homelike," as was afterwards naively explained, they kicked out the panels of the doors, smashed the windows, riddled the walls and cut up the floor for kindling wood.

The provision for housing the wage-earners is often inadequate. The operatives in remote settlements are forced to lodge in rotting, neglected habitations, even though they be rent free. The choicest of these rickety abodes was described by a girl whose only home it had been for fourteen years: "I reckin hit'll set up thar a right smart while yit, but hit's pow'ful cold en leaky." They herd, dirty and disorderly, in filth and semi-idleness, in leaky hovels without other furniture than the barest necessaries.

No porch, no doorstep even, admits to these barrack-like quarters, only an unhewn log or a convenient stone. Board shutters, stretched sagging back, leave the paneless windows great gaping squares. The big, sooty fireplace is decked with an old-time crane and pots and kettles or with a stove in the last stages of rust and decrepitude. A shackling bed, tricked out in gaudy patchwork, a few defunct split-bottom chairs, a rickety table and a jumble of battered crockery keep company with the collapsed bellows and fat pine knots by the hearth. The unplastered walls are tattooed with broken mirrors, strips of bacon, bunches of turkey feathers, strings of red peppers and gourds, green, yellow and brown. The bare floors are begrimed with the tread of animals, and the muddy outline of splayed toes of all shapes and sizes betoken inmates unused to shoes and stockings. The back door looks upon an old-fashion moss-covered well with its long pole and a bucket at the end hung high in air. On the nearest limbs, a few patched garments flap ghostlike in the breeze.

The kitchen often serves as bedroom for the family. A chest of drawers, a bald, decrepit hair trunk, a mirror and splint chairs, a table, a few cracked dishes and a gourd complete the household equipments, while outside the cabin hangs the biscuit tray, and a few peaches or apples dry in the sun. Not uncommonly the cooking is done in the yard in a big pot or over glowing coals. At every door children squat around a tin plate of syrup, dipping in it big hunks of corn-pone and smearing their yellow faces more widely with each mouthful. The sweet "pertatur" roasted in the ashes is always ready. In the cracker's kitchen lard is the universal solvent. The tyrant of his home, the key to his habits, the blazon of his civilization is the frying pan!

The country mills are archaic in their management and in the habits of the operatives. Life is regulated by the sun and the factory bell, which rings for rising, breakfast and work. The hours of labor vary from seventy to seventy-two a week. The workers were "borned in the country" and seldom visit even the neighboring town. In complete isolation, dead monotony and dense, undisturbed ignorance, their toilsome lives run out. Now and then a strolling minister enlivens the little barnlike church on the hilltop. All purchases are made on the order system at the "company's store." Though it is not compulsory for the operatives to deal there, distance from market constitutes compulsion, and the buyer is at a disadvantage from the absence of competition and the loss of the educational comparison of values and management of his funds. Women often work a lifetime without touching a cent of their pay. One forlorn old maid lamented, "I hain't seed er dollar sence Confed money gave out. Hit 'u'd be good fur sore eyes ter see er genewine dollar." Like so many machines, the unsophisticated creatures drudge on, never questioning the prices paid. As the cracker neither adds nor multiplies, it is only by being refused further credit he is made to realize that his supplies depend upon his own efforts.

The genius for evading labor is most marked in the men. They often subsist entirely upon the earnings of meek wives or fond daughters, whose excuses for this shameless vagabondism are both pathetic and exasperating. One young wife claims that her stalwart husband has "been er'cuttin' wood." The father of two little children in the mill does no work at all " 'cep'in' hit's haulin' light wood." A straggling potato row, a scant corn patch on the hillside, an attenuated cow, a few chickens, one pig and woods full of pine knots for fires bound the Georgia countryman's earthly aspirations except as to clothing, tobacco and whiskey, which his spouse's wages supply. Men habitually abandon work on pretence of "makin' er gardin.' " A little girl, who with her sister's help supported a family of six, when asked why her father did not assist, excused him on the plea, "Dad does our gard'nin' "—the garden being a plat ten by twelve! Said a candid wife, "Why, bless yer heart, honey, my ole man'll let a purp eat the grub often his plate 'ca'se he's too darned lazy ter holler 'Git!' " Grouped around the single store of the village, lounging, whittling sticks and sunning their big, lazy frames, sit a score of stalwart masculine figures, while their offspring and their womankind toil in the dusty mill.

The daily life being so simple, the expenditures of the cracker are proportionally small. A weaver by ten months' work earned $140, supported herself and an invalid sister and laid by $40 in a year. Bacon, cornpone, "greens," molasses and coffee are the regimen, with milk occasionally, and in "hog-killin' " time, feasts of spare rib and sausage. The corn that waves over Georgia fields furnishes in various suculent forms the staple diet of the native and, transmitted into other elements, supplies his bacon and whiskey, while the stalks serve for fuel. At corn-shuckings the cracker courts his sweetheart. Of these identical shucks the family bed is made.

The usual attire of the women is all unbleached cotton or a neat check or gingham, the serviceable product of their own looms. The style of dress has not altered a seam in thirty years. A peculiar lankiness characterizes the plain, round skirts, accentuated by the spare, angular form. The whole array [is] made more incongruous by that homeliest head gear, the slat sun bonnet, universal badge of the female cracker. From the end of the tunnel formed by the uncompromising pasteboard slats a shrewd, hard, yellow, cadaverous face peers out. When the covering is removed, the scant hair is revealed caught straight back from the brow and skewered into an untidy knot. The inborn taste for color breaks out in flaring ribbons, variegated handkerchiefs. Occasionally one of the plainest old souls, seized with desire for modern finery, after protracted "tradin'" and naggling, becomes possessed of a fashionable bonnet, gay with yellow or pink flowers and cheap lace, which is donned with her best cotton robe and brogans.

The men wear baggy jeans trousers, often homemade, strapped up almost under the armpits or else without suspenders and dragging about the hips. The shirt is of unbleached homespun without collar or cuffs. A low battered, soft felt hat or a third-hand beaver completes the costume. The favorite occupation of the men is to spit, stare and whittle sticks. In the mills the boys are dressed in trousers a world too big, father's or grandfather's lopped off at the knees and all in tatters. Girls are clad in cotton gowns through whose rifts the skin is visible.

Shoes and stockings are possessed by all except the most miserable of the women. They are, however, put away "for Sunday," and so the simple owners walk barefooted four or five miles to church or camp-meeting with the precious articles wrapped in a handkerchief. Within sight of their goal, they sit down in a bend of the snake fence, dust off their tired feet and, donning the prized hosiery and shoes, march with pride into the assembled congregation. Three of four cotton gowns, as many "bunnits" made of the scraps, a little homespun for underwear may all be bought for $6, and with a blanket shawl for winter the wardrobe is complete. "You do your own washing?" was innocently demanded. "Is I a nigger?" quoth she, witheringly. Hard-earned funds are wasted on trumpery, pinchbeck jewelry, cotton lace, coarse high-tinted flowers, satin shoes for the dusty highways and costumes of indescribable hues. It is pathetic to see this ignorant groping for beauty in their hard and colorless lives.

Twenty-eight percent of the cotton operatives are seriously out of health. Women and children baptized in suffering and sacrifices stand eleven and twelve hours six days in the week tending complex machinery or walking miles up and down long frames in a steaming atmosphere where human flesh becomes limp and helpless. A most potent factor in this abuse is that the fathers will not work and the little ones must. Mary Belle Surrelle Jones, a wizened midget of eight, whose father is dead, began work in the factory at five years old. She went to school a little but does not know her letters and uses unlimited quantities of snuff. Let a loquacious scrap of nine years tell her own story: "I wur eight yur ole come er Chewsdy when maw drawed my fus pay. Don' have money much offen; maw she gimme er quarter laist buthday. Maw's hur in er mill, en paw's her, en Sailly she he'ps maw spool 'ca'se she haint' big 'nough ter piece ainds. Sailly she's six, en maw hain't got nary one ter leave her wid, so she bring her ter mill. No, 'm, I hain't got no book-learnin'. Yais, 'm, I dips. Oversser 't other mill he says, 'Calline, dip snuff,' says he, 'ca'se ef yer don't, blue dye'll pizen yer!' "

The inevitable hardships everywhere so disastrous to the workers in textile fabrics fail to account for the feeble constitutions and wrecked health of so many of these Southern toilers. The malaria lurking about water-courses ravages the mills on the streams and invades the houses of the employees, usually close to the bank. Drainage is neglected and epidemics stalk relentless. The use of snuff is a withering curse, applied with a softened twig dipped into the snuff and rubbed on the teeth. All down the alleys of the factories are women and little girls with the inevitable stick in their mouth. The invariable signs—a carrot-like cuticle, livid lips, black-rimmed eyes, flabby, morbid flesh—proclaim the victim of the poison.

Among the older women drunkenness is not uncommon. For want of legal interference the child is sacrificed either to the dire need or to the avarice, self-ishness and lazy neglect of its parents: when five or six years old the juveniles follow the mothers to the mills, where they are incarcerated till premature old age and helplessness bring about their dismissal. Unmarried women of thirty are wrinkled, bent and haggard. Sickly faces, stooping shoulders, shriveled flesh suggest that normal girlhood never existed, that youth had never rounded out the lanky figure, nor glowed the sallow cheek. A slouching gait, a drooping chest, lacking muscular power to expand, a dull, heavy eye, yellow, blotched complexion, dead-looking hair, stained lips, destitute of color and revealing broken teeth—these are the dower of girlhood in the mills.

Take a little maid whose face is buried in her sunbonnet and who, when asked her age, responds, "I'm er-gwine on ten." Push back her bonnet. A sad spec-tacle reveals itself. Out of a shock of unkempt hair look glassy eyes ringed with black circles reaching far down her yellow cheeks. Her nose is pinched, the fea-tures aborted, the yellow lips furrowed with snuff stains. The skin is ghastly, cadaverous, the flesh flabby, the frame weak and loose-jointed. The dirty legs and feet are bare. A tattered cotton slip clings to the formless limbs. "When do you go to school, my child?" "Hain't never been thar," the waif responds when shyness has yielded to cajoleries. "Never at school! Can't you read?" "No." "Where is your father?" "Him done dade." "And your mother?" A backward motion of the thumb to the mill is the only response. "What is your name?" "Georgy Alybamy Missippy Kicklighter." "What do you do all day, Georgy?" "Wuks." The same backward turn of the thumb. "How long have you been working?" "Ev'ry sence I was mighty nigh er kitten. I hain't been nowhar 'cep'n in mill he'pen' maw sence I was five year ole." "You look sallow. Does anything ail you?" "I be pow-ful weak." "What does the doctor give you?" "Don' give me nothin'. Maw, she gimme groun' pease. She 'low them's better 'n doctor's truck fur agy." This is the product of three generations of mill workers, the grandmother, mother and child drudging side by side. None of them could read or write, none had ever been four miles from their shanty and the factory.

The adult operatives in the older manufactories cannot assign a date at which their apprenticeship began, remembering only that they were "pow-ful young." Girls from fifteen to twenty-five recollect no other playground than the country factories, having been brought there in their mothers' arms in the early dawn and taken home again under the stars. Babies have been reared amid machinery, their cradle often a box of bobbins, their coverlet the hanks of yarn. The precious hours of infancy merge into weary drudgery as soon as the young limbs can be bound to the wheels of toil. Demoralized by a lifetime of travail amid unsanitary conditions, underfed and badly housed, without education, incentives or ideals, the limited mental development of the cracker is scarcely a reproach to him. Though ignorant, he is rarely stupid.

Few of the older operatives know how old they are. Their age is referred to as a tangible or inflammable possession. "Maw tuk hit away" or "Hit burned up when the house was set afire." "How old are you?" usually elicited a comical look of uncertainty. "Now yer got me," was the constant rejoinder. Of 328 women and girls, fifty-six were unable to state even approximately where they or their parents first saw the light. The only seasons in the vocabulary are "cotton-hoein'," "horg-killin'" or " 'tween craps." Such homely phrases indicate an intimacy with the processes of nature. Imagining every stranger a "Yan kee," they are offish and suspicious till reassured, for sectional animosities still smolder.

Large numbers of poor, illiterate white children never enter a schoolroom. Parents, insensible to the advantages of education, make no attempt to have their children attend school, and generation after generation remains untaught. In proximity to cities, where good public schools are maintained nine months of the year, the outlook is more favorable, but even here the privileges of enlightenment are unavailable for the poor crackers, whose wretched little cabins being built beyond suburban limits and the tax collector's arm, their offspring are debarred municipal tuition. The heading, "Working Women in Cities," printed in big capitals, was submitted as a test to a brawny lass of twenty-four. Her mind ran on a recent religious revival, for in good faith she spelt out the words, "Work now for Jesus!" A spinster of thirty-three apologized for breaking down on a more difficult test line offered. "Kin pernounce almos' ary word, but some cain't speak 'em plain," she averred deprecatingly. An emaciated shadow of nineteen cannot read and knows nothing but the factory routine.

Of 330 white women and children tested, from eight to seventy years old, fifty-six, or seventeen percent, read words of four or five syllables, some fluently, some hesitatingly. Seventy, or twenty-one percent, read headings of two syllables with varied degrees of ease from readiness to slow spelling, and all this class could at least write their names. One hundred and four, or thirty-one and one-half percent, read monosyllabic sentences, but in most cases stumblingly and with infinite pains. None of this group could write at all or even spell their own name unless the appellation was very simple. Practically they were wholly illiterate. The remaining one hundred, or thirty percent, embracing children, girls and adults, did not know the alphabet and were in benighted ignorance. Sixty-one and one-half percent of the Georgia cotton operatives neither read nor write!

Some years ago in a newly opened Atlanta factory, with a large contingent of rural workers, occasion arose for the eighty women in the spinning room to sign their names. Only two could do so; these were two colored girls employed as sweepers. Save a rare copy of the Scriptures, neither books nor journals are found in the cracker's possession. Free libraries being, so to speak, non-existent in the South, a priggish sort of Sunday-school narrative is the chief literature of the industrial population. Illiteracy is often a misfortune, sealing a beautiful nature from higher possibilities.

The nomenclature of this uncanny folk is curious and significant. Masculine baptismal titles are numerous, "Johnny Smith" being not a tow-headed, freckle-faced urchin, but a spinster of uncertain age. Infantile nicknames cling to adults, and old hags are still "Babe" and "Honey." "Savannah" and "Atlanta," "Georgia" and "Alabama" sleep side by side, and occasionally one puny offshoot is crushed beneath the names of several states.

Women sometimes curse and brawl. Ribaldry, however, is not the outcome of depraved instincts, but of a silly sensationalism, a bravado to win notoriety, an affectation more than a trait. The normal Georgia cracker under all her nicotine stains overflows in simplicity and unperverted goodness. Roughness of speech and manners covers a gentle, loyal heart and unswerving integrity. Neither in countenance nor in demeanor is there brutality or degradation. Under the vulgarity of the worst natures abide a gracious cordiality, an originality and a freshness. The cracker of the factories is clothed with flesh and blood. The pathos and tragedy of this life are real.

$\lceil 21 \rceil$

At the house we found a rosy-cheeked little granddaughter, not yet three years of age, with a snuff-dip in her mouth. I had seen plenty of women with snuff-sticks protruding from their lips. There were tears in her eyes. She had just been punished for tipping over the snuff-box.

CLIFTON JOHNSON, 1903

CLIFTON JOHNSON (1865–1940), author and illustrator of more than fifty childrens' books, was born at Hadley, Massachusetts. This selection is from Clifton Johnson, "Among the Georgia Crackers," in *Outing*, XLIII (October, 1903), pp. 522–531.

Crickboro is a typical small village in the northern part of Georgia. There are perhaps a dozen houses in the hamlet, with others scattered at intervals along the roads of the vicinity. Most of the houses are one story in height; and all are small. Some of the poorer ones have only board shutters at the window openings. Nearly all the barns and outbuildings are of logs, and occasionally there is a log house. In the midst of the village, or settlement, as it is called, are four or five little stores. They have no show windows and are as simple and rustic as they well could be. Sunrise is their opening time; at noon they are locked while the owners go home to dinner; and in the dusk of early evening they close for the night.

Up a steep hill just east of the village is the Baptist Church, with the cemetery close by. The soil on the hill is full of stones, and whenever a new grave is dug quite a heap of them is thrown out. A half mile up the road from the village is a second house of worship, commonly called "the Hardshell Church," or, as its adherents would say, "the Old Primitive Bapist Church." It is a brown, ramshackle structure without turret or bell, and extremely rough inside and out. Until recently services had been held at the Hardshell Church once a month, but the itinerant preacher was drowned in the winter while crossing a flooded river. "He and another man," said my informant, "got in a ferry skiff and started to pull hit over to the other side of the river by holdin' on with their hands to a wire rope that was stretched acrost. But the current was so swift hit jerk the boat out from under them. One man, he hung on to the wire an' got to shore, but the preacher, he was drownded."

At the church in the village they have Sunday-school every Sabbath, and preaching every second Sabbath. Sunday afternoons, the young folks to the number of thirty or forty are accustomed to gather for "a sing" in one of the homes; and once a year there is "an all-day sing" at the church. This all-day sing draws together the people for ten or twelve miles around. They come on foot, on saddlehorses, and in all sorts of vehicles.

Every church in the region has its annual all-day sing, and this is perhaps the greatest pleasure of the year. There are, however, various lesser pleasures, especially in winter. Then they have parties with an accompaniment of dancing, if girls enough are present who do not belong to the church. But most of the young women join the church at fifteen or sixteen and after that will not indulge in so doubtful an amusement. Yet they have no hesitation in taking part in "Stealing Partners," "Twistification," and "Fancy Four"—games which do not differ much from dancing except in name.

"The way we play 'em is this"—said a young fellow who enlightened me on the subject; "there's music to all of 'em, and while the fiddle's a-goin' we skip aroun' and try to knock with the music. In Stealing Partners we all have partners but one boy, and he picks out any girl he want and swings. That leave another boy without a partner, and *he* have to pick out a girl and swing her, and so on.

"For Twistification, we all gets in line, boys on one side, girls on the other, with room for a couple to march up between us in dancing step. At the end of the line they swing, and we all promenade. Then we form the line and start again.

"Fancy Four is a good deal like Twistification, only two couples instead of one do the dancing and promenading. Of co'se, these games ain't regular dancing. That wouldn't be allowed at most houses. They're Christian dancing."

Corn and cotton are the principal crops of the region, and the fields were busy with workers plowing, strewing fertilizer, and getting the seeds into the ground. The corn is hand-planted and much of it is dropped by the sun-bonneted women walking up and down the furrows. In the autumn the corn ears are picked, and the stalks are left standing in the fields until spring, when they are chopped off with heavy hoes and either piled up and burned, or toted to the borders of the fields, where they are out of the way. Bee-keeping is a common industry. The hives are spoken of as "gums." Usually they are simply oblong, upright boxes of home manufacture; but in earlier times, sections of hollow black-gum trees served the purpose—hence the name.

On the outskirts of the village, I one day stopped to speak with an elderly man working with three boys and a pair of mules in a wayside cotton field. Mr. Shenton—that was his name—was doing more directing than actual working, and when I greeted him he desisted from his labor, and mounted the rail fence to visit more at ease.

"What's land wuth up in your beat?" he inquired.

I gave him an estimate and he said. "The best land we got hyar won't sell for more than fifteen or twenty dollars an acre, except some slopes suited for peaches. Those bring as much as fifty dollars an acre. Won't you come over to the house an' set a while? I ain't well an' I depen' mos'ly on the boys, my gran'sons, to work the craps."

At the house we found his wife standing in the doorway, smoking her pipe; and beside her was a rosy-cheeked little granddaughter, not yet three years of age, with a snuff-dip in her mouth. I had seen plenty of women with snuff-sticks protruding from their lips, not only when they were about their homes, but when walking on the roads and riding on the trains. I had not, however, previously encountered so youthful a snuff-taker. There were tears in her eyes. She had just been punished for tipping over the snuffbox.

"I reckon that chile use ten cents of snuff a week, with what she dip an' waste too," said the woman. "Tobacco do cost. The person what don't use hit at all had ought to get rich. Ellen. Ellen!" she called, "come and take cyar of this baby;" and the little one's mother came out on the porch, and sat down with the child in her lap.

"This baby was always po'ly until las' winter," Ellen explained, "an' the doctor say she couldn't live, so we let her have what she want. Hit seem like she crave for tobacco, an' she learn to dip snuff an' she learn to chew. Most all the women an' girls hyar use snuff. The boys an' men dip some, but generally they jus' chew an' smoke. The boys learn to chew when they air little, an' they keep on chewin' till they air settled married men. Then they begin to smoke a pipe. The girls learn to dip snuff when they go to school, though hit ain't allowed if the master know hit. But the smaller girls think they got to do like the big girls, and there's lots o' snuff-dippin' at recess an noontime, when the teacher don't see hit. I don't remember how ole I was when I begun to use tobacco, but I remember hit made me sick. Paw let us get a chew from his box whenever we want hit. I don't chew none now, and I have try to give up my snuff, but hit seem to be like usin' opium, or drinkin' spirits—yo' cain't stop."

The afternoon was waning and the hens were flapping up to their roosting-place in the limbs of a cedar close by the porch. "Well, I got to be gettin' at my work," remarked Mrs. Shenton. "Hit's a right smart of a job to take cyar of this house; but Ellen she do most of the work now. I done quit it. All our boys and girls gone excep' Ellen and if she leave too, we'd give up the place an' go travelin' an' visitin' about among our children."

When I bade the family "good by." I was urged to call again and to come in some time to dinner. This invitation to dinner I accepted a few days later. I was a little early and Mr. Shenton was out in the field relaying a zigzag fence; but his wife welcomed me to a chair on the porch and assured me he would be in when the "dinner train" went along. It seemed that a train passed about twelve o'clock, and as soon as it hove in sight every one in the fields promptly started for the house.

The dinner train presently rumbled past and Mr. Shenton came hobbling in from his fencing and the boys soon followed, riding on the mules. We had fresh pork for dinner. A neighbor had "killed a shoat last week of a Saturday," and, in accord with the usual custom in warm weather, had shared the meat with all the families living near. While we were at the table I spoke of an event of importance that had recently been discussed in every newspaper in the country. The family had not heard of it. Mr. Shenton said, "The papers, they got fill up with so much depredation of one kind an' another, I stopped a-takin' of 'em."

After we had eaten and adjourned to the porch, Mr. Shenton made some mention of the war and said, "Johnston whipped the very wax out of Sherman right over hyar about three mile."

"Our place was right atween the two armies," added Mrs. Shenton. "I was to home and I had one little boy with me. Some of the bullets come right through the wooden walls and we sat in the fireplace during the fightin'. The soldiers had took all there was to eat in the house. They didn't leave nary a thing, cooked or uncooked. But I didn't want to eat that day. The little boy he got hungry and begun to fret toward night, and a soldier what come in give him some hardtack."

Mr. Shenton had served in the Confederate army under Bragg. His opinion of that leader was not very flattering. "Why!" said he, "if Bragg whipped the fight, he'd run."

"Whar my ole man suffered the worst was at Vicksburg when Grant had 'em besieged thar," affirmed Mrs. Shenton.

"We was eatin' mule beef toward the last," said the veteran, "an' I know I paid twenty-five dollars for a biscuit. Grant no need to have been so long about takin' the place, but he seem boun' to charge in jus' one place, an' we concentrate our men thar, an' had the advantage."

"I think no one aroun' hyar come home from the war worse off than Reuben Snell," remarked Mrs. Shenton.

"Yes," corroborated her husband, "his mind not been quite right since."

"For one thing," Mrs. Shenton continued, "he won't never tech no money. He say money burn him, an' he won't shake hands with no one who's been a handling of it. He has bad spells, an' when one o' them spells come on he begin to smell gunpowder, an' to feel bad. Then he call on God to help him an' he feel better. While he have those spells he preaches, though I never did hear him but once. That time he took the almanac, and he say, 'I'll preach a big un.' He cain't read a speck, an' he held the almanac upside down, an' he say, 'My tex' is 'Broad is the road that lead to destruction.' an' he preach quite a sermon.''

Reuben Snell lived far back in the woods. I was passing his place one day, and stopped for a drink of water. Reuben himself drew some fresh from the well, and handed me a gourd full. He was a pallid, peculiar-looking man, and I was not surprised when he said, "I been sick an' full of pains. My arm is thataway I cain't wind the clock steady. I wind a little, and my arm 'bleeged to drap. The devil, he 'flicts a heap of people so they cain't hardly git along.''

The house was a little affair of two rooms. There was a loft over them, but it was too low for any use except "storing ole loose plunder."

Mrs. Snell sat knitting in the kitchen doorway. "Whar do you live out when you're to home?" she asked.

"I live in Massachusetts," I replied.

"Oh, in Boston," she commented. All through the South I found Boston was considered the equivalent of Massachusetts, if not all New England. "That's sort o' north from hyar, ain't it?" Mrs. Snell went on. "I ain't got no larnin' an' I cain't quite place it exact; but hit's a good piece from hyar, I reckon. Thar was a man come hyar onct from New York or Injiana or somewhere back North."

Mrs. Snell did her cooking over an open fire. "Me 'n' Reuben like biled victuals on the fireplace the best," she explained; "and Reuben since he been like he is, and not got his mind right, he won't eat corn bread baked on the stove. I bake it in a skillet on the hearth. I putt my bread in, and putt on the led and heap coals and ashes on the led and hit bakes nice."

"Peaches are powerful good for hogs," remarked Reuben. "We tote in great loads to 'em, and they get plumb fat. Our hogs use to run in the woods befo' this new law was made, and that save us from havin' to feed 'em, a heap. Hit's the devil's law, this law agin lettin' your hogs run."

Mrs. Snell now rose and prepared to go out and give her chickens their evening feed. She limped and used a cane. "Hit's my foot," said she. "We been havin' bad weather hyar till lately. Hit sot in an' rained an' rained an' rained. Hit's tolerable muddy when hit rains an' I slipped in the mud an' give my foot a sprain."

As she picked her slow way across the yard, I started back to the settlement, through trees feathering into leafage, in a forest brightened with blossoming shrubbery—dogwood, honeysuckle, "ivory" and redbud.

The Color Line

ESPITE their many disadvantages, blacks had made considerable progress by the turn of the century, when blacks had reduced their rate of illiteracy from 92.1 per cent in 1870 to 52.4 per cent and increased their landownership by 1.5 million acres. By 1900 seven colleges for Negroes had been established in Georgia, most in Atlanta. The black minister, E. R. Carter, chronicled the progress of his race in 1894. [Document Twenty-two] Whites began to view black progress with alarm. Forrest Pope, a working man in Atlanta, wrote in 1906: "All the genuine Southern people like the Negro as a servant, and so long as he remains strictly in what we chose to call his place, everything is all right. But when ambition, prompted by real education, causes the Negro to grow restless and bestir himself to get out of that servile condition, then there will be sure enough trouble . . . and I will kill him!"

A dramatic outbreak of lynchings, reflecting the poverty and frustrations of many white Georgians, paralleled the collapse of the cotton economy and the failure of Populist reforms in the 1890's. Scholars have shown a direct relationship between the per acre value of the cotton harvest and the number of lynchings in nine cotton states of the South each year during this period. When the price of cotton was high, lynchings were few; when the price was low, lynchings increased. Between 1889 and 1918 Georgians lynched at least 386 people—more than any other state—and 360 of those were blacks. Two convicted black murderers were snatched from the courthouse at Statesboro in 1904: "The mob swerved into a turpentine forest, pausing first to let the Negroes kneel and confess. The Negroes were bound to an old stump, fagots were heaped around them and each was drenched in oil. When the fagots were lighted, the crowd yelled wildly. When it was all over, they began to fight for souvenirs." [Document Twenty-three]

Because most blacks were poor and uneducated, often confused by vagrancy laws, crop liens and contracts, they were at a disadvantage in legal proceedings against whites; because blacks did not serve on juries, they tended to receive harsher justice than whites for similar criminal acts. [Document Twenty-four] A Negro's fine might be paid by a white "friend" in return for a period of labor or he would be sent to the chain gang. After the Civil War the State began to lease its prisoners to private companies who wished to make money from cheap and unrelenting labor in quarries or brick yards. By 1900 Georgia was leasing some 2500 prisoners, about eighty-five per cent of them black, for terms up to twenty years at the rate of $20 per year per man. [Documents Twenty-five and Twenty-six]

In 1906, when reformers at last staged a successful revolt against the regular Democrats, most white people had come to believe that subordination of the Negro would be essential to a recovery of freedom for themselves—because the threat of Negro domination had been used to stifle reform and justify electoral fraud for two generations. Tom Watson, the embittered Populist who had been defeated for reelection to Congress in 1894, recanted an earlier appeal to black voters and now pledged to support any gubernatorial candidate who would pledge to disfranchise the Negro. In the aftermath of a lurid campaign punctuated with denunciations of blacks as criminal and unfit for full citizenship, Atlanta exploded in a four-day race riot. In September, 1906, a mob of five thousand whites killed ten blacks and wounded sixty more. [Document Twenty-seven] Walter White, a thirteen-year-old black boy who later became a civil rights leader, recalled hearing the cries of the mob: "In that instant . . . I knew who I was. I was a Negro, a human being . . . to be hunted, hanged, abused, discriminated against, kept in poverty and ignorance. . . . I was a Negro!"

In 1908 a constitutional amendment disfranchised the Negro. To vote, a person would have to be a Confederate veteran or descended from one, of good character and citizenship, who could read or write any part of the U.S. or Georgia constitutions or the owner of forty acres of land or property worth $500, with all poll taxes paid back to 1877. Disfranchisement closed the door of progress to half of Georgia's population, for inevitably the whole system of public service and justice would become unresponsive to the needs of people who could not vote.

Segregation, a relatively late development, paralleled the collapse of the South's farms and the movement of displaced whites and blacks into Southern cities. As long as there was no pressure or opportunity for blacks to cross accepted lines and as long as old traditions of social relations prevailed, there was no need for rigid segregation laws. But as the lives of blacks and whites began to converge, especially in the cities where landless whites and blacks were competing for jobs but also in rural districts where black and white sharecroppers lived side by side, lines began to be drawn to separate the races. The first statewide segregation law—a comprehensive bill that separated whites and blacks on the railroads—was passed in 1891. Cities began to pass municipal ordinances against blacks about 1900. As Ray Stannard Baker observed in 1908, blacks began to move into a separate world: "After I began to trace the color line, I found evidence of it everywhere . . . in the theaters, white hotels and restaurants, schools, parks, the city prison. In court, two Bibles are provided. A Negro is never, or very rarely, seen in a white man's church. When he dies, he is buried in a separate cemetery." [Document Twenty-eight] Most Georgians were poor, but blacks tended to receive less than their separate but equal share.

⸂ 22 ⸃

*The Black Side of this beautiful, enterprising city of Atlanta has sur-
mounted obstacles, leaped over impediments, gone ahead, purchased the
soil, erected houses of business and reared dwellings. The Negro is now
engaged in many enterprises, pursuits, professions and occupations.*

EDWARD R. CARTER, 1894

EDWARD R. CARTER (1858–1944), a Negro minister in Atlanta and temperance lecturer, published a history of the progress of his race in Atlanta, with laudatory biographies of his patrons
and sponsors. Excerpts follow from this book, *The Black Side, a Partial History of the Business,
Religious and Educational Side of the Negro in Atlanta, Georgia* (Atlanta, 1894).

Notwithstanding the effort to close every avenue which leads to trade-learning
against the Negro, because of the unfriendly relations existing between most of
the whites and blacks and the continual effort to debar the Brother in Black
from entering into any lucrative business, the Black Side of this beautiful, enterprising city of Atlanta has surmounted obstacles, leaped over impediments, gone
ahead, purchased the soil, erected houses of business and reared dwellings. We
would not have our readers believe that we think ourselves utterly friendless,
for there are among us white brothers who will do us any favor or show us
unlimited courtesy, yet Southern custom and public sentiment [hinder] them
from carrying [out] to any great extent these higher feelings.

   In presenting to the public the history of the Negroes here, I give a brief
sketch of the oldest living Afro-American in this city, Andrew Montgomery.
He lived during the dark days of slavery and bore the cruel treatment character-
istic of those days. Andrew Montgomery was born at Buck Creek, Jackson
County, in 1808. At quite an early age he came to this city, then called Terminus.
At this time there were not more than fifty colored persons here and of that only
two were not slaves. These were Mary Combs and Ransom Montgomery. Mary
Combs was the first colored person to own property in this city. Her property
occupied the place where Wheat Street meets Peachtree Street. This property
she sold and with the proceeds purchased her husband. Ransom Montgomery,
brother to Andrew, was the second person of color who possessed a share in

Atlanta soil. He obtained his freedom by a noble act—the saving of the lives of more than one hundred passengers during the burning of the bridge over the Chattahoochee River while a passenger train was crossing it. The State of Georgia made him a free man and gave him land lying near and around the Macon round-house. During the days of Terminus, whites and blacks worshipped in the same house, the whites using it in the mornings and allowing the Negroes to use it in the afternoons, requiring them to use portions of scriptures like "servants obey your masters," etc., or, to use Father Montgomery's words, "the Negroes had to consider themselves the shoe soles and the whites the upper leather!"

In 1867, the Constitutional Convention met in Atlanta for the purpose of revising the Constitution of Georgia and reconstructing the government generally. It was the year of jubilee for the Black Side. Nearly all public affairs were under their control. All over the state, as well as at Atlanta, began the organization of leagues for the purpose of inspiring and encouraging the Republican party in the state. This league trumpet could have been heard from the mountains to the seaboard. In Atlanta could be seen the sable sons of Ham, who a few days previous handled a plow, saw, shovel or pick, crowding into the legislature and senate hall for the purpose of making laws for the government of their former owners! In nearly every seat in the old capitol hall were seated the ebony-faced men, once slaves, now free men and statesmen. While the brothers in black were rejoicing in theirselves over their freedom, they were at the same time trembling in their boots, so great was the hostility between the two races.

Most of the hostility is now over. The white man is glad that the black man is free and the black man is glad that the white man is free. All he asks is a citizen's privilege, the rights of a taxpayer and free access to the public positions of the city. I doubt whether there are other people who pay as much taxes as the Negro in this city for the support of its government and who share so little recognition in the government.

James Tate, who is now one of the most successful wholesale and retail merchants of the Black Side, in 1866 commenced a grocery business on Walton Street. His total stock at that time amounted to $6. He now carries a stock of more than $6000 in a neat, two-story brick building on Decatur Street. This man was the first of the Black Side to open and teach a school in this city.

The next event of importance in the history of the Black Side in Atlanta was the establishment of Atlanta University, chartered in 1867, not properly opened until 1869. All around [Atlanta] tower colleges, universities and seminaries for the Black Side. There are departments where youths can be taught to read, spell and cipher and given practical geometry without having a book placed in their hands. Atlanta, for the Black Side, is the classic city!

The Negro now is engaged in many enterprises, pursuits, professions and occupations. The storehouses of Tate and Murphy occupy conspicuous places on Decatur Street, while on West Mitchell Street are to be seen the two-story warehouses of N. Holmes and W. H. Landrum. On West Hunter Street is the handsome storehouse, with residence above, of M. V. James. The neat storehouse, and dwelling of P. Escridge on Wheat Street deserves special mention. Going in another direction we arrive at the storehouse and dwelling of I. P. Moyer on Peters Street. Here he carries on a flourishing business. Also on the same street are the storehouses and dwellings of King and R. N. Davis. Such are some of the brick buildings owned by the Black Side of Atlanta.

Returning to Wheat Street, we come to the large fancy grocery of F. H. Crumbly, where he does business on an extensive scale. On the same street are business houses of Pace and C. C. Cater, the storehouse and residence of T. M. Goosby and Son, the bookstore of Hagler and Company. Next in line is the pharmacy of Doctors Slater, Butler and Company. Then, on Fraser and Martin streets are the storehouses of Watts, Graham, Emery and Epps and Jones.

Briefly we mention some other enterprises carried on by the Black Side of our businesslike city of Atlanta. Among the most prominent is that of J. McKinley, which consists in rock-quarrying and dealing in sand and brick. He employs at times more than 150 laborers, white and colored. Another, the Cooperative Southview Cemetery Company. The Georgia Real Estate and Loan Company, the Atlanta Loan and Trust Company demonstrate to the world what the Negro will do if given a chance and let alone.

Just here may also be mentioned the professional pursuits. As lawyers we have the erudite Robert Davis and the cunning, shrewd M. E. Loftin. In dentistry the famous Robert Badger. There is the firm of Doctors Asbury, Taylor and Company, known as the Friendship Drugstore. Then, that of Doctors Strong and Lockart. In the educational line, the scholarly, linguistic Professor William E. Holmes, Professor H. Crogman, who is considered by all as a deep thinker, an able instructor and eloquent speaker, Professor St. George Richardson, learned principal of Morris Brown College. In the public schools, we have as principals the refined, cultured, gentlemanly instructor W. B. Matthews of the Houston Street School, the business-like and oratorical E. L. Chew of the Gray Street School, the eloquent F. Grant Snelson of the Mitchell Street School and the witty, deep-thinking, progressive, self-made Carl Walter Hill of the Martin Street School. Our successful tailors are the polite, artistic G. M. Howell, the venerable William Finch, the successful Rufus Cooper, A. W. Finch, who does a flourishing business, and the steady B. B. Brightwell.

In April, 1881, two Christian women from Boston, Massachusetts, came to Atlanta. Miss Sophia B. Packard and Miss Harriet E. Giles rapped at the door of

Friendship Baptist Church. In the basement of the church, the first term of work lasted only three months. During the summer these white ladies visited the homes, Sunday schools, gave Bible readings, organized a mission band and an educational society. The ensuing October the second term of school opened with an increased number of sixty-nine. The American Baptist Home Mission Society of the North agreed to take charge of the work. The third teacher came in December, 1882. The students were now taught sewing, cooking, house-cleaning and laundering. In February, 1883, nine acres and five frame buildings upon a height in one of the loveliest parts of the city was purchased. In 1884 the name of the school was changed to Spellman Seminary in honor of John D. Rockefeller's father-in-law. (Mr. Rockefeller gave the largest donation toward the purchasing the property and erection of the first brick building.) Sixty-six young ladies have satisfactorily finished the academic course.

Floyd H. Crumbly's father was a slave, his mother a free woman. In 1876, Floyd was 18 years old and living in Atlanta. A recruiting officer of the U.S. Army was seeking recruits and young Crumbly enlisted for five years. After his return from the army, Mr. Crumbly was employed by Charles H. Morgan, a prosperous grocer to clerk in his store. He remained in the employ of Mr. Morgan for some years and then resolved to go into business for himself. With only $10, with which he paid the first month's rent [and] $300 worth of goods [purchased] on credit, he entered the business of a grocer. Business prospered, and at the end of six months Mr. Crumbly began to buy the place he had been renting. In eighteen months he had finished paying for the place and began to buy the place next door. On one of these lots he has erected a handsome two-story building.

J. Robert Davis was born at LaGrange, Georgia, in 1867. His parents came to Atlanta in 1871. He was placed in the Storrs School, then under Miss Amy Williams of Rochester, New York. Robert was admitted into the junior preparatory class of the Atlanta University. At the age of seventeen, he was fitted for college. He went to Lincoln University, Chester County, Pennsylvania, October, 1884. Having come from a Southern school, his admission to a Northern institution non-plused him and he left Lincoln University after spending about three months there. In January, 1885, he registered at Howard University, Washington, D.C. He passed through the college department to within five months of completing his senior year, when some discrepancy arose in which he would not yield. He left his class and went to Fernandina, Florida, where he took charge of a public school. In the autumn of '89 he matriculated in the law department at the University of Michigan. In September, 1891, he applied for admission to the bar of Atlanta. He is destined to make his mark!

Augustus Thompson was born at Jackson, Mississippi, on July 8, 1837. His mother was a slave, but his father was a freeman. His mother with four children, including himself, were willed to a Mr. Julius Sappho of Madison, Georgia. So in 1840 they moved to Madison. (The father could not accompany his wife and children, because the removal of a freeman to another state caused him to be enslaved.) In 1855 he was apprenticed to the blacksmith trade. He was employed at Athens by the Confederate Gun Factory Company and in the Augusta Machine Works. On 1865 he worked as blacksmith for the Augusta Cotton Factory. From 1866 to 1870 Mr. Thompson worked for the Georgia Railroad, at one time as car-builder. He next moved to Union Point, where he was blacksmith of that entire line of railroad. In 1870 he came to Atlanta and soon obtained work in the state road shops as a boiler manufacturer. Mr. Thompson began a business for himself on South Pryor Street, rear of No. 69.

William Finch was born in the county of Wilkes at Washington, Georgia, of a slave mother. [In 1848] he went to Athens to stay with Chief Justice J. H. Lumpkin. He afterward went to the war, where he passed through the hottest of the struggle. In gratitude to the Union for his freedom, Mr. Finch made a beautiful U.S. flag which he presented to the 144th New York Regiment. Deeply interested in the welfare and elevation of his people, he opened and taught the first school for the Negro in his part of the state. He was apprenticed to the tailor's trade at the age of fifteen and in 1866 he went to Augusta to engage in the business. Hoping to better his financial affairs, he came to Atlanta and opened business in this city. He came to Atlanta $50 in debt. By sobriety and close attention to business, he cancelled the debt, educated his children and purchased land on Edgewood Avenue, on which he erected a cozy cottage, now worth $6000. Mr. Finch was at the time a member of the city council, the only Negro who has ever enjoyed that honor in this city. He was the originator of the plan to have public schools for Negro children. He tells a little anecdote concerning his being able to keep horses. Riding along the streets one day he was asked by a white friend, "How is it, Finch, that you are able to keep horses and to ride while I have to walk?" To which Mr. Finch replied, "Do you drink beer, smoke, chew tobacco, and, if so, how much does the use of them cost you? I do neither. This is why I am able to keep horses and ride. The money you spend foolishly I save!"

R. H. Burson first saw the light of day in Morgan County, Georgia, 1840. He was a slave of slave parents, but his treatment was never cruel. In 1852 he was sold to Mr. S. Burson of Morgan County, his former master's son-in-law. His chief duty while a lad was to carry his master's children to and from school. He would gather all the disconnected leaves of the pupils' books lying around the schoolhouse. On reaching home, he sewed the loose leaves together, making, as he said, a book, and was it not a book? The children were kind to him and gave him the necessary assistance, so it was not long before he could spell every word of his homemade book.

A few miles from Watkinsville, in a poor region known as Farmington, in an humble cabin, Jeremiah B. Davis was ushered into this world, April 15, 1857, the son of slaves. After freedom, Jeremiah lived with a white man whose son took pleasure in teaching him and each day would give him a lesson to prepare for the next. When he was seventeen, he became apprenticed to carpentry under one Mr. Mack of Athens. He served this trade nine years. Rev. C. H. Lyon, pastor of the Baptist Church at Watkinsville, now urged him to enter the Atlanta Baptist Seminary. Arranging and locking his tool chest, he made ready for his departure. His possessions amounted to only $15. After paying his railroad expenses for himself and tool chest, Jeremiah had left the pitiful sum of $2.50. Arriving in this city, he succeeded in obtaining board and lodging for $8 per month. Entering school, he paid his tuition of $1. Having brought his tool chest, he was prepared to follow his trade Friday afternoons and Saturdays. By this means he kept up his expenses for three years. The president [of the college then] made him janitor of the building, allowing him as salary $12 per month, including tuition. Thus he completed the course with honor. He assumed charge of a church in the western portion of this city. For this church he served in the capacity of janitor as well as pastor, and for this little weather-beaten structure he purchased lamps, filled and lighted them, but rang not the bell, there being none to ring. [After] eight years, he has erected a handsome $3000 brick structure, having added 240 souls to his flock!

Professor William Henry Crogman, who occupies the chair of Latin and Greek in Clark University in this city, was born in 1841 on the beautiful island of St. Martin in the West Indies. In his fourteenth year he left that island with a gentleman, B. L. Boomer, at that time first mate on a vessel. Mr. Boomer, very much interested in young Crogman, after returning home in Massachusetts, sent him to the district school. He afterwards followed the sea with Mr. Boomer's brother, visiting many lands. In 1868 he entered Pierce Academy, Middleboro, Massachusetts. While attending this school he had to encounter that fiendish race prejudice which everywhere in this country ostracizes the Negro. In the fall of 1870, he was employed at Chafin University, Orangeburg, South Carolina, and taught there three years. He came to Atlanta in 1873.

Irwin W. Hayes was born at Tennille, Washington County, May 5, 1865. At the age of eight he was hired upon a farm four miles in the country and was assigned the work of a shepherd boy, watching cattle upon the pastures. At the end of two years he secured a position at Sandersville which enabled him to attend school at night. At the age of twelve he entered the common school. Next he obtained employment in the National Hotel at Macon as bell boy at night and during the day attended high school. In Savannah he embarked upon the steamer *Halcyon* as cabin boy. During his two years stay with this vessel, he recited daily to the captain and in this way completed all the principal English studies. October, 1883, he matriculated in Clark University at Atlanta.

Thomas Goosby was born November 10, 1840, in Oglethorpe County. He was born of slave parents, but he fared well in the hands of a good, Christian owner who possessed a heart. In his early life he worked on the farm and at the carpenter's trade. During the war he worked at shoe-making. December 1, 1865, Mr. Goosby received his first wages, which consisted of one pound of meat and twenty-five cents per day. Mr. Goosby moved to Atlanta in 1866 and at once obtained work at his trade, carpentry, receiving $1.25 per day. He was employed in the erection of the Kimball House, also the state capitol. In 1889 with his son as partner, Mr. Goosby commenced grocery keeping. He owns a most cozy cottage home on Wheat Street. Mr. Goosby pays taxes on more than $6000 worth of real estate. He is a man of fine parts, gentle, faithful, earnest, respected.

Elijah Richard Graves was born [at] Richmond, Virginia, 1855. In his mother's veins flowed Anglo-Saxon, Indian and African blood. At the time of Hood's raid through Georgia, young Graves refugeed from Atlanta to Macon and then joined the U.S. hospital train, which was then going through the country taking up the dead and wounded soldiers. Leaving the train at Nashville, he returned to Atlanta. He was then adopted into the family of Festus Flipper. Mr. Flipper sent him to Storr's School. Mr. Graves has had a checkered career. He at one time joined a minstrel troup at Athens, which soon dissolved. Not having the means, he had to walk the entire distance to Atlanta! He began to work at the baker's trade, but, his lungs being weak, he feared the constant dealing in flour might more seriously affect them, so he took up the vocation of candy-making. His neat little cottage on Magnolia Street, near which is located his place of business, is attractive and inviting.

Jackson McHenry is a born orator. Words of wisdom fall from his lips like an April shower. Like his brethren, he is hedged in by race prejudice. Assistance is shut out from them wholly because of color. A great number of colored men in this city, of industry and energy, would be lifted to wealth and distinction were it not for Southern sentiment. He came to Atlanta in 1868 with seventy-five cents in his pocket. He soon began blacksmithing with his brothers. Desiring to do better, he took his earnings and purchased an ox and cart and began hauling and selling wood. After a time he was able to dispose of his ox and secured a mule. Finally he sold the mule and obtained a horse. Then, accepting a position as office porter under H. I. Kimball at $40 a month, he gave the team to his brothers. He was engaged as janitor for the financial committee of the

[Republican] legislature at a salary of $30. He pursued this till the Democratic administration, after which he obtained the agency for the Wheeler and Wilson Sewing Machine Company, receiving $75 per month and ten percent on every machine he sold. In 1891 he was made head janitor of the custom house, for which his salary is $800 per year. In 1870 he was nominated for councilman, but was defeated. Eighteen seventy-six found him a nominee for the legislature and he received the largest number of votes ever given a colored man. He has been a delegate to every district convention, also a member of the state central committee.

Willis Smith was born in Walton County in 1835. Deprived of liberty, he had not the opportunity to gain an education. By some means he obtained a Webster's spelling book and with the aid of an old man called "Uncle George Peters," Willis was soon able to spell anywhere in the book but could not read a sentence! Willis went to war in 1860 as attendant for Mr. Calvin Naul and remained during '61, '62, '63 and '64. In 1866 he came to Atlanta. When he arrived he was penniless. He borrowed $5 from his sister and with it set himself up in the business of selling pies and cakes, but this proved a complete failure. Having a knowledge of carpentry, he engaged a job. In 1869 he began bridge-building and house-building. He was soon able to purchase a piece of land. In 1874 he began car-building and worked at that till 1881, when he became the junior partner of Mr. Harrison Coles in the undertaker's business.

William E. Holmes was born in Augusta, January 22, 1856. His parents were slaves, his father belonging to one family and his mother to another. His mother was hired out [for] fourteen years [to] a contracting carpenter. There being but one child on his premises, he took a liking to William and made a pet of him. He ate at his table, slept in his bed and accompanied him in his walks. In this kind treatment, his wife and son vied with him. Books and papers were not kept from him. During the last years of the war his mother sent him to school, carefully concealing his books under his clothes to avoid arrest, for instruction of Negro youth in slavery was forbidden. All over the South they were preparing in this secret way a host to raise up their people. Had this not been the case, our race would never have made such progress in so short a time. From 1865 to 1871 he continued his studies under some of the best teachers from New England. He went to Chicago and was favored with the personal training of Dr. William R. Harper at Yale University and for two years pursued his study of German. He is secretary of the Atlanta Baptist Seminary. The degree of Master of Arts was conferred upon him by the University of Chicago, June 11, 1884. He is worth about $5000.

$\begin{bmatrix} 23 \end{bmatrix}$

"We want blood!" yelled a voice. The mob swerved into a turpentine forest, pausing first to let the Negroes kneel and confess. The Negroes were bound to an old stump, fagots were heaped around them and each was drenched in oil. When the fagots were lighted, the crowd yelled wildly. When it was all over, they began to fight for souvenirs.

RAY STANNARD BAKER, 1904

BORN IN MICHIGAN, Ray Stannard Baker (1870–1946) graduated from Michigan Agricultural College in 1889. In 1892 he became a reporter for the Chicago *News-Record*. Six years later, he was employed by *McClure's*, a muckraking magazine of the era whose writers included Lincoln Steffens and Ida M. Tarbell. In 1940 Baker received a Pulitzer prize for his biography of Woodrow Wilson. The following is from R. S. Baker, *Following the Color Line* (New York, 1908), pp. 175–190.

Statesboro, Georgia, where two Negroes were burned alive under the most shocking circumstances on August 16, 1904, is a thrifty county seat located about seventy miles from Savannah. Since 1890 it has doubled in population every five years, having in 1904 some 2500 people. Most of the town is newly built. A fine, new courthouse stands in the city square, and there are new churches, a large, new academy, a new waterworks system and telephones, electric lights, rural free delivery—everywhere the signs of improvement and progress. It is distinctly a town of the New South, developed almost exclusively by the energy of Southerners and with Southern money. Fully seventy percent of the inhabitants are church members—Baptists, Presbyterians and Methodists—and the town has not had a saloon in twenty-five years and rarely has a case of drunkenness. There are no beggars and practically no tramps. A poorhouse, built several years ago, had to be sold because no one would go to it. The farms are small, for the most part, and owned by the farmers themselves. There are schools for both white and colored children, though the school year is short and education not compulsory.

About forty percent of the population of the county consists of Negroes. Here as elsewhere there are to be found two very distinct kinds of Negroes. The first of these is the self-respecting, resident Negro. Sometimes he is a landowner, more often a renter. He is known to the white people, employed by them and trusted by them. On the other hand, one finds everywhere many of the so-called "worthless Negroes," perhaps a growing class, who float from town to town, doing rough work, having no permanent place of abode, not known to the white population generally. The turpentine industry has brought many such Negroes to the neighborhood of Statesboro. Living in the forest near the turpentine stills and usually ignorant and lazy, they and all their kind, both in the country districts and in the city, are doubly unfortunate in coming into contact chiefly with the poorer class of white people, whom they often meet as industrial competitors. He prowls the roads by day and night, he steals, he makes it unsafe for women to travel alone. When he commits a crime or is tired of one locality, he sets out to seek new fields, leaving his wife and children without the slightest compunction.

About six miles from the city of Statesboro lived Henry Hodges, a well-to-do planter. He had a good farm, he ran three ploughs and rumor reported that he had money laid by. Coming of an old family, he was widely related in Bulloch County and his friendliness and kindness had given him and his family a large circle of acquaintances. The South is still, so far as the white population is concerned, a sparsely settled country. The farmers often live far apart. The roads are none too good. The Hodges home was in a lonely place, the nearest neighbors being Negroes, nearly half a mile distant. No white people lived within three-quarters of a mile. Hodges had been brought up among Negroes, he employed them, he was kind to them. To one of the Negroes suspected of complicity in the subsequent murder, he had loaned his shotgun. Another, afterwards lynched, called at his home the very night before the murder, intending then to rob him, and Hodges gave him a bottle of turpentine to cure a "snake graze."

On the afternoon of July 29, 1904, Mr. Hodges drove to a neighbor's house to bring his nine-year-old girl home from school. No Southern white farmer, especially in thinly settled regions like Bulloch County, dares permit any woman or girl of his family to go out anywhere alone, for fear of the criminal Negro. "You don't know and you can't know," a Georgian said to me, "what it means down here to live in constant fear lest your wife or daughter be attacked on the road or even in her home. Many women in the city of Statesboro dare not go into their backyards after dark. Every white planter knows that there is always danger for his daughters to visit even the nearest neighbor or for his wife to go to church without a man to protect her." It is absolutely necessary to understand this point of view before one can form a true judgment upon conditions in the South.

When Hodges arrived at his home that night, it was already dark. The little girl ran to join her mother, the father drove to the barn. Two Negroes, perhaps more, met him there and beat his brains out with a stone and a buggy brace. Hearing the noise, Mrs. Hodges ran out with a lamp and set it on the gate post. The Negroes crept up—as nearly as can be gathered from the contradictory stories and confessions—and murdered her there in her doorway with peculiar brutality. Many of the crimes committed by Negroes are marked with almost animal-like ferocity. The Negroes went into the house and ransacked it for money. The little girl, who must have been terror-stricken beyond belief, hid behind a trunk. The two younger children, one a child of two years, the other a mere baby, lay on the bed. Finding no money, the Negroes returned to their homes. Here they evidently began to dread the consequences of their deed, for toward midnight they returned to the Hodges home.

During all this time the little girl had been hiding there in darkness, with the bodies of her father and mother in the doorway. When the Negroes appeared, she either came out voluntarily, hoping that friends had arrived, or she was dragged out. "Where's the money?" demanded the Negroes. The child got out all she had, a precious five-cent piece, and offered it to them on condition that they would not hurt her. One of them seized her and beat her to death. The Negroes then dragged the bodies of Mr. and Mrs. Hodges into their home and set the house afire. The two younger children were burned alive. When the neighbors reached the scene of the crime, the house was wholly consumed, only the great end chimney left standing, and the lamp still burning on the gate post.

The murder took place on Friday night. On Saturday, the Negroes, Paul Reed and Will Cato, were arrested with several other suspects, including two Negro preachers. Both Reed and Cato were of the illiterate class. Both had been turpentine workers, living in the forest, far from contact with white people. Cato was a floater from South Carolina. Reed was born in the county, but a worthless and densely ignorant Negro. Not within the present generation had a lynching taken place in the town, and the people were deeply concerned to preserve the honor and good name of their community. In the midst of intense excitement, a meeting of good citizens, both white and black, was called in the courthouse. Speeches were made by Mayor Johnstone, by the ministers of the town and by other citizens, including a Negro, all calling for good order and the calm and proper enforcement of the law.

And the regular machinery of justice was put in motion with commendable rapidity. Fearing a lynching, the Negroes who had been arrested were sent to Savannah and there lodged in jail. A grand jury was immediately called, indictments were found and in two weeks—the shortest possible time under the law—the Negroes were brought back from Savannah for trial. To protect them, two military companies, one from Statesboro, one from Savannah, were called out. The proof of guilt was absolutely conclusive, and, although the Negroes were given every advantage to which they were entitled under the law, several prominent attorneys having been appointed to defend them, they were promptly convicted and sentenced to be hanged. "Let the law take its course," urged the good citizen. "The Negroes have been sentenced to be hanged, let them be hanged legally. We want no disgrace to fall on the town."

In the meantime, great excitement prevailed. The town was crowded for days with farmers who came flocking in from every direction. The crime was discussed and magnified. It was common talk that the "niggers of Madison County are getting too bigoty," that they wouldn't "keep their places." Fuel was added to the flame by the common report that the murderers of the Hodges family were members of a Negro society known as the "Before Day Club," and wild stories were told of other murders that had been planned, the names of intended victims even being reported. On the Sunday night before the trial, two Negro women, walking down the street, are said to have crowded two respectable white girls off the sidewalk. A crowd dragged the women from a church where they had gone, took them to the outskirts of the town, whipped them both violently and ordered them to leave the county. As the trial progressed and the crowd increased, there were louder and louder expressions of the belief that hanging was too good for such a crime. Although Reed and Cato were sentenced to be hanged, the crowd argued that lawyers would get them off, that the case would be appealed and they would go free.

[As] the intense, excited crowd gathered around the courthouse on this Tuesday, the 16th of August, other influences were also at work. We look upon a militia company as a sort of machine, but it is not. It is made up of young men. Most of these young men of Statesboro and Savannah really sympathized with the mob. Among the crowd, the Statesboro men saw their relatives and friends. Some of the officers were ambitious men, hoping to stand for political office. What would happen if they ordered the troops to fire on their neighbors? And "the nigger deserved hanging" and "why should good white blood be shed for nigger brutes"? At a moment of this, clear perception of solemn abstract principles and great civic duty fades away in tumultuous excitement.

The mob had no center, no fixed purpose, no real plan of action. Captain Hitch of the Savannah Company, a vacillating commander, allowed the crowd to pack the courthouse, to stream in and out among his soldiers. He laid the responsibility, afterward, on the sheriff, and the sheriff shouldered it back upon him. This mob crowded up, testing authority. It joked with the soldiers, and, when it found that the jokes were appreciated, it took further liberties. It jostled the soldiers—good-humoredly. "You don't dare fire," it said, and the soldiers made no reply. "Your guns aren't loaded," it said, and some soldier confessed that they were not. (The officers had ordered the men not to load their rifles.) The next step was easy enough. The mob playfully wrenched away a few of the guns, those behind pushed forward and in a moment the whole mob was swarming up the stairs, yelling and cheering. In the court room, sentence had been passed on Reed and Cato and the judge had just congratulated the people on their "splendid regard for the law." Then the mob broke in. A brother of the murdered Hodges, a minister from Texas, begged the mob, with tears streaming down his face, to let the law take its course. "We don't want religion, we want blood!" yelled a voice. The mob was now thoroughly stirred. It ceased to hesitate. It was controlled wholly by its emotions. The leaders plunged down the court room and into the witness chamber, where the Negroes sat with their wives. The mob dragged them out.

Hanging was at first proposed, and a man even climbed a telegraph pole just outside the courthouse, but the mob, growing more ferocious as it gathered volume and excitement, yelled its determination: "Burn them! Burn them!" They rushed up the road, intending to take the Negroes to the scene of the crime. But it was midday in August, with a broiling hot sun overhead and a dusty road underfoot. A mile from town, the mob swerved into a turpentine forest, pausing first to let the Negroes kneel and confess. Calmer spirits again counselled hanging, but someone began to recite in a high-keyed voice the awful details of the crime, dwelling especially on the death of the little girl. It worked the mob into a frenzy of ferocity. "They burned the Hodges and gave them no choice. Burn the niggers!" "Please don't burn me," pleaded Cato. "Hang me or shoot me. Please don't burn me!"

Men were sent into town for kerosine oil and chains, and finally the Negroes were bound to an old stump, fagots were heaped around them and each was drenched with oil. Then the crowd stood back, while a photographer took pictures of the chained Negroes. Citizens crowded up behind the stump and got their faces into the photograph. When the fagots were lighted, the crowd yelled wildly. Cato, the less stolid of the two Negroes, screamed with agony, but Reed bore it like a block of wood. They threw knots and sticks at the writhing creatures, but always left room for the photographer to take more pictures. When it was all over, they began to fight for souvenirs. They scrambled for the chains before they were cold. Pieces of the stump were hacked off, and finally one young man gathered up a few charred remnants of bone. The members of the mob were known, but none of them was ever punished.

All the stored-up racial animosity came seething to the surface, all the personal grudges and spite. As I have already related, two Negro women were whipped on the Sunday night before the lynching. On the day following the lynching, the father of the women was found seeking legal punishment for the men who whipped his daughters, and he himself was taken out and frightfully beaten. On the same day two other young Negroes of the especially hated "smart nigger" type were caught and whipped, one for riding a bicycle on the sidewalk, the other, as several citizens told me, "on general principles." On Wednesday night an old Negro man and his son, Negroes of the better class, were sitting in their cabin some miles from Statesboro, when they were both shot at through the window and badly wounded. Another respectable Negro named McBride was visited by a white mob, which first whipped his wife and then beat, kicked and shot McBride himself so horribly that he died the next day. Four white men were arrested, charged with the murder but never punished.

But what of the large Negro population of Statesboro during all this excitement? The citizens told the "decent Negroes": "We don't want to hurt you. We know you. You are all right. Go home and you won't be hurt." Go home they did, and there was not a Negro to be seen during all the time of the lynching. From inquiry among the Negroes themselves, I found that many of them had no voice to raise against the burning of Reed and Cato. This was the grim, primitive eye-for-an-eye logic that they used, in common with many white men. But all the Negroes were bitter over the indiscriminate whippings which followed the lynching. These whippings widened the breach between the races, led to deeper suspicion and hatred, fertilized the soil for future outbreaks.

$$\begin{bmatrix} 24 \end{bmatrix}$$

The Negro received the regulation "Georgia justice" in the courts, that is, once accused, the Negro is guilty, especially so if the controversy is with a white person, and must prove himself innocent. Justice to the Negro in the courts depends largely upon his standing among his white friends.

ATLANTA UNIVERSITY STUDY, 1904

UNDER the direction and inspiration of William E. B. DuBois, professor of economics between 1897 and 1910, Atlanta University published a series of studies on living conditions among blacks. Research indicated that in the black belt and white belt, there was comparatively little crime; it was in the counties where the races met on numerical equality and competed economically that most crime was charged against blacks. These brief reports on justice in the courts of several Georgia cities appeared in the Atlanta University study *Notes on Negro Crime, Particularly in Georgia* (Atlanta, 1904), pp. 43–48.

Augusta: It seems to me that so many Negroes are arraigned in the courts who are innocent apparently that it is hard to answer the question as to the cause of crime.

Marshallville: I know of no special instance where Negroes have been treated unfairly in the courts, but I think the general understanding is that the white man's word goes before anything else.

Baxley: So far as a Negro is concerned, it matters not how good a law-abiding citizen he may be or how intelligent he is, nor the amount of property he may own and pay taxes on. He has no voice in the court house except as a witness or to be tried.

Fort Valley: The persons whom I asked seemed to think that the Negro of this county received the regulation "Georgia justice" in the courts, that is, once accused, the Negro is guilty, especially so if the controversy is with a white person and must prove himself innocent.

Newborn: Sorry to say that in our courts, a Negro's color is a brand of guilt. This refers to our county and circuit courts. Justice courts in rural districts are a mere farce. Justice to a Negro against a white man is less than a game of chance.

Dawson: During the August or adjourned term of the Superior Court of Terrell County, 1902, one —— was charged with vagrancy. He was a barber by trade and ran a colored barbershop. One of the police on that beat fell out with him and swore out the above warrant. The said —— produced eighty-five men who swore that he shaved them from once to twice a week and cut their hair from once to twice a month and that he sometimes did other work, such as putting down carpets, when called upon. The trial judge declared that he had never heard of Negroes shaving twice a week and did not believe any such thing, that was as many times a week as the average white man shaved and that the Negro's beard does not grow as fast nor come out as fast as white men's and therefore he doubted the veracity of the witnesses. The case was compromised by the said —— paying the sum of $65.

At the November term of the Superior Court held in Dawson, 1903, a boy fourteen years of age was charged of helping a man or tenant steal cotton seed from his landlord. The man had pleaded guilty at the August term of the City Court and had been fined $100 or one year on the gang. The fine was paid by the landlord and the man was kept on the place. The boy refused to plead guilty and appealed his case to the Superior Court. The grand jury found a true bill and he was tried at the November term of court. At the trial the man who pleaded guilty swore that he was a cropper and worked on halves and that the boy and his father lived about three miles from him and that he learned that the boy was to be sent to town early the next morning and that he had gone to the old man who was a cripple and asked him to let the boy come by his home and carry a package to town for him and the boy's father consented as it was not much out of the way. He swore that he had the cotton seed sacked and out by the roadside when the boy came along and that the man put them on the wagon and told the boy to sell them and bring him the money. He did as he was told. He also swore that the boy did not know whether he had stolen the seed or not nor where he had gotten them. The boy's parents swore to the same facts. The boy was found guilty and sentenced to twelve months in the gang.

At the August term of the city court in Dawson, 1903, there were twenty-five young men convicted of gambling on the evidence of one who was excused because he turned state's evidence. He is known as a spotter. When he admitted his guilt the solicitor got up and recommended him to the judge as a hard work-ing Negro whom he knew and who had worked for him on his place. He was excused with only a nominal fine. The other twenty-five received sentences ranging from $30 to $75 and from six to twelve months on the gang.

In the Americus city court, April term, 1904, one X—— borrowed $2 and agreed to pay $3 for the same by working it out when called upon to do so. Before Y——, from whom he borrowed the money, was ready for him or called for him, he was working out another debt which he had contracted with another party. He could not go to Y—— just at the time wanted. Y—— swore out a warrant for cheating and swindling and sent X—— up for eight months on the gang.

Sylvania: They have no voice in court. They are not treated fair in the courts at all.

Thomaston: The criminals do not, in my judgement, at all times have fair and impartial trials. Yet they are treated as fair as the average Negro in the South.

Jewell: The subject is a young man of the little town in which I teach. Christmas this young man shot a boy, for which crime he has not been punished. Of course everybody in the town knows that he is a desperate character and that he can give no cause for the crime of which he is surely guilty. And yet when tried in court he was released. The criminal is a servant for one of the wealthiest families in the county, and, of course, they did their best to prevent his being brought to justice in the county court. The Negro was arrested and taken to court for trial, and as plain as the case was all the so-called best white people of the little town of Jewell met at Sparta on court day and through their influence the jurymen were bribed and the result was that a verdict of not guilty was brought out by the jurymen, even when they knew that he was a murderer. Now, I think the court did the very worst thing that could have been done for the young man. By all means justice should have been meted out to him, not so much for his own salvation as for that of many others who will certainly be influenced by his example. I know of three other cases where the criminals failed to receive justice in the courts, simply because they rendered good service to white people as servants. My opinion is that the white man who makes himself a protection for the Negro's crime in one instance is simply encouraging crime in all directions. My experience is that much of the crime among Negroes arises from the corrupt way in which the courts sometimes deal with criminals. Either one Negro of a certain town has been punished innocently and the others revolt, or one has not been punished for the crime he did commit and so many others are encouraged to commit worse crimes.

Athens: The races in this section work very harmoniously together, and I know of no instance where the courts have not dealt justly with the Negro. As a whole, one of the worst faults the Negro has is the concealment of crime, no matter how low the crimes are. An intelligent, law-abiding citizen in this section gets the full benefit of the law.

Montezuma: In some cases even-handed justice is meted out to both races alike. But in many cases the white man uses his power to dethrone justice.

Sasser: As to their treatment in the courts of my county, I can without hesitation say there is some partiality shown. Do not let it be publicly known that I said we are illegally treated, that is that we do not have a fair trial in every instance in the courts of my county. It would cause me to have enemies among the whites, and they perhaps might set snares for me.

Claxton: I haven't found out definitely how they are treated in the courts. I can safely say they are tried by white juries, white lawyers and white judges, so you can judge.

Wadley: I don't visit the county courts, but as far as I can learn and read in the papers Negroes don't stand any chance in them, and in our town before the Mayor it is the same.

Carnesville: The Negro has very little rights here. All the white man is after is the almighty dollar. Outside of that the Negro is no more thought of.

Marietta: All the officials and jurors are white, but considering the fact that our Judge X—— has presided over the court for a number of years in a very impartial manner I feel that our criminal class here is very fairly dealt with.

Calhoun: To my knowledge Negroes are justly treated in the courts in this county.

Kingston: Now as far as courts are concerned, we do not believe that justice is altogether handed down to us. We believe that when a crime or crimes are committed that each court should do justice irrespective to creed, nationality or color. We believe that the law should not only be enforced after election but before as well.

Waynesboro: They are treated as a rule as all Southern courts treat the Negro.

Shady Dale: Last year a crowd of twenty went to arrest a Negro for a debt of $22. They found six Negroes gathered there for a hunt. The man they sought got away. The six Negroes arrested were fined from $60 to $120. The white men were upheld by the law, yet they had no warrant and met no resistance.

Vienna: Of course, no one would expect the Negro to be dealt with justly in the courts. The judge, jury and lawyers are all whites, hence no sane man would believe that the Negro receives justice before such a prejudiced body. But so far as white men are concerned, I think the Negro is treated fairly well in the courts, that is as well as could be expected from white men. It would not be natural for such a race as the whites, that has the superior advantage, to give the Negro justice.

Rome: Our people as a rule get the worst of it in courts, according to my observation.

Abbeville: I do not know how the Negro stands here in the courts, but I think he has a very poor chance since the jury down here is ignorant and full of prejudice.

Folkston: We are doing very well here with the whites, only we are denied the right of jurymen on account of color.

Geneva: The case of a Negro always is committed, and if he hasn't got some white man on his side he is gone to the gang.

Thomasville: The courts on the whole here are inclined to give the Negro prisoners justice. In our last court forty percent of the accused were acquitted. Some of the charges were very serious, but absence of sufficient evidence seemed to have been recognized by the jurors, who seemed impartial.

Jasper: In the fall of 1903 white folks treated the colored folks very badly by white capping. They dynamited and rocked several of the Negroes' houses in this county. You know the colored people don't get justice in the courts.

Midville: Justice is only measured out to him according to the views of that white man who is in favor of him. The Negro's word in the courts has but little weight. A Negro's word or justice to the Negro in the courts of my county depends largely upon his standing among his white friends. If a Negro has a case against a white man, it is generally held on docket until it becomes cold and thrown out. On the other hand, if a white man has a case against a Negro he is fined or imprisoned.

Blairsville: They are treated fairly well. They neither lynch nor take the lives of the Negro as they do further south, but we are slaves for them in a sense.

Waco: Of course, they are not treated altogether fairly in the courts, for they have no colored jurors here.

Crawford: For the most part there is a decrease in the commission of crime. We think the manner in which the law is administered has much to do with the commission of crime on the part of the Negroes. A white man here can do almost anything wrong in violation of the law; if a Negro is defendant in the case, justice steers clear of the Negro's side. The crime for which Negroes are most strictly held to account is that of breaking contracts. They are invariably hunted for and when found are handcuffed or tied with ropes, brought back, severely whipped. Now and then one is killed (self-defence or accidentally) and the murderer goes free. Negroes can run blind tigers, live in adultery and gamble on the plantation or here in the town unmolested, but he must not miss a day from work. It did actually occur in this county that a white man killed a Negro at a Negro dance without provocation. He was never bothered about it. Some time afterwards the same white man took a mule from a white farmer. He was caught, tried and convicted of horse stealing and sentenced to the chain gang.

Jefferson: There are from forty to fifty misdemeanor convictions a year in our courts. The major part of them get white men to pay their fines, for which they work double the time. These white men run kind of force labor farms. The Negroes' treatment in court is usually fair, as there is no indignant public sentiment against these petty crimes. The offender, after his arrest, is generally taken by the arresting officer to some white man, who is the Negro's choice. There a bond is made and the fellow put to work. When court convenes, the Negro and his employer appear, and after some legal formality the offender is fined. The fine is paid and the criminal goes back to work. These Negroes are nuisances to the respectable Negroes of the communities. They often give much trouble at the churches and other public gatherings, with the boast "that captain so-and-so will stand to me in anything." I am not a pessimist, but owing to the demand for labor in this county and the means employed by the large landowners to secure it, I truly believe misdemeanor crimes are on the increase.

Pendergrass: The Negroes in general are in a bad shape here. There are about eighty criminals here out on bond, some for murder, some for selling whiskey, some for gambling, some for carrying concealed weapons, some for shooting, and most of them are guilty, too, but their captain (i.e. employer) takes their part in court. They generally pay about $25 and work the Negro from one and a half to two years, and the Negro never knows what it cost. Some that are guilty come clear, some not guilty are found guilty just the same, for they can only swear and make a statement. The whites trade in them like slavery times or like horses. Some get their rights and some don't. There is no justice in court for the Negro, except he has money, and they will make him lose it.

Steam Mill: The crime of the Negro is increasing. It is two-thirds greater than ever before. The cause of this is that they are given the full extent of the law on the weakest evidence. There is such a demand down in south Georgia for turpentine hands and sawmill hands that every man who has got a sawmill or a turpentine farm in the county is bribing the courts and the lawyers to convict the Negro regardless of the evidence of the crime, because he wants to buy him for his labor, for he can shoot and force him to labor. Therefore, ninety-eight percent of the convicts of the county prison are made up of the Negro race. We have got more overseers and white bosses than we had forty years ago.

Waynesboro: They always get justice, I believe, when it is a Negro vs. a Negro, but when it is a white man vs. a Negro there seem at times to be some variations. This is putting it very mildly, too.

Adairsville: There is very little mercy shown the Negro in our circuit courts. There seems to be a premium placed on his conviction, however simple and light the charges may be. This I am at a loss to answer for, but as a general rule the pressure is upon him, and he generally gets defeated in the courts all the way from the district to circuit courts. Of course this depends on whom the Negro is in law with. If it is with another of his color, probably he may get justice. But if there is any chance for his color to figure in the matter, he is more than apt to meet squarely and promptly with sudden defeat. We have good men on both sides, some white and some colored, who strive with each other for good, and if it were not for these two classes of men this county would present a sad picture.

Both races would indulge more in cruel hatred for each other. I don't want to say too much right along here, but the Negro is not accorded his rights as a man, either in court or in his domestic and commercial relations, not to say a word about his political privileges.

Lavonia: Of course you are acquainted with procedure of the courts with the Negroes in the South. "To be black" goes a long way in reaching a verdict and determining the fine or punishment. But it is not so bad here as in some other counties, and under these adverse circumstances the Negroes are forbearing, plodding their way onward, some with wisdom and others with indiscretion.

Oconee: Crime is increasing among the whites. The whites indulge Negroes in it a great deal. A Negro kills another and he escapes punishment by getting away or some white man pays a small fine for him and he takes him and works him. The white man is already anxious for him to get into something in order that he can tie him. This is what some of them call controlling labor. There are hundreds of Negroes working on farms and public works with some white man on his bond or working out fines. A Negro seldom comes clear, no matter how weak is the evidence produced against him. It does not pay to go to court.

Brunswick: It is very difficult, if not impossible, to convict white men in the courts of crimes committed against Negroes, nor are Negroes given a fair trial when charged with offenses against the whites. Where Negroes only are involved, money or a pull will generally secure the acquittal of the Negro who has it.

Adrien: Our county is very rough in many ways to work in to the disadvantage of Negroes. We can't get a fair trial in a court of justice, and crimes can't be estimated fairly on account of injustice. Especially if it is a case between the Negro and a white man, there is no hope for the Negro.

Douglasville: As to the treatment of the Negro in the courts, I should judge from my own observation of the proceedings of the courts for the past three years that they are generally impartially dealt with according to the evidence. For the three years that I have been here, I don't remember any Negro complaining as to unjust treatment of his race in court. This town and county from my observation and judgement is an exception to most of the towns and counties that I have lived in.

Baxley: Most of the crimes committed by white men are nolprossed or light fines laid when proven guilty, but there is no hope for the acquittal of a Negro. And if he is proven guilty (which is no trouble to do), he is given a long sentence or a very heavy fine. In this county we have no colored jurors, and possibly this accounts for the Negroes suffering so very much in the criminal courts.

Tifton: In the courts, he is usually a criminal and stands friendless before the law.

[25]

The convict is stripped. Then he is bent over the barrel. He begs and and pleads and struggles. Another brings down, swish! an instrument of leather three inches wide, three feet long upon the naked man on the barrel. The man on the barrel screams a horrible, shrill scream of unutterable pain. From the bluest of skies the soft sun of Georgia looks down upon the frightful scene.

CHARLES EDWARD RUSSELL, 1908

CHARLES EDWARD RUSSELL (1860–1941) published the following article, "A Burglar in the Making," in *Everybody's Magazine* in June, 1908.

They started for the farm near Milledgeville that the state of Georgia provides for the reception of its convicted law-breakers, for it has no penitentiary nor prison. The next day, shaved and shorn and clothed in the stripes that are the badge of the convicted wrong-doer, George found himself standing in a long line of other men similarly clad, black men and white men, placed on exhibition, while an agent for the contractors passed along and appraised their muscles and estimated their worth. For the state of Georgia, having no penitentiary nor prison nor other means of caring for its offenders, practices upon them a very strange device. It sells them for the terms of their sentences into the hands of private and irresponsible persons, and it was for these persons that the man was now going up and down the line, selecting the likeliest and choicest.

George was chosen. He was taken to a convicts' camp at a place that I shall call Gehenna. It was one of many convict camps, some better, some worse. The company that had bought of the state of Georgia this particular batch of slaves was engaged in making brick. Its camp was remote from the cities and ordinary ways of men. Nobody knew what went on there and nobody cared.

It was morning when George, with a fresh detail of purchased slaves, arrived at Gehenna. With the first glance at the camp a chill struck to his heart. There was something most forbidding about the wild and desolate spot, made more hideous with the ragged, dirty structure and the black chimneys of the brick-

211

yard. In one corner was a high stockade with guard pens about it and men with rifles on guard. Within the stockade were wretched, dark, dilapidated and most filthy huts in which other men were doomed to sleep and eat. About the factory yard were men at work, in the broad stripes of the convict, some preparing the clay, some wheeling the yellow, damp, new bricks to the furnaces to be baked. George noticed that all these men were very badly clad, and some went almost naked. Beyond the brick kiln the land sloped into a swamp, a promising breeding place for disease.

George and the others of the new gang were led to one of the filthy sheds, where they received a breakfast of one slice of boiled salt pork and one piece of greasy corn bread. There were no knives nor forks, and George took the pork into his fingers. He felt something move under his fingers. He saw what it was that had moved. It was worms. Struggling hard with himself, he managed to swallow a little of the corn bread (after he had carefully examined it), and with the rest of the gang he was marshalled into the yard.

His work was to wheel loads of those fresh clayey, yellow brick from the place where they had been shaped to the place where they were to be baked. When he went the first time to the place where the bricks were to be shaped, he was amazed to see that the persons engaged in removing the bricks from the drying belt were women. He remembered then that the state of Georgia has no prison for convicted women, and that they are rented to slave brokers just as the men slaves are rented. The work that these women were doing seemed very laborious. With bended backs they must toil hour after hour, lifting the heavy bricks and piling them. A man with a rifle stood and watched the women.

From the place where bricks were shaped to the place where bricks were burned there wound through the yard a path about 400 feet long. George was told that by this path he must take upon the wheelbarrow each time from fifty to seventy bricks and that he must deliver at the furnaces not fewer than 105 loads in the day, sixty loads from sunrise to noon and forty-five loads from the end of the noon hour to sunset. He was also told that his work would be checked up every few hours, and that if he were found to be falling behind he would with good reason be sorry. Each of the unbaked bricks weighed between five and six pounds. That made usually a wheelbarrow load of more than 300 pounds. George weighed 110 pounds!

He has not proceeded far with that first day's work when he has an opportunity to learn exactly what are the good reasons for regretting a failure to complete an apportioned task. There is a commotion in the yard, and two of the guards appear, leading forward a convict to a place where a great barrel lies on its side. A big, authoritative man comes forward and gives orders. The convict is stripped. Then he is bent over the barrel. Two Negroes hold his arms and his head. Two others hold his legs. He begs and pleads and struggles. The Negroes hold him fast. Another man stands by with an instrument. It is made of sole leather about three inches wide, three feet long and 3/8ths of an inch thick. It has a stout wooden handle. The man lifts the instrument high in the air. He brings it down, swish! upon the naked man on the barrel. The man on the barrel screams aloud with sudden agony. He does not shout nor exclaim, he screams a horrible, shrill scream of unutterable pain. The other man raises the instrument and brings it down, swish! again. Again the man on the barrel screams. A blow and a scream, a blow and a scream. Presently it is a blow and a sob. The man on the barrel is crying. Again a moment and his blood trickles down his side. He is screaming, sobbing, crying now—and bleeding. The blows fall upon his bruised and bloody back. He wriggles and twists about. The Negroes can hardly hold down his head and his legs. The other men stand and gaze. The guards hold their rifles, and from the bluest of skies the soft sun of Georgia looks upon the frightful scene, and the sweet spring air from the Southern woods blows over it.

From sunrise to noon the man has wheeled fifty-seven loads of fresh brick. The regulations of this hell on earth require that in such a time he shall wheel sixty loads. So, having thus transgressed, power and law and justice as administered in the state of Georgia exact from him this penalty until he screams and cries and sobs—and bleeds. He walks with difficulty. George learns that the offender is a cripple. He has chronic rheumatism, so that is why he offends concerning the three loads missing from his tally between sunrise and noon.

So grinds on the first day. For dinner they have each a piece of boiled salt pork, a piece of greasy corn bread. Although he is nearly famished, having worked all morning in the open air, George looks upon the food before him and at the recollection of his breakfast, his stomach revolts upon him and he turns sick and faint. But he gulps down the corn bread and, at last, turning the salt pork to the light and shredding it with his fingers, he manages to swallow a little of it. The rest is begged by the hungry man next to him. For supper he has boiled salt pork and a piece of corn bread. He learns then that the state of Georgia does not furnish these viands; they are provided at the sole charge and cost of the company to which his slave labor has been sold.

A light begins to dawn upon him. He perceives that he is no concern of the state of Georgia and no concern of the company to which he has been sold. Between the two he is the lost and forgotten outcast and pariah. The state turns him over to the company and does not care. The company can get all the convicts it wants and does not care. Nobody cares. Why then should the convict care what war he makes upon the society that has thrust him into a pit and left him there?

The days that followed that first day were to George like days in a madman's dream. He must learn to face the salt pork and its animated contents. He must harden himself against the daily whippings. He must harden himself against the incessant brutality, vile smells and abominable sights. While all else is being hardened in him, shall his soul escape? At night he crawls, sore and weary, into his horribly bestenched prison house, where whites and Negroes, young and old, veteran criminal and novice, decent and vile, herd together indiscriminately. Every few days his stomach, which will not become accustomed to the salt pork and greasy corn bread, rebels and rejects the poisonous stuff, and then he works on in the sun ready to drop of weakness and weariness.

Once he falls in a faint at his task and his companions in misery carry him to his filthy bunk, and even the camp doctor admits that he can work no more that day. And so he lies there, and a million insects that inhabit his bed crawl over him and feed upon him, and for weakness he can hardly lift his hand to brush them from his face. So he lies there two days, three days, four days, five days, delirious part of the time, happily unconscious part of the time. The doctor comes and glances at him and goes his way. The slave contractor's agent looks in at the door and curses him.

At last he comes back from the shadow-land and the insects drive him to his feet, and he puts on the broad stripes and staggers into the yard. And then his wheelbarrow is put into his hands again and he begins to wheel brick. But they do not exact of him that day nor for many days the 105 loads. Even in the brick-yards of Gehenna there is a limit to brutality.

Many were the horrible sights he witnessed and shuddered at in those days before the crushing of the system had atrophied in him the last nerve of conscious revolt and he had arrived at the state in which he did not care. Three times in one day he saw that same old man whipped, the man that had rheumatism in his back, for no fault but failing to make the required number of loads. After the third whipping he was too sore to move and had to be helped to his cot. He lay on his filthy bunk with no covering but a cotton sheet, and between the chinks of the wretched wall of that hut the night wind blew sharply upon him. His rheumatism now grew worse. To see him struggling along the path with his barrow of heavy brick was a pitiable sight, but after a time George didn't notice it. He was sinking into a lethargy of indifference. He had learned to eat his salt pork now—sometimes. And when he could not, his companions would beg it of him.

The whippings went on. Nobody cared, except those that were whipped. George learned, after a time, that the men in charge were obliged by the rules to report to the state prison commissioners every case of punishment, with the cause thereof and the name of the person punished. But in fact not one case in

214

twenty was ever so reported. He knew that because, writing a neat hand, he was employed to copy the reports and had monthly before him the evidence of the dereliction.

The deputy warden that represented the state in charge of the camp was also in the pay of the company, which paid him three times as much as the state paid him and to which his obligation was in the same proportion. To the contracting company his use seemed to be to extract from the convicts the utmost labor at the least cost. To the state his duty was much vaguer. The contracting company was obliged by its contract to feed and clothe the slaves. The function of the state seemed to be that it kept the convicts from running away. Simply that and nothing more. Nowhere appeared the slightest suggestion that any of these unfortunates were men—in spite of follies and weaknesses and sins like our own, still men to be pitied and helped and reformed and redeemed.

There were rules, George found, of the most beautiful and humane character, rules evidently designed by kind-hearted men to prevent cruelty and to secure some measure of comfort to the convicts, but all the rules were merely a jest among the persons in charge of the camp. No one pretended to observe them. Thus it was prescribed that the contracting company should furnish ample food of good quality, good and sufficient clothing, good and clean beds. All these rules were as if they had never existed. In that remote and seldom-visited spot the deputy warden was the unquestioned master and seemed to have no limit to his sway except the interest of the contractor.

All the conditions seemed framed and designed to make life wretched for the victims of this horrible system. In the beginning the contractor had bought the labor of the convicts for $11 a head for each year. Now competitive bidding had increased the price to $225 a head a year, and even more, and besides the contractor bore the expense of feeding and clothing. That he might secure a profit on such a bargain it was necessary that the men should be driven through long hours to the utmost capacity of their endurance. And that was why the deputy warden was on the contractor's payroll.

Once in a long time an inspector from the state prison department came to visit the camp, but his coming was invariably known in advance, and the men were set to work to clean up the barracks and whitewash the stockade, and, when the inspector came, for that one meal the men had decent food and the whip was out of sight. The inspector went among the convicts to receive complaints, but a deputy warden or a yard boss went with him everywhere, listening to every word said to him, and the convicts knew too well what would be the consequences to them of any complaint. They were in a trap.

In the middle of George's second year, some incidents came to vary the monotony of horror, the whippings, the tugging at the wheelbarrow, the struggle

215

to and fro in the hot sun or the cold rains. Old faces disappeared as men died or as time won for them an exit from the doors of hell. New faces appeared as fresh relays of slaves were brought up to feed the insatiable contract. Once a convict stood for a moment by the margin of the swamp and then plunged into the water. Instantly blazing rifle shots awoke the echoes, and guards ran and shot and shouted. Covered with mud, the fugitive was dragged back to be beaten first and then loaded with heavy shackles that for weeks he must wear. Once the man that was working next to George complained of terrible pains in his chest and stomach. A yard boss ordered him back to work. At last he fell in a faint. That night he died. His death was entered as due to sunstroke. Some of the men got pneumonia and died. Sometimes they stood for hours to their knees in icy water while they worked in the swamp. Always they were ill-clad, ill-nourished and in no state to withstand the cold. The shoes were rotten and worthless even when new. In the winter men with bare protruding toes walked in the slush. Some had no underclothes, some had no socks.

The time wore by and George came to the end of his term. He had learned to be as sullen, as defiant, as hardened, as reckless as the indurated men about him. When at last the doors opened to set him free, he went back to Atlanta and turned burglar.

For the year ending May 31, 1907, the state of Georgia had 2464 convicts, of whom 1890 were contracted into servitude to various private persons and corporations, and 574 were employed on the county roads. This is a system that multiplies criminals, breeds brutality, encourages crime and puts upon one of the fairest states in the Union a hideous blot.

$\begin{bmatrix} 26 \end{bmatrix}$

The convicts ate while lying down, chained to their bunks, and they were chained in their bunks on Sundays, too. They were made to sleep in the clothes they worked in . . . wet clothes just the same. For supper the convicts were given a piece of corn bread, a piece of meat and a potato. There were no bathing facilities, only a creek.

L. R. MASSENGALE, 1908

EXPOSURE of the chain gang scandal in the Atlanta *Georgian* led to a formal investigation by the state legislature. In July, 1908, state representatives reported the barbarities of the chain gang that they had seen. The reports were published in the Atlanta *Georgian* in a series of articles between July 23rd and July 30th.

Members of the Georgia legislature who had visited Georgia convict camps to inspect them went before the Felder investigating committee on Wednesday and told of starvation, cruelties and inhuman practices in the camps. In spite of the fact that the convict bosses had been tipped off from some quarter and were expecting the committees from the legislature, the following instances of mistreatment of prisoners were discovered and related to the committee.

Representative S. A. Wootten of Wilkes: "At the Sumter County road camp I found two or three convicts working on the gang although they were physically unable, through disease, to work. They were emaciated and yet the authorities in charge of them didn't know they were sick, they said. One old man was ruptured and several were suffering with venereal diseases. In their sleeping quarters the bedding was very filthy. The bed ticks were as black as they could be and did not have the appearance of ever having been washed. I saw no bathing facilities. The convicts were a dirty, woe-begone looking set so far as clothing went. Two or three of the convicts had iron picks riveted to their ankles, these picks being about two feet long, regular road picks. There were sores on their legs caused by friction of these picks against the legs, only the pants leg being between the skin and the pick."

Representative L. R. Massengale of Warren: "At the Floyd County camp the rules were violated. They had no mess hall. The convicts ate while lying down, chained to their bunks, and they told me they were chained in their bunks on Sundays, too. They were made to sleep in the clothes they worked in, and if they came in from the works wet with rain it made no difference. They slept in the wet clothes just the same. For supper the convicts were given a piece of corn bread, a piece of meat and a potato, and if they ate it all for supper they got no breakfast. The only breakfast they got was the remains from the supper the night before. There were no bathing facilities, only a creek. At the Lookout Coal and Coke Company's camp I saw a convict whose arm had been broken in the mines. The bone stuck out above the wrist, through having been badly set or not set at all, yet he was still working in the mines. When I tried to talk with the convicts a warden was sent down within earshot. At the Coweta County road camp I found in a little rough plank room, where horse and mule feed is kept, a Negro dying with consumption. The room was cold and bare, and the Negro was lying on the floor, too weak to talk. He had been there about two weeks, and when I was there the doctor had not been there for three days."

Representative E. E. Cook of Chattahoochee: "At the mines of the Lookout Coal and Coke Company I walked up to an old darky fifty or sixty years old. He said they are required to get out so many tons of coal per day and in the mine they were working the vein would not yield that number and he had been whipped for failing to make the required tons. While he was telling me this, Warden M. O. Maxwell, who was standing by, began to curse him violently, saying, 'God damn you, nigger, you go on and tell what you please, but I'll put you back in the mines, God damn you!' And he went on so violently that I walked away from the place. Maxwell was the state warden, and he seemed very nervous and exceedingly anxious for us to get away."

Representative R. M. Moore of Cherokee: "At the Stanley turpentine camp several convicts came shoving up to me and urged a boy to tell me something. 'Go on and tell him,' they said, and finally I was told by a dozen of them that the boy was whipped every day. No matter what he did, he couldn't please the warden and he got a whipping every day. I looked at the whipping register and found that only two whippings were recorded. I asked the warden about the whippings, and he said, 'Look at the record.' At least a dozen convicts told me the boy was whipped every day. At this camp it looked as if they were expecting us. Convicts had on new shoes, and new blankets had been brought out from town and thrown over dirty old mattresses."

Representative R. M. Young of Troup: "At the camp of Pinson & Allen, in Miller County, I found a blind Negro in the stockade, and he had nearly burned the stockade down, whether with a fire to warm himself by or to cook with I do not know. The building where the convicts are quartered is built of rough

218

boards, without any weather strips at all. Conditions were filthy. I picked up a piece of the bread and I would not feed that kind to my dog. I asked the riding boss how many convicts he had now and how many he formerly had, and found out that they had sold a number for $35 a month each. The cook told us they cooked only one meal per day. They had no vegetables in camp, no syrup for weeks, maybe months."

J. A. Cochran, an ex-convict, was called. He had worked at the Milledgeville camp in 1901 and the Chattahoochee camp in 1902. "The doctor went to an old Negro and said he would have him whipped because he said he was sick. The Negro looked sick, but the whipping boss gave him twenty-five licks, and he was ordered to get into the wagon and go to the field. The old man was unable to climb in and was thrown in like a dead horse. At the field he fell between the rows. Redmond, the boss, cursed him and sent two other Negroes after him. They picked him up and he looked like he was dead. They dropped him and refused to pick him up again. They buried him in a day or two. The Negro was in the hospital when the doctor ordered him to be taken to the field. The Negro gave him no impudence. He just begged them not to have a dying man whipped."

"A darky was pitching brick," said Cochran. "Captain Jim Casey came round and ordered them to work harder. They took a Negro over a barrel and whipped him. He staggered over on a lumber pile. They put him in a wheelbarrow and took him to the hospital and then somebody went after Dr. Green. When the doctor came, the Negro was dead. They held a coroner's inquest and the verdict was the Negro drank too much water. The guards around the camp formed the coroner's jury. The only reason the Negro was whipped was because he couldn't keep up with the required work. If you'll go to the camp, you'll find them working there with the sweat running down into pools on the ground. A white boy from Atlanta came to the camp and on Christmas day he took lockjaw. He stayed there three days and nights with lockjaw. He was never visited by a doctor. We were told the doctor was 'having Christmas' and had no time to wait on convicts. Warden Casey, himself, in 1903, whipped seventeen Negroes in one day for not doing their task. He gave them from fifteen to twenty lashes each." Cochran described the "swapping" of convicts. The convicts would be "trotted around" like horses at a sale. "There's a man there worth $200," they would say. "All you could smell was whiskey and all you could hear was cussin'," said Cochran. "It's nothing but a drunken mob, that's one reason it's so bad out there."

The Felder investigation committee had its eyes opened Thursday to the real Georgia convict lease system. The star witness was C. D. Wortham, formerly a guard at the Chattahoochee brick camp, who said that he had been discharged because he had reported to the prison commission some of the atrocities that were committed while he was there. The spectators in the crowded committee room leaned forward in their chairs and at times the breathless silence was broken by smothered groans at tales of heart-rending scenes in the Georgia convict hells.

C. D. Wortham was sworn. He was at the Chattahoochee Brick Company from February, 1900, and was there nearly two years. He was yard man, paid by the state. Wortham described the whipping of Pete Harris, who afterward died. "Dr. Green had examined the sick Negro and marked him as all right and he was given twenty-five or thirty lashes by Captain Casey. Two or three Negroes were holding him. He was whipped twice that day, once when he was put to work at 7 in the morning and again after he had given out at work, about 4 o'clock that afternoon. I found the Negro with flies in his mouth and his pulse nearly stopped. I told them he was dying and they didn't credit it. He was taken into the hospital and I had several men help me to revive him. The Negro died in about ten minutes. Next morning five men from up around the cotton mills came to the camp. Coroner Stamps and Dr. Green came, Captain Casey told the coroner to put those five men on the coroner's jury. The inquest was held. Two Negro convicts, great pets because they entertained Captain Casey's company, testified that the Negro had eaten a hearty dinner!"

Arthur W. Moore was sworn. He worked at Chattahoochee Brick Company for eight years, left about fifteen months ago. "The convicts are overworked. It is too hard for them. I've seen 'em fall and faint. I've seen them whipped while at work. They are kept in a trot or they get the strap. I've seen five or six whipped at once because they didn't do enough work to please Captain Casey. The food is pretty bad sometimes. The rules are not observed. They wash the bed clothes about once a year. There was a fireman, Tim Goings, given thirty lashes once and two or three minutes later he was given about thirty more. I've seen eight or ten whippings a day, and there were a lot I didn't see. They'd average five a day, easy."

M. A. Keith, who had served time at the Durham coal mines for killing a man in Atlanta but was pardoned, was the next witness. "I worked in the mine from daylight to 8 o'clock at night, sometimes 11. They put me entirely out from under the state's control under men employed by the company. I knew I was being worked illegally, but I had no appeal—no one to whom I could appeal. I worked in the mine from daylight to 8 o'clock at night, sometimes 11. They worked other convicts illegally this way, out from under the state's control. I saw them whip a white man 103 licks for falling behind seven pounds one day in his task of coal. This man fainted after he was whipped. I have seen one white boy, named Wynne, whipped to death. It was in 1906. He was eating supper. The warden had a lot of hogs in the stockade. This boy had made some coffee and had thrown some of it on one of the hogs. It was reported to the warden, who gave him sixty-nine licks. He never got out of the hospital. He was frail, not over sixteen years old. He had been sent up from Cobb County for stealing two cans of potted ham. They stripped him naked. They whipped him with a big strap. A bunch of Negroes held him down on the ground. He went into the hospital and died. There was no coroner's inquest. I made the report under instructions that he had died of consumption." He said the convicts were handed out raw bacon and a piece of corn bread for breakfast as they came out of the stockade, and they had to eat it on the way to the mines. He said the straps weighed six pounds and were sometimes rolled in the sand to make them take the skin off. "There never was one of the prison commissioners or their inspectors went through that mine or any other camp I ever worked in."

Ephriam George Gaither, a Negro ex-convict, was called. He had worked at Sugar Hill camp and Chumley Hill, October, 1900 to September, 1901. He saw a young fellow, sixteen years old, in for three months, shot down by a guard. The buckshot load tore off the side of his face. He ran off through the woods. Dogs were put on his trail, and they soon stopped barking. The guards came back and said, "That nigger is gone over the mountains." Then the convicts saw a bitch dog carrying a human arm about in her mouth near the works. They went over and held some kind of an inquest and buried the body, but only the guards were on the jury. The dogs ate half the body before the camp authorities took notice of it. He told of guards bending a convict over the railroad track and beating him until he could barely whisper.

The mob began to gather shortly after 8 o'clock. "Let's clean the black devils out—teach them a lesson!" The mobs followed the fleeing Negroes. A Negro was seen running up the street, and the crowd started in fierce pursuit, crying, "Lynch him! Lynch him!"

ATLANTA JOURNAL, 1906

THIS account of the Atlanta race riot, written in the inflammatory, yellow-journalism style of the period, is abridged from news reports in the Atlanta *Journal*, September 20–23, 1906.

About noon on Saturday, Mrs. Lizzie Chafin, the wife of a farmer and dairyman, noticed a strange Negro in the neighborhood. He came down the road and stopped in front of her house, a pretty cottage on the Flat Shoals Road. The place is lonely. Seeing her on the veranda, he asked, "Does Mr. John Brown live near here?" Mrs. Chafin said that he did not. "Can I have a drink of water?" he persisted. Mrs. Chafin grew suspicious. "There is a spring near here," she replied. "You might use that." While she said this, Mrs. Chafin made as if to bring down a double-barreled shotgun which was hung on the wall of the house. The Negro saw this, moved on and disappeared. About 3 o'clock, she had occasion to go into the barn on an errand. In part of the barn is stored the feed for the cows and horses. This place has a sort of latticework and through this latticework Mrs. Chafin saw a black forehead and two gleaming eyes. "What are you doing there?" she cried. There was no answer. "Why don't you go away from here?" Mrs. Chafin demanded. "Because I don't want to!" was the impudent response. With that, the forehead and eyes disappeared and the full form of a Negro—the same that had appeared earlier in the road—emerged from the door.

The Negro, crouched in some tall weeds near the barn, steadily approached her. There was no longer any doubt of his design. Mrs. Chafin screamed, turned and fled toward the house. Her screams attracted the attention of the nearest neighbor, Frank Armstrong, a dairyman. He grabbed his gun and started on the run toward the Chafin home. Mrs. Chafin ran into the house, through the hall and to the front veranda. She snatched the shotgun from the wall and returned with it. When she reached the back veranda, the Negro was nearly to the steps. He turned and fled. The Negro was now running swiftly across the field. He soon got into a dense strip of woods behind the house. When she had run a hundred yards or so and had lost sight of him, she gave up the chase. She ran back to her house. Her husband, who had arrived in her absence, was frantic. The news of the attempted outrage spread. Mr. Armstrong and other neighbors, to the number of fifty or more, armed themselves. They did not consult the city or county authorities, but formed a searching party. Later a messenger was sent to the Federal prison and the bloodhounds there were borrowed.

At 7 o'clock Saturday evening, shortly after supper, Mrs. Mattie Arnold, 25 years of age and the wife of an upfitter for the Ladder Specialty Company, became thirsty and went out to the back porch, which is enclosed in latticework. The well stands in the corner of the porch within two feet of the rear door. "Come on, honey, and go with me." These words were hissed into the ear of Mrs. Arnold, with her arm in his vice-like grasp, by Henry Green, a Negro ex-convict, who crept upon the rear porch. Green was shortly afterwards captured by two white men on the railroad tracks several blocks away. At Marietta Street and Bellwood Avenue, a large number of infuriated citizens quickly assembled, and many threats of violence were openly made. After a narrow escape from the hands of angry citizens, he was hurried to the Tower by County Officer Dunbar. It is stated that the Negro was recently released from the chain gang.

About 8 o'clock, Mrs. Alma Allen, a young woman, eighteen years of age, was attacked by a fiendish Negro on the back veranda of the home of her step-father at 182 Davis Street. Miss Allen had been eating bananas and went to wash her hands, when she was struck on both shoulders from the rear. Turning around, she recognized the form of a burly Negro and immediately screamed. Her sister, hearing the cries, rushed upon the porch just in time to see her sister thrown to the floor through the back door. The screams of the two young ladies attracted the attention of the next door neighbor, Dr. W. Dodge Hearn, a dentist. Dr. Hearn rushed to the place and found Miss Allen lying on the floor across the back door entrance. The Negro had disappeared. About 8 o'clock, Mrs. Mattie Holcombe, wife of F. N. Holcombe of 215 Magnolia Street, was severely frightened when she went to a window of her home for the purpose of closing the blinds and discovered a Negro just outside in the yard. Mrs. Holcombe screamed and the intruder made good his escape.

It was a more than good Saturday night crowd. The usual habitués thronged Decatur Street. The Negroes filled the mullet stands, eating-houses and saloons.

With the Negroes in these saloons were a few white men—the white men in front, the Negroes in the rear. The whole street stunk—stunk is the word! Odors of mullet, of week-old beer, of corn and rye whiskey, of frying grease, of barber shops, of humanity. Drunken and maudlin Negroes, men and women, with the criminal white types, lounged on the sidewalks or staggered through the crowds. They drank from great schooners of beer or swallowed corn whiskey at a gulp. Smoke-wreathed air and the foul odor of liquor pervade the place.

Most of the dives are underground, one block from Decatur Street. They are strung out all in a row. They are small holes in the wall of one-story frame shanties. Rosa Edwards of 96½ Decatur Street conduct[s] the most typical of the dives. She has nine beds strung out in a row at the wall. Some have curtains, others have not. One may sleep there, if he can, for ten cents. The beds go down into the kitchen. Rosa serves beer if one orders it and drinks it with food. Steaks at ten cents and sandwiches at five cents are the rule. Langford's White Midway on Piedmont Avenue, east of Decatur Street, has Coney Island "skinned a block." Langford, a white man, runs a Negro skating rink. He has police protection and keeps an orderly place. Besides his rink, he has minstrels, a merry-go-round and side shows.

The mob began to gather shortly after 8 o'clock. News of [the] assaults upon white women, one after another, aroused the people and, though there was no concerted action, the people, as if by common agreement, gathered at Broad and Marietta streets. As news of each additional outrage spread, the anger of the men increased. [By] 9:30 o'clock, probably a thousand people had gathered, and they seemed to naturally gravitate towards Decatur Street, the hotbed of Negroes and crime. At Pryor Street they were stopped and held for some minutes by Mayor Woodward, who was on the streets. He feared trouble and addressed the crowd, urging them to disperse and go to their homes and their families. The words of the Mayor held the crowd for the minute, but soon the news of another reported assault became general.

In the meantime, many of the crowd had armed [themselves] with sticks and clubs and bottles, in fact any weapon of assault possible to obtain. "To Decatur Street!" yelled some excited man. "Let's clean the black devils out—teach them a lesson!" The shout struck a responsive chord and soon a hundred men and boys were crying "To Decatur Street!" The mob was then at the intersection of Pryor Street, and a dozen policemen were holding them in check. Captain Mayo was in command, and he was doing his best. He realized the danger if the crowd encountered the Negroes on "Rusty Row," as Decatur Street had been called. And until after 10 o'clock, Captain Mayo was successful in his efforts. But a passing Negro excited the attention of the crowd. He had been drinking [and] was boisterous. Some man struck the Negro over the head with a stick, another hit him with a barrel stave and still another kicked him. The black man turned to fight. He was knocked down and trampled by a hundred men, and the police were powerless to stop the onslaught.

In the running fight, the crowd had advanced down Decatur Street to the Star Theater. Here the police made another stand, and for five minutes the crowd was held, held until another Negro, unconscious of his danger, appeared, to be cuffed and beaten. The mob was without a leader, but this last experience aroused their fighting blood. Hundreds dashed by the officers, striking Negroes down to the right and to the left. Negroes were gathered at Decatur Street and Central Avenue, and the sight of them increased the anger of the crowd. The whites advanced in lines. The Negroes broke in disorder, fleeing for the most part out Central Avenue towards the old Union Station. The mobs followed the fleeing Negroes, delighted at the rout of the blacks. As the Negroes raced out Central Avenue, the crowd's attention was drawn by a baggage wagon bearing two darkies. They were attacked at once and were forced to leave their wagon, retreating on foot before the crowd. The skating rink, located on Central Avenue, was next noticed by the mob. Fortunately, the officers prevented a concerted attack upon this, though several Negroes in front were battered with stones hurled by the crowd.

Having been checked at the skating rink, the headless mob again turned to Decatur, and, while hundreds were here excitedly discussing affairs, someone fired a pistol. The noise came from the building of the old Young Men's Library between Central Avenue and Pryor Street. Someone said he had been grazed by the bullet, while another claimed to have seen a Negro fire the gun and asserted that it came from the Detroit Barbershop at 47 Decatur Street. With this announcement, the crowd stormed the barbershop and the place was wrecked, the Negroes fleeing in panic. The place was stormed with a volley of rocks, and the Negroes in the chairs, together with the tonsorial artists, disappeared through the rear door. Hundreds of Negroes standing along the walks on either side of Decatur Street were the targets for rock throwers, while as many more were beaten with sticks, clubs, etc. In most instances they escaped to the nearby buildings, falling in basements and chasing up stairs.

No amount of persuasion on the part of the police or the Mayor would induce the mob to disperse and go home. They continued to attack Negroes indiscriminately, in all instances being pulled off by the police. Mayor Woodward turned in a fire alarm from Box No. 42 at Decatur and Ivey streets. At the order of the Mayor, Chief Joyner had his men attach hoses to three different plugs and soon the mob was retreating before several streams of water. Instead of going home, however, the crowd beat a retreat to a point safely beyond the water, and here the rioting was renewed.

The retreat had taken the crowd to Marietta and Peachtree streets, and it was here that the trolley car fights occurred. For an hour the rioting about the trolley cars continued, and many Negroes were beaten up. Probably a dozen trolley cars were halted as they passed through the center of the city. In each instance, hundreds of angry white men surrounded the cars and wreaked their vengeance upon the Negroes. Instantly they pushed themselves in front of the track. While the motormen slackened their cars to keep from running over the people in front, members of the mob reached the rear ends of the platform and cut the rope which released the trolley overhead. The street car employees were powerless to defend the passengers. The men climbed all over the cars, running the Negroes out at the front platforms and through the windows. As soon as a Negro reached the ground, he was caught by the crowds, who threw themselves at their captive, breaking sticks over his head and striking him wherever they could. Many of the Negroes had their hands above their heads. One stroke of a stick and the arms came down and blows that could be heard for nearly a block were rained by the mob. A number of cars were filled with lady passengers and they made their way to the platforms, attempting to prevent the captors from boarding the cars. The ladies were pushed aside and the mob filled the cars. When the cars were emptied, the conductors replaced the trolley ropes and quickly left the scene.

Just after the bars had closed, a white man named G. C. Tomlinson had been badly cut by a Negro on Decatur Street. The news spread like wildfire. A Negro was seen running up the street toward Pryor, and the crowd started in fierce pursuit. Crying "Lynch him! lynch him!" at the tops of the their voices, the men dashed up the street after the fleeing man. By the time the corner of Pryor and Decatur streets was reached there were fully two hundred men running madly. The Negro dashed into North Pryor Street about fifty yards ahead of his pursuers. Reaching Auburn Avenue, he turned into that street and made a break for Peachtree. It was at the hour when the largest number of night crowds was in the center of town, and the two hundred men increased into some four or five hundred.

On Peachtree Street the Negro fled. Cars which were coming into town were quickly emptied of their loads, and men joined in the riot. By the time the English-American Building was reached, there were other mobs which came surging down Peachtree from toward the Grand Building. There the mobs joined and hemmed in the Negro between them. Then the madness of the infuriated pursuers broke loose. Each member hurled himself at the Negro, who twice broke loose, only to be caught again. In front of the Piedmont Hotel, one thousand men, with bricks, sticks and every conceivable impromptu weapon, began their merciless torment upon the defenceless man. Sticks were broken over his head, a beer bottle was hurled at him and broke in fragments on his forehead. The Negro fell prostrated to the ground and then arose again, only to make a futile attempt to escape. One policeman, Officer Carson, dashed up to the Negro's rescue. The mob hurled him back. Above the noise of the shouts and cries arose the universal yell, "Lynch the brute, kill the fiend, hang him, burn him!" A man held a newspaper high above the heads of the crowding, vengeance-wreaking mob. The newspaper bore the headlines of the late assaults of the afternoon.

The mob surged forward and backward again, momentarily irresolute to its purpose and direction. Ladies and their escorts who were on the streets fled into stores that still remained open. Doors were hastily locked and the sea of increasing numbers swelled up and down the street. Officer Carson, meanwhile, had secured the Negro and with drawn club struggled down toward Auburn Avenue. When a store next to the R. M. Rose whiskey house was reached, the officer threw open a door with his night key and carried his prisoner within. How the Negro was ever gotten to the police station is not known.

As the Negro disappeared, Tomlinson [the white man who had been knifed on Decatur Street] hurried down the street. The sight of the wounded man caused the mob to grow wilder in their impulse. Foiled at securing the Negro they had pursued, the frenzied men began an onslaught on every Negro man they found. One Negro found on Luckie Street made a dash for liberty. It was too late. The mob had seen him and started for him. Dodging through the crowds, the Negro dashed to the right hand side of Peachtree, opposite the Piedmont Hotel. Seeing all efforts to escape futile, the Negro sprang to the sidewalk and plunged headlong through the plate glass door to the tailoring house of Tom Weaver. The glass shattered, and the Negro continued his flight to the rear of the establishment, where he jumped through the glass windows. Other Negroes were rapidly found and they were summarily dealt with. No mercy was shown. The Negroes began flocking into stores and buildings, where doors were barred and bolted and the Negroes sought refuge in the rear. The majority were not so fortunate, and they were overwhelmed by the crowds. The Negroes who had been on Decatur Street had just started home, and the crowds saw them. Several Negroes fled to the post office for protection, believing themselves safe on Federal property. But such was not the case. They were pursued and on the very steps of the building a dead Negro was found. Although the mob, or more properly the mobs, showed consideration for the Negro women during the first hour of the rioting, this consideration grew less and less as time wore on and at midnight no quarter was being shown either sex. All Negroes looked alike to the mobs, and the appearance of a black face upon the streets made no difference to the frenzied people.

A Negro fled down Peachtree toward Edgewood. It drew the crowd and they dashed toward the most crowded part of the city. Here cars were stopped and blocked again. The Negroes were subjected to the fury of the now redoubling mob. Ambulance calls were quickly coming in, and the clanging gongs only added to the confusion. At 10:50 o'clock the greatest portion of the crowds had drifted to Edgewood Avenue and Peachtree Street. A corps of city firemen had laid a hose on Decatur and Pryor streets and was flooding the street from Peachtree to Piedmont Avenue. As the mob reached the intersection of Peachtree and Edgewood, the hose was run further up toward Marietta Street, and the stream was turned on them. It drove them back toward Peachtree and Walton streets and another section filled Marietta Street from Broad to Forsyth. Then the police began to arrive.

A closely pursued Negro fled into the refreshment stand of Eunie Moore on the corner opposite the Prudential Building. The place was just being closed for the night, and the mob thought the proprietors were attempting to barricade the store to defend the Negro. Instantly the fury broke loose. The mob splintered the glass fronts of the doors into a thousand pieces. Sticks were thrown into the building, and the mirrors on the walls mutilated. The cigar counter was broken open and the goods flung on the floor. Eunie Moore, who was standing near the front of the stand, was a target for the crowd. When the police arrived, they found him in the rear of the stand, almost crazed from his injuries, with his right arm badly cut and the blood staining his shirt.

The crowd then made its way slowly to Forsyth Street toward Marietta Street. The other division fell back on Walton Street and came into Peachtree again. Here a part surged back up toward the Piedmont Hotel and others joined those between Walton and Marietta streets. The riot call had been sent in a few minutes earlier, and the officers were beginning to arrive. In a few minutes there were twenty-five or thirty patrolmen and officers on the scene. It was a physical impossibility for them to check the crowd. The Negro barbershops on the street were eagerly besieged by the ferocious mobs. A Negro, attempting to flee from the crowd, took refuge in a shop. He was shot to death.

The division on Marietta Street near North Forsyth Street started in pursuit of a Negro, whom they caught in the vicinity of the bridge. He tripped and fell, and the mob was on him instantly. Again the sticks and clubs came into play. The Negro, cut and slashed in the breast a number of times, was left by the crowd. For half an hour he lay on the pavement and finally died while a curious crowd stood about him and looked on.

The mob turned back toward Broad Street. Here a street car was stopped and the men made desperate efforts to secure a Negro who was in the car. Four policemen quickly reached the scene and pulled a white man off, who was attempting to climb through the aperture on the rear platform. The crowd surged angrily around the four officers, demanding that they release the prisoner, shouting that he was "a white man" and that they would kill the officers if they did not turn him loose instantly. Two additional policemen arrived. Men in the mob threw themselves at the police, cursing them and attempting to tear their hands from off the prisoner's wrist. The policemen were compelled to strike back, and it was only the stream of water from the firemen on the corner of Peachtree and Edgewood Avenue that enabled the officers to pass down the street with their prisoner.

As time wore on, the crowds in the center of the city began to disperse but, instead of going to their homes, the men and boys formed themselves in smaller mobs and scoured Atlanta. Different mobs stopped at various houses to inquire if any Negroes were to be found on the premises, while others roamed over the streets, pouncing upon every Negro they could find. Probably a dozen Negroes, boarded the Georgia Railroad train, due to leave Atlanta shortly after midnight, were attacked and put to rout by probably a hundred infuriated men. In their attacks upon the cars, the windows were broken and the property otherwise damaged. It left Atlanta without a Negro passenger aboard, so far as could be ascertained. Negro bootblacks peering from the Kimball House barbershop, located on the Wall Street side of the hotel, attracted the crowd, and a magnificent plate glass window was smashed with rocks which were thrown at the Negroes.

At 12 o'clock the mad throng raised a loud cry to march on toward Peters Street. Down Pryor, up Alabama, they wended their way into Whitehall. And when Whitehall was reached the mob turned with yells and screams, seizing every available piece of lumber and every stone large enough to be used as a weapon. Into Madison Avenue they began to pour, headed for Peters Street. Just as the surging mass reached the viaduct, the crowd was augmented by those who had come down Whitehall Street. As the crowd increased, the yelling increased and in double-quick time Peters Street was one mass of armed men. Crossing the viaduct, the crowd moved as some swollen river and at each Negro establishment the mob wreaked its vengeance. Just a block across the viaduct a Negro woman was standing at the door and here with fury the men did their work. The glass was broken and fell with crashes that could be heard by all, and this was an inspiration to demolish as much as possible of the Negro restaurant. One of the men held a large piece of lumber in his hand, and with this he battered the door. Under the powerful strokes it gave way, and into this place the mad crowd rushed. Back in the distance a few Negroes could be seen, and the Negro woman sought refuge in a closet. As the mob entered, her screams could be heard above the noise of the angered men. Fully satisfying themselves with totally wrecking this place, they moved on, breaking every window pane thought to be the place of business of a Negro.

On and on the mob moved out Peters Street. When they had reached a certain portion of the street, rocks and sticks were thrown against a Negro hut and almost instantly a shotgun was fired from the window, slightly injuring a man. Immediately the fire was returned by those who had revolvers. For a time this checked the movements of the crowd. Then the cry was raised, "Fire arms!" The crowd swarmed to the hardware store of Penson and McCartey and against the protests of a number in the crowd the crash of the large front glass fell, covering those who stood near. Into the store the mob rushed, seizing every available weapon to be found and all the ammunition, well armed with pistols, guns of every description, clubs and rocks.

Halfway down the street, Milton Brown, a Negro employee of the Stocks Coal Company, who lives at Morris Street, turned into Peters Street. Just as he entered, the cry went up that a Negro was in sight and with one mad rush the crowd began to swarm around him. Those who had sticks began to pound him in an unmerciful manner, and he began running up the street. After clearing the crowd, those who were armed began to fire upon him, and he was literally torn to pieces. He ran to a nearby house and fell upon the doorsteps. An ambulance was called, but the response came back that they had no ambulance to send. A police officer came up and stationed himself near the Negro and a nearby surgeon was summoned.

As late as 1 o'clock, when the riot was quieted down and people were going home, the police were confronted with the greatest confusion. The Grady Hospital was not large enough to accommodate the injured. The clang of the ambulance gong was to be heard there continually, and man after man, bleeding from many wounds, was brought there for treatment. All available space at the institution was taken. The police station was turned into a hospital. The police estimated that one hundred men had been taken care of, exclusive of those who had gone to the hospital. The ambulance of that institution was not sufficient, the patrol wagon and private ambulances were pressed into service. The men who were brought in were white and black. Their faces were cut, mashed and bloody, their clothes half torn off their body. Some were shot, some had knife wounds, others were beaten. With them were men arrested on the charge of inciting a riot.

[28]

*After I had begun to trace the color line, I found evidence of it every-
where. In the theaters, Negroes never sit downstairs. White hotels and
restaurants are entirely barred to Negroes. The schools, the parks, the
city prison are separate. In court, two Bibles are provided. A Negro is
never, or very rarely, seen in a white man's church. When he dies, he
is buried in a separate cemetery.*

RAY STANNARD BAKER, 1908

BORN in Michigan, Ray Stannard Baker (1870–1946) graduated from Michigan Agricultural
College in 1889 and began his career in journalism as a reporter for the Chicago *News-Record*
in 1892. Six years later, he was employed by *McClure's*, a muckraking magazine of the era that
also published Lincoln Steffens and Ida M. Tarbell. After Atlanta's 1906 race riot, Baker travelled
to Georgia to survey the race problem. He later became the Pulitzer Prize-winning biographer
of Woodrow Wilson. The following pages are from R. S. Baker, *Following the Color Line* (New
York, 1908), pp. 1–105.

When I first went South I expected to find people talking about the Negro, but
I was not at all prepared to find the subject occupying such an overshadowing
place in Southern affairs. This is not surprising, for the Negro in the South is
the labor problem, he is preeminently the political issue, and his place, socially,
is of daily and hourly discussion. A Negro minister I met told me a story of a
boy who went as a sort of butler's assistant in the home of a prominent family
in Atlanta. His people were naturally curious about what went on in the white
man's house. One day they asked him, "What do they talk about when they're
eating?" The boy thought a moment, then he said, "Mostly they discuss us
colored folks." Not long afterward, I was lunching with several fine Southern
men, and they talked as usual with the greatest freedom in the full hearing of the
Negro waiters. Somehow I could not help watching to see if the Negroes took
any notice of what was said. I wondered if they were sensitive. Finally, I put the
question to one of my friends. "Oh," he said, "we never mind them. They don't
care." One of the waiters instantly spoke up, "No, don't mind me. I'm only a
block of wood."

I set out from the hotel on the morning of my arrival to trace the color line as it appears outwardly in the life of Atlanta. A great many Negroes are always on the streets, far better dressed and better appearing than I had expected to see. Crowds of Negroes were at work mending the pavement. I stopped to watch a group of them. A good deal of conversation was going on, here and there a Negro would laugh with great good humor, and several times I heard a snatch of a song. Much jollier workers than our grim foreigners, but evidently not working so hard. A fire had been built to heat some of the tools, and a black circle of Negroes were gathered around it like flies around a drop of molasses, and they were all talking while they warmed their shins, evidently having plenty of leisure. As I continued down the street, I found that all the drivers of wagons and cabs were Negroes. I saw Negro news boys, Negro porters, Negro barbers, and it being a bright day many of them were in the street—on the sunny side.

It was simply amazing to me, considering the bitterness of racial feeling, to see how lavish many white families are in giving food, clothing and money to individual Negroes whom they know. A Negro cook often supports her whole family, including a lazy husband, on what she gets daily from the white man's kitchen. In some old families the "basket habit" of the Negroes is taken for granted. In the newer ones, it is, significantly, beginning to be called stealing, showing that the old order is passing and that the Negro is being held more and more strictly to account, not as a dependent vassal but as a moral being, who must rest upon his own responsibility. Often a Negro of the old sort will literally bulldoze his hereditary white protector. Mr. Brittain, superintendent of schools in Fulton County, gave me an incident in point. A big Negro with whom he was wholly unacquainted came to his office one day and demanded a job. "What's your name?" asked the superintendent. "Marion Luther Brittain," was the reply. "That sounds familiar," said Mr. Brittain. "Yes, sah. Ah'm the son of yo' ol' mammy." In short, Marion Luther had grown up on the old plantation. It was the spirit of the hereditary vassal demanding protection and support, and he got it. The Negro who makes his appeal on the basis of this old tradition finds no more indulgent or generous friend than the Southern white man, indulgent to the point of excusing thievery and other petty offences, but the moment he assumes or demands any other relationship or stands up as an independent citizen, the white men—at least some white men—turn upon him with the fiercest hostility.

Many Southern men I met had little or no idea of the remarkable extent of advancement among the better class of Negroes. I don't know how many Southern men have prefaced their talks with me something like this: "You can't expect to know the Negro after a short visit. You must live down here like we do. Now I know the Negroes like a book. I was brought up with them. I know what they'll do and what they won't do. I have had Negroes in my house all my life." But curiously enough I find that these men rarely knew anything about the better class of Negroes, those who were in business or in independent occupations, those who owned their own homes. They did come into contact with the servant Negro, the field hand, the common laborer, who make up, of course, the great mass of the race. On the other hand, the best class of Negroes did not know the higher class of white people and based their suspicion and hatred upon the acts of the poorer sort of whites with whom they naturally came into contact. The best elements of the two races are as far apart as though they lived in different continents, and that is one of the chief causes of the growing danger of the Southern situation. Many Southerners look back wistfully to the faithful, simple, ignorant, obedient, cheerful, old plantation Negro and deplore his disappearance. They want the New South, but the old Negro. That Negro is disappearing forever along with the old feudalism and the old-time exclusively agricultural life.

One of my early errands led me into several of the great new office buildings, which bear testimony to the extraordinary progress of Atlanta. And here I found one of the first evidences of the color line. In both buildings, I found a separate elevator for colored people. In one building, signs were placed reading "For Whites Only." In another "This Car for Colored Passengers, Freight, Express and Packages." A few days later an intelligent Negro with whom I was talking asked me, "Have you seen the elevator sign in the Century Building? How would you like to be classed with 'Freight, Express and Packages?' " I found that no Negro ever went into an elevator devoted to white people, but that white people often rode in cars set apart for colored people.

One of the points in which I was especially interested was the "Jim Crow" regulations, the system of separation of the races in street cars and railroad trains. In almost no other relationship do the races come together, physically, on anything like a common footing. In the street cars they touch as free citizens, each paying for the right to ride, the white not in a place of command, the Negro without an obligation of servitude. Street car relationships are, therefore, symbolic of the new conditions. A few years ago the Negro came and went in the street cars in most cities and sat where he pleased, but gradually Jim Crow laws or local regulations were passed, forcing him into certain seats at the back of the car. In Savannah Jim Crow ordinances have gone into effect for the first time, causing violent protestations on the part of the Negroes. There could be no better visible evidence of the increasing separation of the races and of the determination of the white man to make the Negro "keep his place" than the evolution of the Jim Crow regulations. I was curious to see how the system worked in Atlanta. Over the door of each car, I found this sign: "White people will seat from front of car toward the back and colored people from rear toward front." Sure enough, I found the white people in front and the Negroes behind. As the sign indicates, there is no definite line of division between the white seats and the black seats. The very first time I was on a car in Atlanta, I saw the conductor—all conductors are white—ask a Negro woman to get up and take a seat farther back in order to make a place for a white man. I have also seen white men requested to leave the Negro section of the car. At one time, when I was on a car, the conductor shouted, "Heh, you nigger, get back there!" which the Negro, who had taken a seat too far forward, proceeded hastily to do. "We pay first class fares," said one of the leading Negroes in Atlanta, "exactly as the white man does, but we don't get first class service. I say it isn't fair."

I heard innumerable stories from both white people and Negroes of encounters in the street cars. Dr. W. F. Penn, one of the foremost Negro physicians of the city, himself partly white, a graduate of Yale College, told me of one occasion in which he entered a car and found there Mrs. Crogman, wife of the colored president of Clark University. Mrs. Crogman is a mulatto so light of complexion as to be practically undistinguishable from white people. Dr. Penn, who knew her well, sat down beside her and began talking. A white man, who occupied a seat in front, turned and said, "Here, you nigger, get out of that seat! What do you mean by sitting down with a white woman?" Dr. Penn replied somewhat angrily. The white man turned to his wife and said, "Here, take these bundles. I'm going to thrash that nigger." In half a minute the car was in an uproar, the two men struggling. It is significant that one of the features of the Atlanta riot was an attack on the street cars in which all Negroes were driven out of their seats. One Negro woman was pushed through an open window, and, after falling to the pavement, she was dragged by the leg across the the sidewalk and thrown through a shop window. In another case when the mob stopped a car, the motorman, instead of protecting his passengers, went inside and beat down a Negro with his brass control lever.

Another interesting point significant of tendencies came early to my attention. They had recently finished at Atlanta one of the finest railroad stations in this country. The ordinary depot in the South has two waiting rooms of about the same size, one for whites and one for Negroes. But when this new station was built, the whole front was given up to white people and the Negroes were assigned a side entrance and a small waiting room. Prominent colored men regarded it as a new evidence of the crowding out of the Negro, the further attempt to give him unequal accommodations, to handicap him in his struggle for survival. There are in the station two lunchrooms, one for whites, one for Negroes.

After I had begun to trace the color line, I found evidences of it everywhere, literally in every department of life. In the theaters, Negroes never sit downstairs, but the galleries are black with them. Of course, white hotels and restaurants are entirely barred to Negroes. "Sleepers Wanted" is a familiar sign in Atlanta, giving notice of places where for a few cents a Negro can find a bed or a mattress on the floor, often in a room where they are many other sleepers crowded together. No good public accommodations exist for the educated or well-to-do Negro in Atlanta. Indeed one cannot long remain in the South without being impressed with the extreme difficulties which beset the exceptional colored man. In slavery time many Negroes attended white churches. Now a Negro is never, or very rarely, seen in a white man's church.

Of course, the schools are separate and have been ever since the Civil War. In one of the parks of Atlanta I saw this sign: "No Negroes allowed in this park." While I was in Atlanta, the art school, which in the past has often used Negro models, decided to draw the color line there, too, and no longer employ them. Formerly Negroes and white men went to the same saloons and drank at the same bars. In a few instances in Atlanta there were Negro saloon keepers and many Negro bartenders. The first step toward separation was to divide the bar, the upper end for white men, the lower for Negroes. After the riot, by a new ordinance no saloon was permitted to serve both white and colored men. Consequently, going along Decatur Street, one sees the saloons designated by conspicuous signs: "Whites Only." "Colored Only." In the city prison, the Negro is separated from the whites. In court, two Bibles are provided. When he dies, he is buried in a separate cemetery.

The Negro knows he has little chance to explain if by accident or ignorance he insults a white woman or offends a white man. The Negroes fear the white people. My very first impression of what this fear of the Negroes might be came not from Negroes but from a fine white woman. She told this story: "I had a really terrible experience one evening a few days ago. I was walking along when I saw a rather good looking young Negro come out of a hallway to the sidewalk. He was in a great hurry, and, in turning, suddenly, as a person sometimes will do, he accidentally brushed my shoulder with his arm. He had not seen me before. When he turned and found it was a white woman he had touched, such a look of abject terror and fear came into his face as I hope never again to see on a human countenance. He knew what it meant if I was frightened, called for help and accused him of insulting or attacking me. He stood still a moment, then turned and ran down the street, dodging into the first alley he came to. It shows, doesn't it, how little it might take to bring punishment upon an innocent man."

So I went down to police courts. I chose a Monday morning, that I might see the accumulation of the arrests of Saturday and Sunday. The police station stands in Decatur Street in the midst of the very worst section of the city, surrounded by low saloons, dives and pawn shops. A great room upstairs was crowded to its capacity. The docket that morning carried over one hundred names—men, women and children, black and white. I found that 13,511 of the total of 21,702 persons arrested in 1906 were Negroes, or sixty-two percent, whereas the colored population of the city is only forty percent of the total. A very large proportion of the arrests that Monday morning were Negroes. "Where's your home?" the Judge would ask. And in a number of cases the answer was, "Ah come here fum de country." Over and over again it was the story of the country Negro or the Negro who had been working on the railroad, in the cotton fields or in the sawmills, who had entered upon the more complex life of the city.

One has only to visit police courts in the South to see in how many curious ways the contact of the races generates fire. "What's the trouble here?" inquires the judge. The white complainant, a boy, says, "This nigger insulted me!" and tells the epithet the Negro applied. "Did you call him that?" "No sah, I never called him no such name." "Three seventy-five—you mustn't insult white people!" A strapping Negro man was brought before the judge. He showed no marks of dissipation and was respectably dressed. Confronting him were two plainclothes policemen, one with his neck wrapped up, one with a bandage around his arm. Both said they had been stabbed by the Negro with a jack-knife. The Negro said he was a hotel porter and he had the white manager of the hotel in court to testify to his good character, sobriety and industry. It seems that he was going home from work at 9 o'clock in the evening, and it was dark. He said he was afraid and had been afraid since the riot. At the same time the two policemen were looking for a burglar. They saw the Negro porter and ordered him to stop. Not being in uniform the Negro said he thought the officers were "jes' plain white men" who were going to attack him. When he started to run, the officers tried to arrest him, and he drew his jack-knife and began to fight. The judge said, "You musn't attack officers," and bound him over to trial in the higher court.

One thing impressed me especially, not only in this court but in all others I have visited: A Negro brought in for drunkenness, for example, was punished much more severely than a white man arrested for the same offence. The injustice which the weak everywhere suffer, North and South, is in the South visited upon the Negro. The white man sometimes escaped with a reprimand, he was sometimes fined $3 and costs; but the Negro, especially if he had no white man to intercede for him, was usually punished with a $10 or $15 fine, which often meant that he must go to the chain gang. One of the chief causes of complaint by the Negroes of Atlanta has been of the rough treatment of the police and of unjust arrests.

One reason for the very large number of arrests—in Georgia particularly—lies in the fact that the state and counties make a profit out of their prison system. No attempt is ever made to reform a criminal, white or colored. Convicts are hired out to private contractors or worked on the public roads. A very large proportion of the prisoners are Negroes. The demand for convicts by rich saw-mill operators, owners of brick yards, large farmers and others is far in advance of the supply. The natural tendency is to convict as many men as possible: it furnishes steady, cheap labor to the contractors and a profit to the state. Undoubtedly this explains in some degree the very large number of convicts, especially Negroes, in Georgia. Some of the large fortunes in Atlanta have come chiefly from the labor of chain gangs of convicts leased from the state.

My curiosity, aroused by the very large number of young prisoners, especially Negroes, in Judge Broyles's court, led me next to inquire why these children were not in school. Just as in the North the tenement classes are often neglected, so in the South, the lowest class—which is the Negro—is neglected. Several new schools have been built for white children, but there has been no new school for colored children in fifteen or twenty years. So crowded are the colored schools that they have two sessions a day, one squad of children coming in the forenoon, another in the afternoon. (The colored teachers, therefore, do double work, for which they receive about two-thirds as much salary as the white teachers.) Because there is not enough room for Negro children in public schools, the colored people maintain many private schools. The largest of these, called Morris Brown College, has nearly 1000 pupils. This "college" is in reality a grammar school. Many children also find educational opportunities in the Negro colleges of the city—Clark University, Atlanta University and Spellman Seminary—which are supported partly by the Negroes but mostly by Northern philanthropy.

The mass of colored people still maintain a more or less intimate connection with white families. To one who has heard so much of racial hatred as I have since I have been down here, a little incident that I observed the other day comes with a charm hardly describable. I saw a carriage stop in front of a home. The expected daughter had arrived, a very pretty girl indeed. She stepped out eagerly. Her father was halfway down to the gate, but ahead of him was a very old Negro woman in the cleanest of clean starched dresses. "Honey!" she said eagerly. "Mammy!" exclaimed the girl, and the two rushed into each other's arms, clasping and kissing, the white girl and the old black woman. Often I have heard Negroes refer to "my white folks" and similarly the white man still speaks of "my Negroes." The old term of slavery, "master," has wholly disappeared and in its place has risen "Boss" or sometimes "Cap" or "Cap'n." To this, the white man responds with the first name of the Negro, "Jim" or "Susie" or, if the Negro is old or especially respected, "Uncle Jim" or "Aunt Susan." To an unfamiliar Northerner one of the very interesting phases of conditions down here is the panic fear displayed over the use of the word "Mr." or "Mrs." No Negro is ever called "Mr." or "Mrs." by a white man. That would indicate social equality. In the same way a Negro may call Miss Mary Smith by the familiar "Miss Mary." But if he called her "Miss Smith" she would be deeply incensed. The formal "Miss Smith" would imply social equality.

The worthless and idle Negro, often a criminal, comparatively small in numbers but perniciously evident, has lost his "white folks" and he has not attained the training or self-direction to stand alone. He works only when he is hungry, and he is as much a criminal as he dares to be. He is usually densely ignorant, often a wanderer, working today with a railroad gang, tomorrow on some city works, the next day picking cotton. The great middle class of Negroes, who do the manual work of the South, have their "white folks" for whom they do washing, cooking, gardening or other service, so that they have a real place in the social fabric and a code of self respect. They are crowded into straggling settlements like Darktown and Jackson Row, a few owning their homes but the majority renting precariously. Poverty here, however, lacks the tragic note that it strikes in crowded Northern cities. A banjo, a mullet supper, an exciting revival give the Negro real joys.

Above these, a third class, few in numbers but most influential in their race, are the progressive, property owning Negroes who have wholly severed their old intimate ties with the white people and who have been getting further and further away from them. One day, walking in Broad Street, I passed a Negro shoestore. I did not know that there was such a thing in the country. I went in to make inquiries. It was neat, well kept and evidently prosperous. I found that it was owned, organized and controlled wholly by Negroes. The manager was a brisk young mulatto named Harper, a graduate of Atlanta University. I found him dictating to a Negro stenographer. There were two reasons, he said, why the store had been opened. One was because the promoters thought it a good business opportunity. The other was because many Negroes of the better class felt that they did not get fair treatment at white stores. At some places—not all, he said—when a Negro woman went to buy a pair of shoes, the clerk would hand them to her without offering to help her try them on, and a Negro was always kept waiting until all the white people in the store had been served. Since the new business was opened, he said, it had attracted much of the Negro trade, all the leaders advising their people to patronize him.

The cotton picking season was drawing to its close when I left for the black belt of Georgia. There is no better time of year to see the South than November, for then it wears the smile of abundance. The fields were lively with Negro cotton pickers. I saw bursting loads of the new lint drawn by mules or oxen, trailing along the country roads. All the gins were puffing busily. At each station platform cotton bales by scores or hundreds stood ready for shipment and the towns were cheerful with farmers white and black, who now had money to spend. The heat of the summer had gone, the air bore the tang of a brisk autumn coolness. Many Negroes got on or off at every station with laughter and shouted good-bys.

I reached Hawkinsville, a thriving town of some 3000 people, just south of the center of Georgia. Pulaski County, of which Hawkinsville is the seat, is a typical county of the black belt. More than half of the inhabitants are Negroes. There the race question, though perhaps not so immediately difficult as in cities like Atlanta, is with both white and colored people the imminent problem of daily existence. The entire county has only 8000 white people and 12,000 Negroes. At Hawkinsville I met J. Pope Brown, the leading citizen of the county. For five years he was president of the State Agricultural Society; he has been a member of the legislature and chairman of the Georgia Railroad Commission; and he represents all that is best in the new progressive movement in the South. Mr. Brown took me out to his plantation, a drive of some eight miles. In common with most of the larger plantation owners, Mr. Brown makes his home in the city. After a while I came to feel a reasonable confidence in assuming that almost any prominent merchant, banker, lawyer or politician whom I met in the towns owned a plantation in the country.

I concluded that the movement of white owners from the land to nearby towns was increasing every year. A traveller in the black belt sees many plantation houses, even those built in recent years, standing vacant or else occupied by white overseers. Thousands of small white farmers, both owners and renters, remain, but when the leading planters leave the country, these men grow discontented and get away at the first opportunity. Going to town, they find ready employment for the whole family in the cotton mill or in other industries. Hawkinsville has a small cotton mill and a community of white workers around it. A natural segregation of the races is apparently taking place. I saw it everywhere I went in the black belt. The white people were gravitating toward the towns or into white neighborhoods and leaving the land, even though still owned by white men, more and more to the exclusive occupation of Negroes. Many black counties are growing blacker, while not a few white counties are growing whiter. One of the most active causes of this movement is downright fear—or race repulsion expressing itself in fear. White people dislike and fear to live in dense colored neighborhoods, while Negroes are often terrorized in white neighborhoods.

One of the most significant things I saw was the way in which the white people were torn between their feeling of race prejudice and their downright economic needs. Hating and fearing the Negro as a race, though often loving individual Negroes, they yet want him to work for them. They can't get along without him. Generally speaking, the race hatred in the South comes chiefly from the poorer class of whites who either own land which they work themselves or are tenant farmers in competition with Negroes and from politicians who seek to win the votes of this class of white men. The larger landowners and employers of labor, while they do not love the Negro, want him to work and work steadily and will do almost anything to keep him on the land—so long as he is a faithful, obedient, unambitious worker. When he becomes prosperous or educated or owns land, many white people no longer "have any use for him" and turn upon him with hostility, but the best type of the Southern white man is not only glad to see the Negro become a prosperous and independent farmer but will do much to help him.

Mr. Brown's plantation contains about 5000 acres, of which some 3500 acres are in cultivation, a beautiful rolling country well watered, with here and there clumps of pines and dotted with the small homes of the tenantry. As we drove along the country road we met or passed many Negroes who bowed with the greatest deference. Some were walking, but many drove horses or mules and rode not infrequently on top buggies, looking most prosperous. Mr. Brown knew them all and sometimes stopped to ask them how they were getting along. The outward relationships between the races in the country seem to me to be smoother than it is in the city. I was impressed with the fact that nearly all the houses used by the Negro tenants were new and much superior to the old log cabins built either before or after the war, some of which I saw still standing, vacant and dilapidated. Mr. Brown has other methods for keeping the tenantry on his plantation satisfied. Every year he gives a barbecue and "frolic" for his Negroes with music and speaking and plenty to eat. A big watermelon patch is also a feature of the plantation and during all the year the tenants are looked after, not only to see that the work is properly done but in more intimate and sympathetic ways.

Cotton, as in all this country, is almost the exclusive crop. In spite of the constant preaching of agricultural reformers, like Mr. Brown himself, hardly enough corn is raised to supply the people with food, and I was surprised here and elsewhere at seeing so few cattle and hogs. Sheep are nonexistent. In Hawkinsville, though the country 'round about raises excellent grass, I saw in front of a supply store bales of hay which had been shipped in 400 miles—from Tennessee! At the time of my visit, the Negroes were in the cane fields with their long knives, getting in the crop. We saw several little one-horse grinding mills pressing the juice from the cane, while near at hand, sheltered by a shanty-like roof, was the great simmering syrup kettle, with an expert Negro at work stirring and skimming. And always there were Negroes 'round about, all the boys and girls with jolly smeared faces, and the older ones peeling and sucking the fresh cane.

How does the landlord—and a lord he is in a very true sense—manage his great estate? It requires about 100 families, or 600 people, to operate Mr. Brown's plantation. Of these, ninety percent are colored and ten percent white. I was much interested in what Mr. Brown said about his Negro tenants, which varies somewhat from the impression I had in the city of the younger generation. "I would much rather have young Negroes for tenants," he said, "because they work better and seem more disposed to take care of their farms. The old Negroes ordinarily will shirk, a habit of slavery." Besides the residence of the overseer and the homes of the tenants, there is on the plantation a supply store owned by Mr. Brown, a blacksmith shop and a Negro church, which is also used as a school house.

Three different methods are pursued by the landlord in getting his land culti-vated. First, the better class of tenants rent the land for cash, a "standing rent" of some $3 an acre. Second, a share-crop rental, in which the landlord and the tenant divide the cotton and corn produced. Third, the ordinary wage system: the landlord hires workers at so much and puts in his own crop. Mr. Brown rents 2500 acres for cash, 400 on shares and farms 600 himself with wage workers. The plantation is irregularly divided up into what are called one-mule or one-plough farms—just the amount of land which a family can cultivate with one mule—usually about thirty acres.

Most of the tenants, especially the Negroes, are very poor and wholly depen-dent upon the landlord. Many Negro families possess practically nothing of their own, save their ragged clothing and a few dollars' worth of household furniture, cooking utensils and a gun. The landlord must therefore supply them not only with enough to live on while they are making their crop, but with the entire farming outfit. Let us say that a Negro comes in November to rent a one-mule farm from the landlord for the coming year. "What have you got?" asks the landlord. "Notin', boss," he is quite likely to say. The boss furnishes him with a cabin to live in, which goes with the land rented, a mule, a plough, possibly a one-horse wagon and a few tools. He is often given a few dollars in cash near Christmas time, which ordinarily he immediately wastes. He is then allowed to draw from the plantation supply store a regular amount of corn to feed his mule and meat, bread and tobacco and some clothing for his family. The cost of the entire outfit and supplies for a year is in the neighborhood of $300, upon which the tenant pays interest at from ten to thirty percent, from the time of signing the contract in November, although most of the supplies are not taken out until the next summer. Besides this interest, the planter also makes a large profit on all the groceries and other necessaries furnished by his supply store.

Having made his contract, the Negro goes to work with his whole family and keeps at it until the next fall when the cotton is all picked and ginned. Then he comes in for his "settlement"—a great time of year. The settlements were going forward while I was in the black belt. The Negro is credited with the amount of cotton he brings in and he is charged with all the supplies he has had and interest, together with the rent of his thirty acres of land. If the season has been good and he has been industrious, he will often have a nice profit in cash, but sometimes he not only does not come out even but closes his year of work actually in deeper debt to the landlord.

Planters told me of all sorts of difficulties they had to meet with their tenants. One of them, after he had spent a whole evening telling me of the troubles which confronted any man who tried to work Negroes, summed it all up: "You've just got to make up your mind that you are dealing with children and handle them as firmly and kindly as you know how." He told me how hard it was to get a Negro tenant even in the busy season to work a full week, and it was often only by withholding the weekly food allowance that it could be done. Saturday afternoon the Negro goes to town or visits his friends. Often he spends all day Sunday driving about the country, and his mule comes back so worn out that it cannot be used on Monday. There are often furious religious revivals which break into the work, to say nothing of "frolics" and fish suppers at which the Negroes often remain all night long. Many of them are careless with their tools, wasteful, irresponsible. One planter told me how he had built neat fences around the homes of his Negroes and fixed up their houses to encourage them in thrift and give them more comfort, only to have the fences and even parts of the houses used for firewood.

Toward fall, if the season has been bad and the crop of cotton is short, so short that a Negro knows he will not be able to "pay out" and have anything left for himself, he will sometimes desert the plantation entirely, leaving the cotton unpicked and a large debt to the landlord. If he attempts that, however, he must get entirely away, else the planter will chase him down and bring him back to his work. Illiterate, without discipline or training, with little ambition and much indolence, a large proportion of Negro tenants are looked after and driven like children or slaves.

Conditions in the black belt are in one respect much as they were in slavery times. If the master or lord is "good," the Negro prospers. If he is harsh, grasping, unkind, the Negro suffers bitterly. It gets back finally to the white man.

Scarcity of labor and high wages have given the really ambitious and industrious Negro his opportunity, and many thousands of them are becoming more and more independent of the favor or ill-will of the whites. Therein lies a profound danger, not only to the Negro, but to the South. Gradually losing the support and advice of the best type of white man, the independent Negro finds himself in competition with the poorer type of white man, whose jealousy he must meet. He takes the penalties of being really free. Without the political rights of his poor white competitor and wholly without social recognition, discredited by the bestial crime of the lower class of his own race, he has, indeed, a hard struggle before him. In many neighborhoods he is peculiarly at the mercy of this lower class white electorate and the self-seeking politicians whose stock in trade consists in playing upon the passions of race-hatred.

The present tenant system grows naturally out of slavery. The white man had learned to operate his big plantations with ignorant help, and the Negro on his part had no training for any other system. The white man was the natural master and the Negro the natural dependent and emancipation did not change the spirit of the relationship. Today a white overseer resides on every large plantation and he or the owner himself looks after and disciplines the tenants. The tenant is in debt to him, in some cases reaching a veritable condition of debt slavery or peonage, and he must see that the crop is made. Hence he watches the work of every Negro, and indeed that of the white tenants as well, sees that the land is properly fertilized and that the dikes are kept up, that the cotton is properly chopped and regularly cultivated. Some of the greater landowners employ assistant overseers or "riders," each with a rifle on his saddle. What the Southern planter wants today is Negroes who will "keep their place." Many laws have been passed which are designed to keep the Negro on the land and, having him there, to make him work. The contract law, the abuses of which lead to peonage and debt slavery, is an excellent example. The Negro tenant often has no way of knowing what is in the contract he signs (about half the Negro tenants of the black belt are wholly illiterate). He must depend on the landlord to keep both the rent and the supply store accounts. In other words, he is wholly at the planter's mercy. It is so easy to make large profits by charging immense interest percentages or outrageous prices for supplies to tenants who are too ignorant or too weak to protect themselves. It is easy, when the tenant brings in his cotton in the fall, not only to underweigh it but to credit it at the lowest prices of the week. The criminal laws, the chain-gang system and the hiring of Negro convicts to private individuals are all, in one way or another, devices to keep the Negro at work. This dealing of the strong with the weak is not Southern, it is human.

Often an unscrupulous landlord will deliberately give a Negro a little money before Christmas, knowing that he will waste it in celebration, thus getting him into debt so that he dare not leave the plantation for fear of arrest and criminal prosecution. If he attemps to leave, he is arrested and taken before a friendly justice of the peace and fined or threatened with imprisonment. If he is not in debt, sometimes the landlord will have him arrested on the charge of stealing a bridle or a few potatoes and brought into court. In several cases I know of, the escaping Negro has even been chased with bloodhounds. On appearing in court, the Negro is naturally badly frightened. The white man is there and offers to take him back and let him work out the fine—which sometimes requires six months, often a whole year. In this way Negroes are kept in debt-slavery or peonage year after year, they and their whole family. In one case in particular, I saw a Negro brought into court charged with stealing cotton. "Does anybody know this Negro?" asked the judge. Two white men stepped up and both said they did. The judge fined the Negro $20 and costs, and there was a real contest between the two white men as to who should pay it—and get the Negro. They argued for some minutes, but finally the judge said to the prisoner, "Who do you want to work for, George?" The Negro chose his employer and agreed to work four months to pay off his $20 fine and costs. Sometimes a man who has a debt against a Negro will sell the claim—practically selling the Negro—to some farmer who wants more labor. A step further brings the Negro to the chain gang. If there is no white man to pay him out, or if his crime is too serious to be paid out, he goes to the chain gang, and in several states he is then hired out to private contractors. The private employer thus gets him sooner or later.

Still other methods are pursued by certain landlords to keep their tenants on the land. In one extreme case, a Negro tenant, after years of work, decided to leave the planter. He had had a place offered him where he could make more money. There was nothing against him. He simply wanted to move. But the landlord informed him that no wagon would be permitted to cross his (the planter's) land to get his household belongings. The Negro, being ignorant, supposed he could thus be prevented from moving. There are even landlords and employers who will trade upon the Negro's worst instincts—his love for liquor—in order to keep him at work. An instance of this sort came to my attention at Hawkinsville. The white people of the town were making a strong fight for prohibition. But the largest employer of Negro labor in the county had registered several hundred of his Negroes and declared his intention of voting them against prohibition. This employer actually voted sixty of his Negroes against prohibition, but the excitement was so great that he dared vote no more. He said bluntly, "If my niggers can't get whiskey they won't stay with me. You've got to keep a nigger poor or he won't work." In another instance, also extreme, a planter refused to let his tenants raise hogs, because he wanted them to buy salt pork at his store.

I spent much time driving about on the great plantations and went into many of the cabins. Usually they were very poor, of logs or shacks, sometimes only one room, sometimes a room and a sort of lean-to. At one side there was a fireplace, often two beds opposite, with a few broken chairs or boxes and a table. Sometimes the cabin was set up on posts and had a floor, sometimes it was on the ground and had no floor at all. The people are usually densely ignorant and superstitious. The preachers they follow are often the worst sort of characters. The schools, if there are any, are practically worthless. The whole family works from sunrise to sunset in the fields. Even children of six and seven years old will drop seed or carry water. It would be impossible to overemphasize the ignorance of many Negro farmers. It seems almost unbelievable, but, after some good-humored talk with a group of old Negroes, I tried to find out how much they knew of the outside world. I finally asked them if they knew Theodore Roosevelt. They looked puzzled. "Whah you say dis yere man libes?" "In Washington," I said. "You've heard of the President of the United States?" "I reckon I dunno," he said.

It keeps coming to me that this is more a white man's problem than it is a Negro problem. The white man is in full control of the South, politically, socially, industrially. The Negro is his helpless ward. I saw crowds of young Negroes being made criminal through lack of proper training. It is better to educate men in school than to let them educate themselves to become a menace to society. For the protection of society, it is as necessary to train every Negro as it is every white man. I could not help thinking how pitilessly ignorance finally revenges itself upon that society which neglects or exploits it.

Index